Random Violence

Random Violence

*How We Talk about New Crimes
and New Victims*

Joel Best

UNIVERSITY OF CALIFORNIA PRESS

Berkeley   Los Angeles   London

University of California Press
Berkeley and Los Angeles, California

University of California Press, Ltd.
London, England

"'Road Warriors' on 'Hair-Trigger Highways'" from
Sociological Inquiry vol. 61, pp. 327–45; by permission
of the University of Texas Press.

Library of Congress Cataloging-in-Publication Data

Best, Joel.
    Random violence : how we talk about new crimes and
new victims / Joel Best.
        p.   cm.
    Includes bibliographical references (p. 211) and index.
    ISBN 0-520-21571-0 (alk. paper). —
    ISBN 0-520-21572-9 (alk. paper)
    1. Fear of crime—United States.   2. Crime—United
States—Public opinion.   3. Violence—United States—
Public opinion.   4. Victims of crimes—United States—
Public opinion.   5. Mass media and crime—United
States.   6. Crime in mass media.   I. Title.
HV6789.B47   1998
364.973—dc21
                                                98-6234
                                                CIP

Printed in the United States of America
9 8 7 6 5 4 3 2 1

For Joan,
who worries even more than I do

CONTENTS

ACKNOWLEDGMENTS

This book began in what I thought were unrelated case studies—of freeway violence, hate crimes, victims' rights, and so on. Gradually, over about ten years, I came to see connections among those topics, and I began trying to explore these links. It was a slow process, involving many drafts of many papers, and along the way I received a great deal of help.

Both my previous employer, California State University, Fresno, and my current one, Southern Illinois University at Carbondale, provided research grants to help me collect and analyze data. The National Endowment for the Humanities funded two Summer Seminars for College Teachers that gave me opportunities to discuss social-problems theory with a wonderful array of scholars. I also had opportunities to present pieces of this work at various conferences and campuses, and I benefited greatly from the comments I received on those occasions, although I cannot always remember just who supplied which suggestions.

I particularly want to acknowledge the support—and criticism—of those individuals who graciously read some of what I was writing, listened to what I had to say, or just let me pick their brains. Kathleen Lowney deserves special mention: a participant in my first NEH Summer Seminar, Kathe became my collaborator and confidant, a close friend. She saw promise in this project, even when it was badly jumbled, and she constantly encouraged me to work on it. In addition, I want to thank Lynn Appleton, Jun Ayukawa, Loy Bilderback, Peter Blum, Thomas Burger, Francis Cullen, Bill Ellis, Gary Alan Fine, Sylvia Grider, Beth Hartung Freimuth, Jennifer Horowitz, Mary Hutchinson, Philip Jenkins, Jill Kiecolt, Stan Knapp, Donileen Loseke, Dave Luckenbill, John Lynxwiler, Donna Maurer, Gale Miller, Larry Nichols, Paul Roman, the late Larry Ross, Hillel Schwartz, Kim Sweeney, Tracy Thibodeau, Ronald Troyer, Rhys Williams, and the others who helped me shape this book. Of course, I received more good advice than I took; none of these people can be blamed for the book's shortcomings.

Parts of some chapters draw upon earlier publications: Joel Best, "'Road Warriors' on 'Hair-Trigger Highways,'" *Sociological Inquiry* 61 (1991): 327–45; Kathleen S. Lowney and Joel Best, "Stalking Strangers and Lovers," in *Images of Issues*, edited by Joel Best, 2d ed. (Hawthorne, N.Y.: Aldine de Gruyter, 1995): 33–57; Joel Best and Mary M. Hutchinson, "The Gang Initiation Rite as a Motif in Contemporary Crime Discourse," *Justice Quarterly* 13 (1996): 383–404; and Joel Best, "Victimization and the Victim Industry," *Society* 34 (May/June 1997): 9–17.

PREFACE

This book examines our fears about crime and the way we express them. It explores how we think and talk about what frightens us; it analyzes contemporary concerns over violence and victimization and villainy. It assumes that our fears have consequences, that they shape our thinking and our behavior—sometimes in ways that make things worse. In particular, I argue that focusing on "random violence" distorts our understanding of our society's crime problems, and that this distortion makes it harder for us to address those problems.

There are already many studies of the "fear of crime," but I have made little use of them. Most of these studies measure fear by asking people whether they are afraid to walk alone in their neighborhoods at night, and then try to determine which sorts of people are most likely to say yes. Usually these studies find that older people and women (who are relatively less likely to be victimized) worry a great deal, while young adults and males report low levels of fear (even though they have higher rates of victimization).

The problem with these studies, from my point of view, is that they do not address the texture of our fears. We do not fear "crime"; we fear the carjackers, the sexual predators, the drive-by shooters—the strangers who attack without warning or provocation. We fear sudden, unexpected, undeserved chaos, pointless suffering at the hands of brutal barbarians. I believe that this vision—this fear of random violence—shapes many of our reactions to contemporary social life.

Nothing in this book is intended to imply that some people are not targets of unexpected violent attacks by strangers, or that these victims do not suffer. People close to me have told me about their experiences as victims, and the press informs me daily of others' injuries. I am fully aware that real people suffer real harm, I recognize that many of these victims are permanently damaged, and I view this suffering and this damage as deplorable, as serious social problems.

That said, I do not think that our society has figured out the best way to look at these problems. We tend to view crime as a melodrama in which evil villains prey on innocent victims. This melodramatic vision runs through our popular culture, with bad guys like *The Silence of the Lambs*'s Hannibal Lecter committing grotesque, pointless murders. Why does Lecter kill and eat his victims? Because he is evil; because that's just the kind of thing he does—that's why. Melodrama is the basis for many of our most popular entertainments, but melodramatic imagery also influences more serious discussions of crime; the reports of journalists, the speeches of politicians, and the analyses of academics often adopt an implicitly melodramatic stance. They routinely take the worst examples of criminal violence and imply that they are typical. This melodramatic view distorts the nature of crime, but it also serves other purposes: it increases the journalists' audience; it promotes the causes of both liberal and conservative politicians; it makes the academics' work seem more compelling. And melodrama has other consequences: it frightens and confuses the public, and it makes it harder to design and carry out effective social policies. Because this melodramatic vision is damaging, it deserves critical examination. That is the task of this book.

My goal is to explore how we talk about random violence, in order to understand why we come to fear the things we do. Although I hope to call some of what "everyone knows" into question, this book is not intended as simply an exercise in debunking. Rather, I have a larger purpose: to better understand how our society identifies—and then responds to—crime and other social problems. But such understanding requires critically examining what reporters, politicians, academics, and others say about social problems. If their claims distort the nature of a problem, then—no matter how well-intended the distortion—they lay a poor foundation for social policy, and they deserve exposure and critique.

I have chosen to focus on what I call "new crimes"—crimes that came to widespread public attention during the 1980s and 1990s. In some cases, we insist that there is nothing new about a new crime except that people finally have given it a name and are paying attention to it. In other cases, there is the sense that the crime itself is new, a sign that things are getting worse, that the social order is collapsing, falling to some new low. Because we talk about new crimes as though they are emblematic of contemporary society, they offer a useful way to identify and analyze our fears. New crimes must be brought to our attention; we must be taught what they are and why they should be feared. As a result, claims about new crimes are more explicit than our talk about older, more familiar crimes; talk about new crimes tends to take less for granted, spelling out the nature of the problem.

I begin, in chapter 1, by criticizing the common practice of describing contemporary crime problems as acts of random violence. "Random violence" is a frightening term, one that evokes visions of patternless, purposeless chaos, of a society in collapse. It is also a term that ignores virtually everything criminologists know about crime. If characterizing crime as random violence badly distorts the crime problem, why is the term so popular? The answer lies both in its rhetorical power—we fear random violence—and in how talking about random violence circumvents other, potentially awkward issues.

Chapter 2 focuses on the media's role in identifying and promoting new, short-lived crime problems. News reports describing waves of wilding and freeway violence as new forms of criminal activity attracted widespread attention in the late 1980s, but interest in both crimes soon faded. These cases illustrate the power of the press, its ability to define issues of public concern. But they also reveal the limits of that power; media attention cannot, by itself, maintain active public interest in new crimes.

Producing enduring concern about crime problems requires the efforts of others, such as activists, government officials, and experts. Although freeway violence and wilding did not endure as social issues, two other new crimes that emerged at about the same time—hate crimes and stalking—benefited from the sponsorship of those outside the media. Chapter 3 describes how these crimes inspired new laws and became institutionalized as important crime problems.

Chapter 4 turns to contemporary concerns about gangs. Today's gang imagery borrows heavily from mid-1980s depictions of large gangs in Los Angeles that emphasized the conspiratorial features of gangs. Fears of big, conspiratorial gangs soon spread throughout most of the country. I argue that our ideas about social problems draw upon an available repertoire of imagery, and I try to examine how claims about gangs and other new crime problems mobilize these cultural resources.

In chapter 5, the focus shifts from violence to victims. Between roughly 1960 and 1975, several social changes drew public attention to victims and victimization, making it easier to arouse concern for the plight of what I call the "new victims." Today, claims about victims tend to be grounded in a common set of assumptions, a contemporary ideology of victimization. This ideology has become a powerful resource for those seeking to promote new social problems.

Chapter 6 continues the argument, showing how the ideology of victimization has gained acceptance in law, medicine, and other institutional centers of power and influence. The combination of a seemingly incontrovertible ideology and broad institutional support lays the foundation for a victim industry—a set of social arrangements able to identify and label large numbers of victims.

The focus shifts again in chapter 7, this time toward the language of social policy. Here, I examine the practice of "declaring war" on social problems—the war on crime and the various wars on drugs, poverty, cancer, and so on. This war metaphor obviously has broad appeal. Less obvious are the metaphor's serious, undesirable consequences for social policy. This example reveals how melodramatic imagery shapes not only our fears, but also social policies.

Finally, chapter 8 makes explicit some theoretical assumptions that have guided the rest of the analysis. Sociologists have compiled a great many case studies, each examining how a particular social problem rose to public attention. But individual social problems never emerge in isolation. New problems build, in various ways, upon claims about other, already familiar problems, and the final chapter explores these links among social-problem claims.

Taken together, these eight chapters consider how we talk about crime and other social problems, and why so much of what we say distorts in order to disturb. Melodrama provides a framework for many, perhaps most, public debates about social problems. Advocates portray our world in terms of innocent victims beset by evil villains. This is, of course, frightening, and it is meant to be. But this world offers plenty of challenges, enough so that we do not need to make things seem more frightening than they are. Understanding how and why we create our fears may be the first step toward managing them.

CHAPTER I

Random Violence

BEWARE!
There is a new GANG INITIATION!!

This new initiation of *murder* is brought about by Gang
Members driving around at night with their car lights off.
When you flash your car lights to signal them that their lights
are out, the Gang Members take it literally as "LIGHTS OUT,"
so they follow you to your destination and kill you! That's
their initiation.

Two families have already fallen victim to this initiation
ritual. Be aware and inform your families and friends.

DO NOT FLASH YOUR CAR *LIGHTS FOR
ANYONE!!*

flyer circulated in Chicago, 1993

Tales of gang members driving around, planning to kill whoever flashed
headlights at them, spread from coast to coast during the fall of 1993
(Brunvand 1995; *FOAF Tale News* 1993b, 1993c). Concerned citizens
passed along the story via photocopies, faxes, and, of course, word of
mouth. Employers warned their employees, law-enforcement agencies
alerted one another, and the press cautioned the public. It seemed a
plausible story: everybody knew that there were gang members out
there; the notion that gang "initiation rites" required members to commit terrible crimes was well ingrained; and cars and guns seemed easy

to come by. *It could happen*, people told themselves. *That's just the kind of thing gangs do.*

The previous year's gang-initiation story had been about ankle grabbers at shopping malls (Brunvand 1993; *FOAF Tale News* 1993a). It involved gang members who crawled beneath parked vehicles, waiting for the drivers to return. When a driver paused to open the car door, the gang member would reach out and grab the victim's ankles. There were different versions of what happened next: in one, when the victim reached down to pry the assailant's hands loose, the gang member chopped off a finger as a souvenir; in others, the gang member slashed the victim's Achilles tendon, dropping the victim to the ground—the first step in a robbery, rape, or murder. People believed the ankle-grabbing story, in spite of its improbable elements (e.g., gang members positioning themselves for criminal attacks by crawling under cars, overpowering victims by grabbing their ankles, easily slicing through the tough Achilles tendon, etc.). After all, it was just the kind of thing gang members do.

There is no evidence that either gang-initiation tale was true. Neither seems especially plausible, yet both were widely believed. What explains this credulity? Concern about random, senseless violence has become a central theme in contemporary culture. In addition to gang initiation rites, we worry about serial murders, carjackings, freeway shootings, sexual predators, wilding, hate crimes, kids with guns, stalking, drive-by shootings, copycat criminals, workplace violence, shootings in schools, and other unpredictable threats. Why shouldn't we also worry about ankle-grabbing attacks and lights-out killings?

The notion that our society is plagued by random violence has surprisingly broad appeal. Consider two recent quotations invoking the concept:

> Our greatest fear is of violence from a nameless, faceless stranger. . . . Citizens of all races who are fearful of random violence have good reason for their concern. Storekeepers, utility workers, police officers, and ordinary citizens out for a carton of milk or a family dinner are all increasingly at risk.

We are terrified by the prospect of innocent people being gunned
down at random, without warning and almost without motive, by
youngsters who afterward show us the blank, unremorseful faces
of seemingly feral, presocial beings.

The first quotation is from the liberal attorney Adam Walinsky (1995:
44, 47), the second from the conservative political scientist James
Q. Wilson (1994:26). Although they bring different ideological assumptions to social analysis, and although they recommend different
sorts of solutions for society's problems, both Walinsky and Wilson define random violence as a major social crisis.

Similar warnings abound. The Federal Bureau of Investigation (1994:
237) warns: "Every American now has a realistic chance of murder victimization in view of the random nature the crime has assumed." Senator Daniel Patrick Moynihan (1993:27) charges: "Violent killings, often
random, go on unabated. Peaks continue to attract some notice. But
these are peaks above 'average' levels that thirty years ago would have
been thought epidemic." The criminologist Jerome H. Skolnick (1994:
34–35) notes the intense media coverage given a few violent crimes:

> The message seemed to be that random violence is everywhere
> and you are no longer safe—not in your suburban home, commuter
> train, or automobile—and the police and the courts cannot or will
> not help you. . . . It is random violent crime, like a shooting in a
> fast-food restaurant, that is driving fear.

A sociologist conducting focus groups of women talking about crime
finds that they describe "predatory, extremely violent, criminals who attack at random" (Madriz 1997:112). A reader writes to *Time* magazine
about "the latest episode in the drama of random violence that airs
almost every day in America," calling it a "spiraling epidemic" (Gerol
1994). And a commentator for *U.S. News & World Report* reacts to President Clinton's suggestion that schools begin the day with a moment of
silence:

> Silence is a small, fragile thing. It cannot cure teen pregnancy or
> stop random violence. It cannot banish gangs or drugs. It cannot

rebuild families or restore faith. But it can, at times, replenish the spirit. (Roberts 1994)

In short, references to random violence have become commonplace, indicating a widespread sense that random violence is a significant problem.

In part, this concern with random violence seems grounded in a general sense that crime is both out of control and on the rise. But this generalized sense of dread is heightened by specific fears, fostered by what sociologists call "moral panics"—exaggerated, heavily publicized reports of sudden increases in particular sorts of criminal violence, such as the stories that gangs had begun holding lights-out initiations.[1] And, unlike the lights-out story, which was not true, there is at least some basis for many of the claims that bring new crime problems into the spotlight of public attention.

Consider, for example, the focus on freeway shootings in Los Angeles in the summer of 1987 (Best 1991). The story began when reporters juxtaposed stories of two shootings on L.A. freeways during the same June weekend. When a third shooting occurred a few weeks later, the press declared that they had spotted a trend, and, for three weeks in late July and early August, news stories about L.A.'s "road warriors" riding "hair-trigger highways" attracted national attention. These reports emphasized the randomness of freeway violence: anyone in a vehicle could become the target of an unprovoked attack. However, it soon became obvious that freeway violence was not spreading across the country or increasing in southern California; it was not even all that common in L.A. There simply weren't enough serious freeway shootings to justify continued media coverage, and the moral panic faded almost as quickly as it arose.

Concern over freeway violence was an intense but brief episode. In contrast, other crime problems prove to have greater staying power once they gain our attention. Serial murder, for example, achieved high visibility in the early 1980s (Jenkins 1994). Whereas the press had always viewed reports of multiple murders as good news stories, it traditionally treated such killings as unrelated, aberrant episodes. However, after several notorious cases emerged in the late 1970s and early 1980s, people began to view serial murder as a distinct type of crime, and there were claims about an epidemic of serial murders. One sensational book on the topic began with the words "America is caught up in the midst of what one expert calls 'an epidemic of homicidal mania,' plagued by ruthless predators—lately dubbed serial murderers or 'recreational killers'—who stalk their human prey at random, often for the sheer joy of killing" (Newton 1992:1), while the feminist Jane Caputi (1987:2, 3) characterized serial sexual murder as "sexually political murder, . . . functional phallic terrorism," and "male torturing and killing of women at random." Interest in the topic remains high: dozens of nonfiction books approach the topic from various angles, ranging from popular accounts to academic studies from disciplines as diverse as history, criminology, anthropology, psychiatry, and women's studies; and the diabolical serial murderer, striking at random, is a standard pop-culture icon in novels and movies.

Sociologists usually approach these topics through case studies of particular moral panics, examining the rise and fall of concern about lights-out gang initiations or freeway shootings or serial murders.[2] This book adopts another approach. I want to argue that such recent episodes of intense concern are part of the broader, more general, contemporary concern with random violence. As the examples concerning lights-out initiations, freeway violence, and serial murders suggest, claims about specific moral panics routinely invoke the notion of randomness. Although there are obvious differences among these moral panics (most notably, no killing was ever linked to a lights-out initiation, and there were only a handful of shooting deaths on L.A. freeways in 1987; but there have been hundreds of well-documented killings by serial murderers), these differences are less significant than the general sense that contemporary society is plagued by random violence.

A review of recent press coverage provides evidence of growing concern about random violence. Figure 1 shows the number of articles

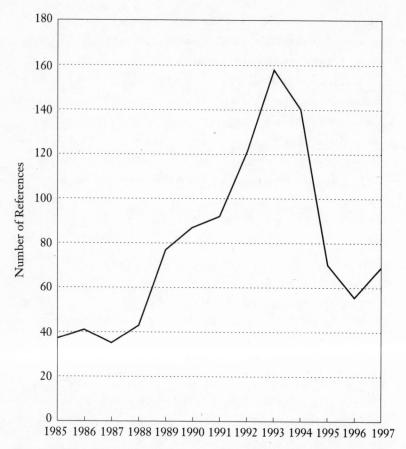

Fig. 1. References to "random violence" in major newspapers and newsmagazines, 1985–1997. SOURCE: NEXIS database for *Newsweek, Time, U.S. News & World Report, Chicago Tribune, Los Angeles Times, New York Times, Washington Post.*

using the expression "random violence" that appeared in seven major newsmagazines and newspapers: *Time, Newsweek, U.S. News & World Report,* the *Chicago Tribune,* the *Los Angeles Times,* the *New York Times,* and the *Washington Post,* from 1985 to 1997.[3] Use of the term rose slightly during the 1980s, then increased markedly after 1989, peaking in 1993. This increased usage corresponds to the rise of several moral panics about new crimes during the late 1980s and early 1990s, including free-way violence (1987), wilding (1989), stalking (beginning around 1990), kids and guns (1991), carjacking and ankle grabbing (both 1992), lights-out gang initiations (1993), and sexual predators (1994), to say nothing of other concerns—such as serial murder (1984–) and drive-by shootings (1985–)—that maintained high levels of visibility. There has been a general concern with random violence, and it is that general concern that is the subject of this book.

THE NATURE OF RANDOM VIOLENCE

Considering our readiness to talk and worry about random violence, we give surprisingly little thought to what the term implies. Warnings about the threat of random violence rarely define the term; instead, they illustrate the problem's nature with typifying examples.[4] These examples can be highly melodramatic: there is an "ideal victim"—usually a respectable person engaged in some innocent activity—who suffers a sudden, unexpected, unprovoked, violent attack by an assailant with no connection to the victim, no good reason to hurt this person in this way. Often the particular example chosen to illustrate the problem is especially horrifying. Consider the first paragraph in a *Newsweek* story on carjackings:

> Pamela Basu had no reason to believe she was in danger. The 34-year-old research chemist was driving her daughter, Sarina, to pre-school on a warm morning last September when two young men approached her gold BMW at a stop sign one block from her suburban Maryland home. They forced her from the car and sped away, but Basu's left arm became ensnared in the harness strap of her seat belt. She was dragged for nearly two miles as her assailants swerved into a barbed-wire fence in an apparent attempt to dislodge her. Before finally ridding themselves of the fatally injured woman, they stopped to toss her 22-month-old daughter from the car. She was found, miraculously unhurt, still strapped in her car seat. (Turque 1992)

This grotesque story offers high melodrama—an upper-middle-class mother attacked and murdered, and her young child endangered, by callous strangers.[5] It justifies *Newsweek*'s title for the piece: "A New Terror on the Road: Carjacking Puts Fear in the Driver's Seat." The example of Pamela Basu suggests that everyone is in danger, that carjacking is random violence; as *Newsweek* warned: "Cars have been commandeered just about anyplace motorists congregate. . . . Routine errands have become a tense exercise in some communities."

Reports of terrible crimes committed by strangers are disturbing, but they do not justify broad generalizations about violence being random. The term "random violence" demands closer inspection. When statisticians speak of randomness, they refer to independent events that occur by chance, in no identifiable pattern. Imagine a set of numbered balls used in a lottery drawing. The balls are stirred into an unpredictable arrangement, then five are drawn. In a random drawing, each ball has an equal chance of being drawn, as does each combination of balls. That is, the number-one ball's chance of being selected is equal to the number-two ball's, and so on, and the combination one-two-three-four-five is just as likely to occur as one-two-three-four-six or any other possible combination. Such is the nature of randomness.

What, then, do we mean by random violence? The term has several implications. Imagine a society within which some number of violent incidents occurs, each incident involving an attacker and a victim. If this violence is truly random, then not only is each individual in that society at risk of being attacked, but all individuals run *equal* risks of victimization, and every individual also is a potential attacker, and everyone is equally likely to attack someone else. Immediately, we recognize that this sort of chaos is not what most people mean when they speak of random violence. Although many claims about random violence imply that everyone is a potential victim, they do not assume that everyone is a potential attacker. Rather, they imagine that attackers are somehow different from their victims, that they are gang members, or psychopaths, or at least males.[6] When most people speak of random violence, they imagine a world in which the general population of potential victims shares the risk of being attacked by these likely attackers. Depending on the crime, the population of victims may be all women (vulnerable to sexual assault), all children (molestation), all gays (homophobic attacks), all drivers (carjacking and freeway violence), and so on. In this sense, we imagine that violence is *patternless:* all potential victims share the risks, so that victimization can happen to anyone: "The list of homicide victims is endless. . . . Grandmothers and college students, prowling street kids and small babies in their walkers, neighbors chatting on city streets, young mothers getting ready for work" (Prothrow-Stith 1991).

What motivates these random attacks? We may acknowledge that violence can be deliberate and purposeful—what criminologists call "instrumental"—as when a bank robber steals money. But other violence seems pointless, meaningless: the bystander shot in a drive-by; the rape victim selected apparently by chance; and so on. This pointlessness is implied when we talk about random violence: gang members are killing motorists who blink their headlights. Why? Because that's what the gang initiation rite requires. Because it's just the kind of thing gang members do—or might do. The notion of random violence, then, refers to the risk that anyone might be attacked for no good reason. This is possible because the attacks are *pointless*, the victims chosen at random. Again, in a world of random violence, no one is safe.

In addition to patternlessness and pointlessness, there is a third theme that runs through claims about random violence: *deterioration.* Warnings about random violence imply that things are getting worse, that there are ever more violent incidents, that respectable citizens run greater risks of victimization than in the past. There are competing explanations for this deterioration: conservatives tend to blame a deteriorating culture (e.g., "the rising tide of immorality"), while liberals usually point to deterioration in the social structure (e.g., "the growing gap between rich and poor"). But, regardless of which causal explanations they prefer, when people worry about random violence, they assume that things are worse today than they were yesterday, and they fear that things will be even worse tomorrow.

In short, when we use the expression "random violence," we characterize the problem in particular terms: violence is patternless (it can happen to anyone); it is pointless (it happens for no reason at all); and it is becoming increasingly common. This is, of course, a very frightening combination. A society that cannot control the growth of patternless, pointless violence seems on the verge of chaos, anarchy, collapse.

Those who speak of random violence rarely examine these three assumptions. For the most part, they assume—and their listeners take it for granted—that patternless, pointless violence is on the rise. However, even a cursory examination of the most basic, familiar criminological evidence calls all three assumptions into question: most violence is not patternless; nor is it pointless; nor is it increasing in the uncontrolled manner we imagine.

PATTERNLESSNESS

We often have a difficult time thinking about patterns in social behavior. I am reminded of this difficulty at the end of each semester, when my students turn in term papers about such social problems as child abuse, rape, incest, and other forms of victimization. Almost every paper features a passage along these lines:

> What sorts of people suffer this victimization? All sorts. The victims are rich and poor, male and female, black and white, of every age.

These papers always make me feel that I've failed: after spending a semester trying to teach my students to recognize and understand the patterns in social problems, I find their papers cheerfully announcing that there are no patterns to be found.

Yet, in spite of my students' eagerness to deny it, the patterns are there. And, if randomness is the absence of a pattern, then violence isn't random. There are thousands of social-scientific studies, enough to fill a small library, proving that violence is patterned.

Consider one example: homicide in the contemporary United States.[7] According to FBI statistics, the U.S. homicide rate in 1994 was 9.0 per 100,000 population. That is, for every 100,000 Americans, there were nine homicides. But not everyone runs the same risk of being a homicide victim; in fact, the risk of victimization—the homicide rate—varies wildly depending on one's age, sex, and race. Consider the pattern among white males in 1990 (shown in fig. 2): during the first fifteen years of life, rates of victimization are low (2.7 or less per 100,000); the figure rises to 12.5 for white males aged fifteen to nineteen, peaks at 18.1 for those twenty to twenty-four, then gradually declines until it reaches about 4.0 for the oldest white males. In other words, the chances of a white male being killed in a homicide are relatively low during childhood, are highest during adolescence and early adulthood, and then decline in middle and old age. This seems reasonable. Few small children become homicide victims: children spend most of their lives under the protection of adults; their greatest risk of homicide is at the hands of an abusive adult caretaker. But adolescents and young adults spend much less time under older adults' supervision, and they take more risks: they experiment with sex and alcohol and illicit drugs; they get into more fights, drive more recklessly, and commit more crimes than older adults; and this independence is more likely to get them killed. As adults mature, they tend to settle down—get married, hold steady jobs, spend more time at home and less on the town—and their risk of becoming a homicide victim falls.

The same general pattern emerges when we add nonwhite males and white and nonwhite females to the graph (see fig. 3; note that, although the graph's vertical scale has changed, the line drawn for white males runs through exactly the same points as in fig. 2): for each group, the risk of being a homicide victim is low in childhood, reaches a peak in adolescence and young adulthood, and then declines with age. However, there are striking differences in victimization rates among the four

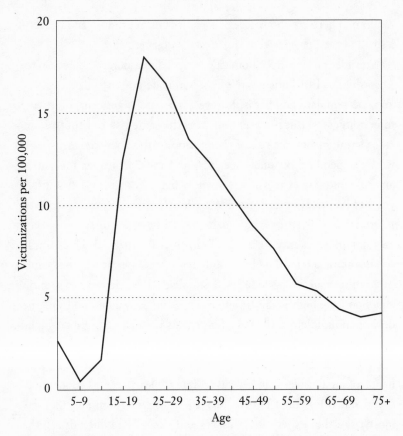

Fig. 2. Homicide victimization rate for white males by age, 1990. SOURCE: MacKellar and Yanagishita 1995.

groups. White females have the lowest rates of victimization: through age nine, white males and females run essentially the same risks; but for whites aged ten and older, females are victimized far less often than males. For instance, the peak age of victimization is twenty to twenty-four for both white males and white females, but the victimization rate for white males is 18.1, about four times greater than the rate of 4.5 for white females.

If white females consistently have the lowest homicide victimization rates, nonwhite males have the highest.[8] In every age category, the

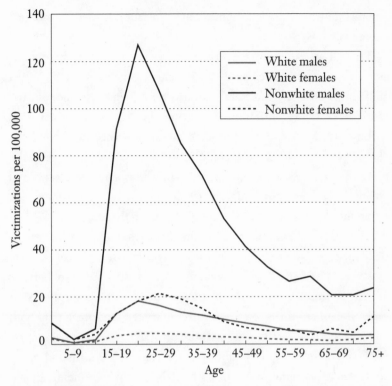

Fig. 3. Homicide victimization rates by age, race, and sex, 1990. SOURCE: MacKellar and Yanagishita 1995.

homicide rate for nonwhite males is three to seven times higher than it is for white males. Again, the age of peak victimization is twenty to twenty-four, but the rate for nonwhite males is 126.8—seven times greater than the rate for white males, and twenty-eight times greater than the rate for white females.

The pattern continues when we look at nonwhite females. Like their white counterparts, nonwhite males and females share similar rates of victimization through age nine; thereafter, females have consistently lower rates of victimization than males. At the same time, nonwhite females run higher risks of victimization—two to five times higher, depending on the age group—than do white females. In most age groups, a nonwhite female's risk of homicide victimization is roughly that of a white male.

Though we can say that everyone runs some risk of being a homicide victim—that homicides kill young and old, male and female, black and white—that broad generalization is fundamentally dishonest, because the risk of victimization varies so markedly. If we were actuaries, writing policies for homicide victimization insurance, we would not charge everyone the same premiums. Rather, we would charge males more than females, nonwhites more than whites, and adolescents and young adults more than children or older adults. To speak of homicide as random violence ignores the clear patterns in these deaths.

This extended example concerns homicide victimization, but essentially the same patterns appear when we examine other sorts of criminal violence. Whether we look at victimization rates for rape, robbery, or assault, or whether we look at homicide offenders, rapists, robbers, or other violent criminals, the basic patterns are the same: males are both more likely to be victimized (with the obvious exception of sexual assault) and more likely to commit violent offenses; adolescents and young adults have the highest rates of both victimization and offending; and nonwhites are more likely to be both victims and offenders than whites (Maguire and Pastore 1996; Snyder and Sickmund 1995; Zawitz et al. 1993). If random violence refers to risks spread evenly among society's members, then contemporary criminal violence is patterned, not random.[9]

POINTLESSNESS

In October 1994, Susan Smith attracted national attention when she claimed that a carjacker had forced her from her Mazda at gunpoint and then driven away, with her three-year-old and fourteen-month-old sons still strapped in the car. More than a week later, the nationwide hunt for the kidnapper and the two boys ended when Smith confessed to investigators that she had deliberately driven the car into a lake and left her sons to drown. Commentators made much of Smith's claim that the carjacker was a black male; they charged that white racism led people to accept Smith's story. But none of these commentators questioned the readiness of the press and the public to believe a story about a carjacker abducting two little boys and stealing a four-year-old compact car from a small town in South Carolina. Why would a carjacker do that? That's just the kind of thing they do.

The fear of random violence means we no longer expect violence to be purposeful. When we hear about Pamela Basu dragged to her death by carjackers, or an innocent passerby shot in a drive-by, or a teenager killed over a pair of gym shoes, we say the violence is pointless, that it lacks any reasonable motivation. No one should die in a fight over gym shoes. When such tragedies occur—and they do—the very pointlessness of the deaths makes them seem even more tragic (O'Neal 1997).

Precisely because they are horrific, these cases become the subjects of extensive media coverage, coverage that transforms them from terrible tragedies—remarkable *incidents*—into typical examples—or *instances*—of carjacking, drive-bys, or the larger problem of random violence. These horror stories make powerful examples precisely because they make no sense: "Random violence provides no such mark of intelligibility and moves with a heightened ambiguity. As explanations contest one another, the status of random crime increases to the level of general societal threat" (Acland 1995:49). Because horror stories capture moments of seemingly random violence, they exemplify what the media claim is an epidemic of random violence bedeviling the larger society. Some people die in terrible, apparently pointless ways. If, instead of viewing those deaths as extraordinary tragedies, we turn them into typifying examples, then we've given shape to the larger problem of random violence.

Whether violence makes sense, of course, depends upon who is making the evaluation. People who commit violent acts have their reasons.[10]

When asked, they may say they attacked their victims because they were angry or because they wanted to maintain their reputation for toughness or because they wanted to intimidate the victim into compliance. Of course, we usually reject the reasons offenders give; we say they are not good reasons, not valid or sensible, that they are senseless from the larger society's perspective. Thus, claims about senseless violence discount offenders' explanations as irrelevant.

There are at least two problems with this line of reasoning. The first is one of perspective. We—the larger society—reject the notion that there is ever a good reason for a drive-by shooting or a lethal fight over gym shoes. This makes violence pointless—but pointless by definition. The logic is circular: violence is pointless because violence is pointless. But from a different perspective, that of the participants in the shootings and fights, the violence may seem sensible—a means of proving oneself or dominating others or getting revenge and so on.

Consider again the very high homicide death rates for young black males in the late 1980s and early 1990s. Criminologists offer a historical account for what happened during that period (Blumstein 1995; Brownstein 1996). When the inner-city trade in crack took off in the mid-1980s, the potentially high profits from dealing drugs created an intense, violent competition for control over the crack marketplace, and competitors spent a portion of their profits to arm themselves, buying more—and more powerful—guns. Gangs sometimes became participants in this struggle. In addition, a growing proportion of youths who were not involved in gangs or the drug trade became concerned for their safety, and they began carrying weapons to protect themselves (Sheley and Wright 1995). Increasingly, minor disputes involved youths who were armed, and who sometimes used their weapons. (According to this explanation, homicide rates began to fall in the mid-1990s as control over the crack market consolidated, reducing the violent competition to control the drug trade.) The net result of these processes was a rising youth homicide rate, particularly in black ghettos. From the view of the larger society, each killing was a pointless tragedy, but for the participants, money, power, and prestige often were at stake.

Of course, it is always possible to identify cases where no one claims that the violence made sense—for example, the uninvolved bystander accidentally killed by a stray bullet fired during a drive-by. There are true, terrible reports of such events. The question is what we should make of these stories. This is the second problem with assertions of pointlessness: when we use, say, the death of an innocent bystander to typify the problem of contemporary violence, we stack the deck. We ignore the killings that occur between rival gangs, between competing drug dealers, between people who have become so angry or ashamed or jealous or frightened of each other that violence escalates. There is a paradox: although we consider homicide to be especially terrible, the most serious crime, most homicides are products of mundane motives; they aren't all that newsworthy and they don't get that much press coverage (Luckenbill 1977). In contrast, the press is drawn to the most bizarre, the most frightening, the most pointless killings. Reporters rush to tell these stories, but then convert them into representative instances of contemporary violence. To call violence pointless is to ignore the situations in which it emerges, and the meanings most violence has for the perpetrators and, often, their victims.

DETERIORATION

Warnings about random violence usually imply not only that things are bad, but that they are getting steadily worse. This is one of the great taken-for-granted assumptions about modern life: society is becoming ever more violent. We describe violence in terms of epidemics and plagues—imagery that conveys a sense of devastation, decline, and deterioration.

In spite of the general readiness to accept these claims about impending societal collapse, the evidence of deterioration is surprisingly

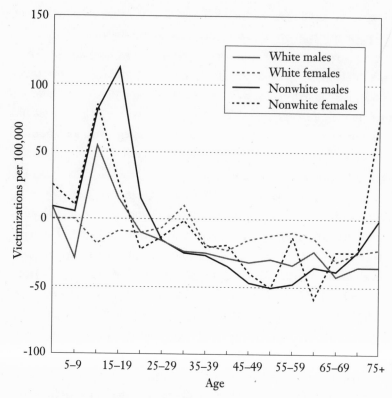

Fig. 4. Percentage change in homicide victimization rates by age, race, and sex, 1980–1990. SOURCE: MacKellar and Yanagishita 1995.

thin and uneven. Again, we can begin by using homicide rates as an index of violence. Figure 4 shows how homicide victimization rates changed between 1980 and 1990. The overall homicide rate calculated by the FBI actually fell during this decade, from 10.2 to 9.4 per 100,000. But this modest decline masks the interesting patterns that emerge when we separate homicide victimization rates by race, sex, and age. In general, young people's homicide victimization rates rose during the 1980s, while the victimization of older adults fell. The groups that showed the largest increases were all young and nonwhite: females aged ten to fourteen (up 86 percent), and males aged ten to fourteen (up 81 percent) and fifteen to nineteen (up 112 percent). And, of these, the greatest increase—both as a percentage and in the number of homicides—involved nonwhite males aged fifteen to nineteen, whose victimization rate jumped from 43.3 per 100,000 (four times the national average) to 92.0 (*nine* times the national average). Again, it is a mistake to describe these recent developments as either random or representing general societal collapse. Most adults' risk of becoming a homicide victim dropped during the 1980s. For nonwhite adults, this decline reflected a longer trend in which homicide rates peaked during the early 1970s. And, although the risks for many children rose during the 1980s, it is important to remember that children's homicide rates are low, so that relatively small increases in the numbers of homicides can produce substantial increases in the homicide rate. The real story of homicide in the 1980s concerns nonwhite males aged fifteen to nineteen and twenty to twenty-four; these groups had marked increases in already high homicide rates. For these young, nonwhite males, deadly violence was a growing threat—a threat linked to ghetto poverty, gangs, the trade in drugs (particularly crack), and the growing availability of guns.

In other words, recent changes in homicide rates do not tell a simple story of random, society-wide deterioration. The pattern is more complicated: declining risks for most adults; higher risks for many children; and terrible increases among nonwhite adolescents and young adults. However, the story shifts if we take a longer view: if we use 1960 as a baseline, homicide rates nearly doubled, from 5.1 per 100,000 to 9.4 in 1990 (see fig. 5). Whites of both sexes and all age groups faced increased risks of homicide between 1960 and 1990, but even during this longer time period, risks declined for nonwhite males over thirty-five and nonwhite females over twenty-five. Spotting patterns in changing risks is complicated; the change in homicide victimization rates depends upon which group is examined over which period, but the data do not reveal the steady, universal increases in homicide risks implied in warnings about random violence and societal deterioration.

There are no readily available data that will allow us to calculate

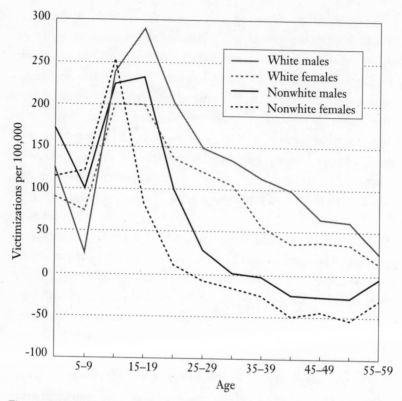

Fig. 5. Percentage change in homicide victimization rates by age, race, and sex, 1960–1990. SOURCE: MacKellar and Yanagishita 1995.

changes in victimization rates by sex, race, and age for other violent crimes. We do have two sets of figures about overall rates of violence, but they contradict each other. The crime rates calculated by the FBI reveal marked increases in the rates of rape, robbery, and aggravated assault; rates for all three crimes more than quadrupled between 1960 and 1990 (Maguire and Pastore 1996). These FBI data—based on crimes reported to the police—are consistent with claims of deterioration, and warnings about random violence often cite rising crime rates. However, because many victims do not report crimes to the police, the FBI's crime rates underestimate the true incidence of crime. Since 1973, the federal

Bureau of Justice Statistics has sought to correct this underestimate by conducting national surveys to measure victimization. The National Crime Victimization Survey (NCVS) uses respondents' reports of victimization to calculate victimization rates. These NCVS data do not confirm the increases shown in the FBI's crime rates; rather, between 1973 and 1992, victimization rates for rape, robbery, and aggravated assault all showed modest declines (Zawitz et al. 1993).

In sum, the commonplace assumption that violence is escalating out of control can be challenged. Although violent-crime rates have risen considerably since 1960, part of this increase may be due to improved reporting. If more victims report crimes, or if police keep more complete records of the crimes reported, the crime rate will rise, even if the actual incidence of crime goes unchanged. We know that reporting rates have risen and police record keeping has improved, while rates of reported victimization have declined somewhat. This suggests that claims about dramatic increases in the overall level of violence are at least exaggerated. Moreover, the changes in homicide victimization (shown in figs. 4 and 5) serve as a reminder that different subgroups within the population may experience very different changes in the level of violence.

Warnings about rising random violence rarely incorporate such subtleties. More often, they typify the problem with a horrific example, add a dramatic statistic or two, and mix them with the taken-for-granted notion that violence is on the rise throughout society. The resulting claim—"the random distribution of risk by a society that is fundamentally out of control" (Furedi 1977:58)—seems so obvious that it needs no close examination. However, the evidence reveals that claims of societywide deterioration are exaggerated and overly simplistic.

THE APPEAL OF RANDOM VIOLENCE

Although random violence has become a central image in contemporary discussions of crime, the notion of randomness distorts what we know about criminal violence. It exaggerates the degree to which violence is patternless, pointless, and increasing. It is imagery calculated to promote fear rather than understanding.

Then why is this melodramatic imagery so popular? The answer, of course, is that melodrama is powerful. The idea of random violence is unsettling, disturbing, frightening; it challenges our most basic assumptions about social order. If violence is patternless and pointless, then anyone—women as well as men, children as well as adults, the middle class as well as the poor—might become a victim. If violence is increasing, then everyone is in growing danger:

> Drive-by shootings are particularly distressing . . . because it may appear that the target was chosen at random and that innocent bystanders may be hit. Any person's concern about his vulnerability is heightened. . . . When there is a sense that more murders are being committed against strangers, any person can conceive of himself as a target. (Blumstein 1995:23)

Rhetoric about random violence implies that everyone has a vested interest in supporting efforts to stamp out the problem. If violence is random, then everyone is at risk, and anyone who is at risk—that is, everyone—has reason to be concerned and to demand action. Typifying a problem with frightening examples, and then democratizing the risk—defining the threat as universal—is a recipe for mobilizing maximum social concern (Fumento 1990).

This widespread concern helps explain why warnings about random violence transcend the obvious ideological divisions within contemporary society. These warnings come from feminists and fundamentalists, liberal Democrats and conservative Republicans. The frightening imagery of random violence can be tailored to fit almost any ideological agenda. But there is another reason why rhetoric about random violence is so popular. By implying that pointless violence is a general, patternless threat to society as a whole, warnings about random violence gloss over the potentially awkward or embarrassing issues of class and race. As we have already noted, there are dramatic racial differences in violence: in particular, African-Americans are far more likely to both commit violent offenses and be victimized by violence than are whites. These racial differences, of course, reflect class differences: rates of violence are highest among the poor, and blacks constitute a disproportionate percentage of the poor.[11] Any discussion of patterns in violence must confront class and race—two of the most awkward topics in American political discourse.

Confronting race and class is awkward for both liberals and conservatives. Liberals fear they will have difficulty arousing sympathy for the poor and minorities, particularly if they propose publicly funded programs to benefit those groups. Opponents of these measures may argue that Middle America has no stake in solving the problems of the poor, saying, in effect, "That's not our problem" or "We've already done enough to help the poor, and we shouldn't have to do more." It is easier to finesse such potential opposition and arouse widespread concern by implying that a problem affects (and the programs to solve it will benefit) everyone. Because references to random violence imply that everyone is at risk, they can help mobilize such general concern. Depicting violence as random, and therefore patternless, also lets liberals circumvent potentially awkward questions about the patterns of violence. In particular, liberals are reluctant to call attention to evidence that blacks commit violent offenses at higher rates than whites. The subject of black criminality may invite all sorts of critiques, ranging from arguments that race somehow biologically fosters criminality to various critiques of black culture and institutions. Moreover, liberals fear both that minority criminality can be used as evidence that social programs don't work, and that focusing on the link between ethnicity and violence will result in a form of "blaming the victim." It is not that liberals lack rejoinders to these arguments—they can respond that social structure, particularly class and racial inequality, should be blamed for crime— but rather that the issue of race is volatile, and it seems easier to ignore it rather than confront it. Talking about essentially patternless random violence offers liberals a way to avoid raising this troublesome subject.

Warnings about random violence serve parallel purposes in conservatives' discussions of crime. For conservatives, it is class, rather than race, that seems awkward to address. Poor people are more likely to both commit violent crimes and be victimized by violence, but acknowledging this seems to invite arguments that more should be done to help the poor by improving job opportunities, increasing social services, and the like. (In an earlier era, conservatives might have found reassurance in the higher rates of criminality among the poor, which could be taken as a sign of the inherent viciousness of the lower orders, but such explanations have lately fallen out of favor.) Most contemporary conservative interpretations locate the causes of criminal violence in culture (Bennett et al. 1996). In this view, violence is part of a web of interlocking social problems, including broken families, teenage sexuality, premarital pregnancy, welfare dependency, substance abuse, delinquency and criminality, and gangs, all caused by and reflecting a damaged or dysfunctional culture. A potentially embarrassing counter to this argument, of course, is that all of these problems are associated with poverty, with social class: might not these "cultural" problems have their roots in social structure? This is where references to random violence offer conservatives a convenient distraction. Random violence is patternless, and claims about patternless random violence gloss over the links between class and crime. Similarly, random violence is pointless, senseless. And pointless crime need not be understood as an act of frustration, rebellion, or some other more or less comprehensible reaction to the barriers of class. Rather, random violence, in its pointlessness, is just further evidence of the criminals' cultural pathology. In this view, random violence is a symptom of a sick culture, and talking about random violence helps conservatives keep the focus on culture, and play to the fears of the middle class, by invoking the sense that no one is safe from the likes of Willie Horton and other predatory criminals.

The political usefulness of the term "random violence" may explain why depictions of crime as random rose during the 1980s. After Ronald

Reagan became president, debates over social issues became increasingly bitter; there were fewer efforts to build bipartisan alliances to confront the problems of race and class. Increasingly, race and class became viewed as political embarrassments, topics best ignored whenever possible. Thus, advocates of virtually every political position found it easy to denounce violence—as long as it could be divorced from its social context.

In sum, there are two principal advantages to describing the crime problem in terms of random violence. First, the phrase "random violence" evokes rhetorically powerful imagery: it demands our attention and concern, because it questions the stability of the social order and makes us fear for our own safety, and for the safety of everyone around us. Second, defining the crime problem as one of ever-increasing, patternless, pointless—that is, random—violence eliminates the need to explain the patterns in crime. Focusing attention on random violence allows ideologues to skip over embarrassing or awkward issues: liberals can avoid talking about race and culture, just as conservatives can avoid confronting issues of class and social structure.

It is easy to see the appeal of framing issues in terms of random violence, but it is less clear that this is an effective way to think about crime problems. Defining violence as patternless not only discourages us from searching for and identifying patterns; it keeps us from devising social policies to address those patterns. Defining violence as pointless eliminates any need to consider and address the motivations for violence. Assuming that violence is increasing causes us to ignore patterns in change, and thereby fail to notice which policies are working. Denouncing random violence may work as crowd-pleasing rhetoric, but it does not offer much help in designing effective anticrime policies.

Obviously, there is an element of chance—randomness—in every social encounter. Incalculable contingencies shape whether we fall in love (and with whom), whether specific investments earn a profit, whether our next automobile trip ends in a fatal accident. We cannot identify, let alone control, many of the factors that shape these outcomes. Still, we know that our individual actions can affect the likelihood of different outcomes: by buckling up, obeying the traffic laws, and not drinking and driving, we can reduce our chances of being killed in a car wreck. And social policy can also influence those outcomes: requiring cars to have seat belts and mandating their use significantly reduced death rates from automobile accidents. As individuals—and as a society—we do not simply throw up our hands in the face of "random traffic accidents." Instead of emphasizing the role of randomness, we search for patterns in risk and devise policies based on the patterns we identify.

In much the same way, if we want to understand criminality and violence, we need to think in terms of their patterns, in terms of the motivations and behaviors of offenders and victims. Random violence is a powerful image, so powerful that it threatens to short-circuit constructive thought about the nature of our society's problems.

THE LANGUAGE OF CRIME

The expression "random violence," then, has become a commonplace in talk about contemporary crime, a sort of cliché of pop criminology, not because it accurately summarizes the nature of crime—it decidedly does not—but because it is rhetorically convenient, arousing intense interest in and concern about crime while diverting attention away from awkward questions of race and class. It is, of course, just one term in the contemporary vocabulary for discussing crime. This vocabulary constantly changes: new crimes (e.g., carjacking) appear and come into vogue, while once familiar expressions (e.g., "garroting" [the nineteenth-century equivalent of mugging] or "soiled dove" [a nineteenth-century euphemism for prostitute]) fall out of favor.

The implications of describing violence as random suggest that the turnover in terms used to talk about crime and other social problems reflects more than a faddish attraction to novel language. People invent new words to describe social problems, sometimes quite deliberately, because those words evoke some connotations and avoid others; consider the different implications of "crippled," "handicapped," "disabled," and "differently abled"; of "drunkard" and "alcoholic"; or of "sexual deviate," "homosexual," and "gay." But it is not enough to create a word; some new words are ignored and soon forgotten. Successful terms get picked up, sometimes self-consciously at first, then used by more and more people, until they seem normal rather than novel. The example of "random violence" suggests that some terms may prove attractive to a broad range of users, and that this broad popularity encourages their adoption and widespread use.

The words we choose when we talk about crime and other social problems are consequential. Describing crime in terms of random violence has implications for how we think about crime, about criminals, and about prospective criminal justice policies. It becomes, therefore, important to stop taking our vocabulary of crime for granted. We need to explore the ways in which this language emerges, spreads, evolves, and influences. Discussions of crime usually focus on criminal behavior, on action. This book, however, concentrates on the importance of the words used to depict those acts.

CHAPTER 2

From Incidents to Instances

*The Media Discover Wilding
and Freeway Violence*

Violence and theft—crime's most basic forms—obviously have long histories. Featured in ancient myths and prohibited under most cultures' customs and laws, they are elementary forms of deviant behavior, apparently timeless. Of course, we understand that the definition of crime changes as social arrangements change, that the demise of feudalism or the rise of cities, or the invention and spread of cars and computers, produces new laws, redefining what is criminal. In contemporary American society, social change seems constant, taken for granted—including changes in the nature of crime. We tell one another about new drugs (or old drugs making a new comeback), about new kinds of criminals, about new outrages against decency and order. "Have you heard what gangs"—or kids, or crooks—"are doing now?" we ask each other. We speak of new types of crime: computer crimes and hate crimes and occult crimes. Each new crime has a history, a moment when it is discovered and recognized, and each shifts in its visibility and incidence as social conditions change. Sometimes, news of a single terrible event is enough to define a new crime problem.

WILDING AND FREEWAY VIOLENCE
AS NEW CRIME PROBLEMS

Consider the case of wilding. The brutal assault and gang rape of the "Central Park jogger" on April 19, 1989, had more than enough dramatic elements for a shocking crime story: the victim was both innocent (a jogger in New York's grand Central Park) and privileged (she was twenty-eight, white, and well educated, and worked as an investment banker); her assailants were working- and lower-class, black and Hispanic, teenage males. The New York media were already giving the story plenty of attention when the mention of a single word expanded the story, making the Central Park assault somehow representative of a much larger crime problem. News stories on April 22 reported that some of the arrested youths told police they had been "wilding":

> "It's not a term that we in the police had heard before," [Chief of Detectives Robert Colangelo] said. . . . "They just said, 'We were going wilding.' In my mind at this point, it implies that they were going to go raise hell." (Pitt 1989)

The term transformed the Central Park assault from a newsworthy *incident* into an *instance* of the broader wilding problem. Wilding seized the media's imagination. What had been a local crime story now received coverage on all three network news broadcasts (on April 24), on ABC's *Nightline* (May 16), and in newspapers nationwide (the *Los Angeles Times* called wilding "a chilling new word . . . in the dictionary of fear" [J. Goldman 1989]). Never mind that no one seemed sure whether "wilding" was actually a term from the youths' vernacular or just a product of a misunderstanding (Acland 1995:49; Benedict 1992: 198–201). After conducting interviews "on the streets," one *New York Times* reporter called wilding "a slang term usually pronounced wil'ing that refers to the practice of marauding in bands to terrorize strangers and to swagger and bully" (Kaufman 1989), and the columnist Jimmy Breslin (1989) claimed that "the word has to be 10 years old," but a

Times editor, J. Anthony Lukas (1989), insisted that "street kids" were not familiar with the term: "Some suspect that the accused actually told the police they were after 'the wild thing'—a euphemism for sex—from the rap song by that name." If the assault on the jogger seemed to embody upper-middle-class fears of the criminal underclass, "wilding" was a perfect word to describe the menace of random violence. Wilding now became a subject for media attention in its own right, with critics debating the meaning and significance of wilding. Commentators argued that wilding resembled fraternity gang rapes, lynchings, the My Lai massacre, or socially approved "pillaging" in sports and the stock market. They blamed wilding on television, rap music, and other violent popular culture, on schools that fail to teach values and a juvenile justice system that fails to rehabilitate youths, on a rape-prone society, racial tensions, pornography, and whatever makes adolescents feel "unwanted and unvalued," making them "morally homeless."[1] Reporters identified a few other incidents of wilding, such as "a band of black schoolgirls wielding pins against white women" (Bernstein 1989). Wilding became a widely understood metaphor that could be used to describe partisan political maneuvers, or to encapsulate everything wrong with American culture:

> Wilding includes a vast spectrum of self-centered and self-aggrandizing behavior that harms others. A wilding epidemic tears at the social fabric and threatens to unravel society itself, ultimately reflecting the erosion of the moral order and the withdrawal of feelings and commitments from others to oneself, to "number one." (Derber 1996:6)

Still, although wilding became an enduring metaphor, media coverage of wilding as a crime problem declined almost as abruptly as it began. The *New York Times* carried thirty-three stories in 1989 (the year of the Central Park assault) that referred to wilding as a crime problem, and another twenty-six stories in 1990 (the year the assailants were tried). However, once the Central Park case was no longer in the news, references to wilding fell to a handful per year.[2] Wilding is an example of a new crime that suddenly entered the spotlight of publicity, then almost as quickly faded into the shadows.

Now consider a second example: freeway violence. On June 24, 1987, the *Los Angeles Times* ran a brief story titled "2nd Freeway Shooting Incident Is Investigated"; it noted that there had been two apparently unrelated shootings on L.A. freeways during the previous weekend (Stewart 1987). This story seems to have established a new crime category (freeway shooting) that, in turn, inspired a June 26 column claiming that there had been "four unrelated freeway shootings over the past 10 months" (Sauter 1987a). The columnist—former CBS News president Van Gordon Sauter—later explained that his column reflected "a desire to seize on a trendoid—the journalistic category reflecting something new, potentially interesting and possibly—just possibly—indicative of a trend" (Sauter 1987b). *Times* reporters were now "watching for a trend." An editor assigned a reporter, Lonn Johnston, to write a feature article on the topic. Completed after a few days, the story "was held [i.e., not published] for a couple weeks" (Bill Billiter and Lonn Johnston, telephone interviews with author, 1989).

Journalists have a rule of thumb: the third time something happens, you have a trend. The July 20 *Times* news story—"Traffic Dispute Results in Third Freeway Shooting"—revived the new crime category (Billiter 1987). The next day, Johnston's feature article appeared, amended with a "new top" referring to the latest incident; this piece shifted the focus from news reports about particular incidents to a general analysis of the freeway violence problem ("a new kind of urban warfare") (L. Johnston 1987). The same day, a *Los Angeles Herald Examiner* editorial cartoon showed a motorist shopping for "the ultimate freeway defense vehicle"—a tank.

The new crime was now established. A July 26 story began: "While police searched for suspects in the latest highway shooting . . . " (Kendall 1987); it was the first of four front-page *Times* articles over five days. (The *Herald Examiner* ran front-page freeway-violence stories on twelve of the fourteen days from July 21 to August 3.) As the story received more attention, the freeway-shootings category began showing elasticity: not all reported incidents occurred on freeways, and not all involved shooting. Some reporters began using broader terms to refer to the problem—for example, "traffic-related shootings" or "roadway violence"—and a variety of incidents were presented as instances of the category, including rocks thrown at windshields (*Nightline*, ABC, July 30) and:

> one copycat has moved from the freeways to the busy Southern California skyways. The pilot of a Cessna says he was threatened by the pilot of another plane, who flew close—alongside—and pointed a handgun. (CBS, August 5, 1987)

Press reports described freeway shootings as a series of incidents— a "sudden evolution," "trend," "wave," "spate," "spree," "upsurge," "fad," "rash,"—an "epidemic," "plaguing Southern California," "reaching alarming proportions." At the same time, some reporters acknowledged that it was impossible to document increasing freeway violence. The category had no official standing; no law-enforcement agency kept records on freeway shootings as such, and the press had no way to accurately measure shifts in incidence. Instead, reporters quoted officials to the effect that freeway violence seemed more common, and referred to a running total of incidents, usually beginning with shots fired at a motorcyclist on June 18 (a case not mentioned in any of the early *Times* stories). By mid-August, this list included over forty incidents.[3]

The media anticipated that freeway violence would spread beyond southern California. CBS's Dan Rather wondered: "Is it a local phenomenon, or does it indicate something in the country as a whole, something in society at large?" (CBS, August 5, 1987). Broadcasting from Chicago, ABC's Peter Jennings noted: "There haven't been any incidents here in the Midwest" (ABC, August 6, 1987). But the *Wall Street Journal* argued that the violence was nationwide: "The nation's freeways now resemble something out of the Wild West" (Gonzales

1987). In its August 17 issue, *Time* noted: "Highway officials in Arizona, Washington, Utah, and Northern California reported armed confrontations last week" (Trippett 1987); three months later, a short item reported that freeway violence "appears to have faded on the West Coast but is all the rage in southern Illinois and is spreading to eastern Missouri" (*Time* 1987). However, these isolated reports were apparently insufficient to maintain media interest in freeway violence as a spreading problem.

Although freeway violence soon disappeared from newspapers' front pages and network news broadcasts, it lives on in popular culture and folklore. The notion that freeway violence remains common in Los Angeles crops up occasionally: in a 1988 exploitation movie (*Freeway*); in an aside in a magazine article describing traffic jams in Japan ("this passivity is better than gunning other motorists down, as in Los Angeles" [Fallows 1989:52]); in the 1991 movie *L.A. Story;* or in humor on the Internet ("Southern California Freeway Shooting Schedule: MONDAYS: Small arms only—.30 caliber and under; TUESDAYS: Ladies' shotgun day; . . . " [*Cartalk* 1996]). In 1990 (Carlton 1990) and again in 1996 (A. Goldman 1996), the media reported new waves of violence on L.A.'s freeways; on occasion, they announced similar waves of freeway shootings in other cities—for example, Detroit (*New York Times* 1989).[4]

There are obvious similarities between wilding and freeway violence. Both received intense, albeit short-lived, media attention. In both cases, the media took one or two particular crimes, argued that those incidents represented a new crime problem, named the problem, and began covering the story. Both new crimes quickly became widely familiar, and, almost as quickly, media attention shifted away from both. This trajectory of short-lived media attention demands analysis.

CRIME WAVES

When people talked about wilding and freeway violence, they described them as terrible, intense new crime problems—what we usually call *crime waves.* We view crime waves as sudden increases in criminal activity, increases that demand explanation. Perhaps the rise in criminality reflects changes in the population—say, an influx of immigrants. Or perhaps it reflects changing social arrangements—more children raised in single-parent families, or more adults frustrated by their inability to find work. Whatever the explanation, there is a straightforward assumption that crime has, in fact, increased.

On the other hand, criminologists usually doubt claims about crime waves.[5] Crime waves, they say, are really waves in media attention: they occur because the media, for whatever reason, fix upon some sort of crime, and publicize it. Crimes that might ordinarily receive little notice suddenly become the subject of editorials, feature articles, op-ed pieces, columns, editorial cartoons, talk-show commentary, and late-show monologues—the full treatment used to focus attention on social problems. In this view, crime waves really are just waves of crime news.

Crime waves seem to have been a nineteenth-century invention. For many reasons—including rising literacy, urbanization, faster communication, and, especially, improvements in printing technology—it was in the nineteenth century that newspapers assumed their essentially modern form, emphasizing reports of current—and especially sensational—events. Crime news offered grist for this mill: each new crime had the potential to be covered as a new outrage, perhaps a warning of impending societal collapse.

It is important to realize that most early crime reporting focused on the particulars of the case at hand. For example, the 1836 ax murder of Helen Jewitt, a New York City prostitute, was perhaps the greatest nineteenth-century crime story, if only because it helped define the nature of the penny press (the new, cheaper newspapers aimed at a mass urban audience) (Leonard 1986; Schiller 1981; Tucher 1994). Newspapers across the country carried stories about the Jewitt case; they described the brothel where the crime occurred, presented detailed biographies of Jewitt, speculated about the identities of her clients and the crime itself, and covered the arrest and trial of the man accused. As a gruesome crime with overtones of sex and scandal, Jewitt's murder received the most thorough coverage possible at the time. Yet this coverage remained focused on the particular crime; the press did not generalize about the "threatened prostitute" problem or warn about a wave of random ax murders.

Identifying a crime wave requires something more: generalizing beyond the particulars of the case, characterizing the incident as an instance of some new trend, some larger social problem. When the press links a particular crime, such as the assault on the Central Park jogger, to the larger crime problem of wilding, it adopts a popularized version of the sociological imagination, discovering public issues in private troubles (Mills 1959). This analytic move occasionally appears in nineteenth-century crime coverage: in 1865, for example, Boston newspapers warned about a wave of garroting (muggings in which the assailants often choked their victims into submission) (Adler 1996). But this was the exception; most nineteenth-century crime news—even reporting on the most visible, sensational crimes, such as Jewitt's murder—remained focused on the particulars of the case at hand rather than generalizing to a larger problem.

In contrast, consider how readily today's media link particular cases to larger social problems. The sensational news of O. J. Simpson's arrest quickly inspired competing claims that the Simpson-Goldman murders exemplified the problem of domestic violence, or stalking, or the violence inherent in professional football, or police malfeasance, or the instability of interracial marriages, and so on. We *problematize* events, turning particular criminal acts into examples of types of crime.[6] This sort of problematizing provides the premise for countless talk-show episodes in which the guests on the stage represent some alleged phenomenon (e.g., men who have sex with their baby-sitters, men who have sex with their mothers-in-law, and on and on). Even extraordinarily unusual episodes are interpreted as having larger significance. For example, take the exotic case of Charles Stuart, the successful white Boston suburbanite who, in 1989, murdered his pregnant wife and shot himself while they were in their car, then reported the crime from his car phone, blaming a black assailant. Broadcasters' access to recordings of Stuart's call to the police—coupled with the novelty of a crime being reported by car phone and the callousness of the apparently pointless murder of a pregnant woman—turned the crime, and the Boston police's aggressive search for the black killer, into a national news story. But it was the revelation that Stuart had killed his wife and faked the crime report, and Stuart's suicide once he came under suspicion, that invited problematization. Critics now saw the Stuart case as a glaring example of white racism; the readiness of the police and the press to believe Stuart's report now exemplified the way racism shapes how we think about and respond to crime. Even sociologists problematized the Stuart case; Charles Derber (1996:3, 6) called it an example of "white wilding," and called Stuart an "ultimate wilder." As this example suggests, few criminal acts lack the potential to be defined as instances of some larger crime problem.[7]

In addition to generalizing from particular cases, claims about crime waves imply changing levels—increases—in criminality. We talk about crime waves as though there are fashions in crime: people didn't used to commit this crime (or commit it so often), but now they do. The press treats increasing crime as news, evidence that things are getting worse. Reporting that crime is stable—or even declining—makes a less compelling story. Of course, it is always difficult to assess claims of increasing crime: once people start paying attention to a particular crime, treating it as a more serious matter, victims are more likely to report it, the authorities become more determined to respond to it, official definitions of the offense often become broader, and, inevitably, rates for that crime, as measured by reports to the police, rise. Reports of both rape and family violence since the 1970s display this pattern: both forms of violence have long histories; both traditionally had unknown but doubtless substantial proportions of unreported cases; both became the focus of policy reforms that encouraged victims to report cases, provided improved services for those victims, expanded the definition of the crime, and made it easier to prosecute cases; both became the focus of extensive media campaigns denouncing the offense and sympathizing with the victims; and both showed increased numbers of reported offenses. It is difficult to interpret these increases. Do they indicate—as is sometimes suggested by reformers seeking to keep the spotlight of public attention focused on these offenses—real increases or waves of violence against women? Or might they reflect successful campaigns to make victims more willing to report cases and the authorities more conscientious about processing those reports? If a larger proportion of cases gets reported, the number of reported cases can go up, even as the actual incidence of crime falls. But our readiness to accept claims about crime waves makes it far easier to assert that things are getting worse, that the social order is deteriorating. Arguments that an increase in reported offenses actually represents increased reporting due to more effective social policies are too subtle; they confuse many (who ask how news of higher rape rates could possibly coincide with a decline in the incidence of rape), and they infuriate advocates (who rely on claims of a growing threat to maintain public outrage).

Our two examples—wilding and freeway violence—illustrate media-created crime waves at the end of the twentieth century. Both began with specific crimes—a gang rape in Central Park, a couple of unrelated shootings on L.A. freeways. In both cases, the press argued that these particular crimes were part of a larger pattern—instances, rather than mere incidents. The press named the new crimes, characterized them as crime waves, and, for a few days or weeks, kept attention focused on them.

THE TEMPLATE
FOR SOCIAL-PROBLEMS NEWS

Media reports of crime waves reflect the conventions of contemporary journalism. Reporters and editors expect that news stories about particular crimes will adopt the standard formulas for newswriting—that is, who-what-when-where presented with the story's most important aspects first, followed by increasingly specific items as the story develops. But there are additional conventions that govern the reporting of stories about social problems, a sort of template for social-problems coverage. Specifically, reports about social problems *describe* the nature of the problem, *explain* its causes, and *interpret* its meaning. Press coverage of the 1987 freeway-shootings problem in Los Angeles illustrates how the press applies this template to a new crime problem.

Describing the Problem

Descriptions of early freeway shootings emphasized that the incidents often began with mundane traffic disputes, that they seemed random, without clear motive, irrational. Stories spoke of copycats and "triggermen out for a cruel joke" (NBC, July 29, 1987). The result, reporters suggested, was a wave of freeway violence, with freeways becoming "shooting galleries," "scenes of combat," "war zones," or a "terror zone."

If freeway shootings were random and senseless, then they could be described as lacking any sort of relevant context. For instance, the first network news story about freeway violence (CBS, July 24, 1987) introduced a typifying example to describe the problem. The story began:

ANCHOR DAN RATHER: Southern California authorities are dealing with, literally, murderous rage. As Jerry Bowen reports, it has made driving on the freeways unsafe at any speed. [video: logo of car in crosshairs; labeled "Freeway Shootings"]

RADIO TRAFFIC REPORTER (?): . . . an earlier stall here at the number two lane is gone now, but traffic's not any better . . . [video: aerial view of freeways; labeled "Los Angeles"]

REPORTER JERRY BOWEN: It's always been crazy on the southern California freeways—a real zoo—but these days the animals are armed and dangerous. [video: ground views of freeway traffic]

JIANG NAN: As I was turning on Atlantic Boulevard, and I hear gunshot. At first, I thought it was not a gun, it was my tire pop. The next thing I known I [unclear] blood, so I feel pain. [video: close-up of Nan speaking, lying in a hospital bed]

BOWEN: Nineteen-year-old Jiang Nan was shot by another motorist last month during a race for a freeway exit. [video: shots of Nan in bed from farther away]

Three nights later, Nan reappeared in an ABC story (July 27):

REPORTER KEN KASHUIHARA: Jiang Nan was shot in the arm because, he says, he honked his horn at another driver. [video: Nan walking, bandaged]

NAN: You can't go around people, shooting people because people just honk your horn. You know. That's not right. [video: close-up of Nan speaking, sitting in car's driver's seat; labeled "Jiang Nan—Victim"]

CBS and ABC used Jiang Nan's experience to exemplify the randomness of freeway violence. In contrast, the *Los Angeles Times* story about the same incident offered more information about its context:

> Alhambra Police Detective Jim Varga said Sunday's shooting occurred after two cars approached the New Avenue freeway on-ramp in Alhambra at about the same time, and the drivers "began jockeying for position to see who would get on first."
>
> Once on the freeway, occupants of both cars threw paper cups and other items at each other, and the other driver tried to prevent Nan from changing lanes, Varga said. When Nan headed for the Atlantic Boulevard exit, the gunman opened fire, striking Nan in the arm. (Stewart 1987)

This description makes the shooting seem less random, less an irrational response ("shooting people because people just honk your horn"), and more like the escalating "character contests" that often precede interpersonal violence (Luckenbill 1984). Though the press did not offer detailed accounts of every incident, reports showed other cases of free-way violence emerging from a context of conflict. Some reporters tried to restrict the concept of freeway shootings to random incidents: "In-vestigators believe that as many as four of the recent shootings in-volved gang activity or narcotics and may not have been examples of random roadway violence" (Kendall and Jones 1987:20). In other words, nonrandom shootings on freeways were not "freeway shootings." (In 1987, the media attributed five deaths to freeway violence, but Centers for Disease Control researchers, after eliminating cases involving prior disputes, found only two [one on a freeway] [Onwuachi-Saunders et al. 1989].)

If freeway shootings were random and on the rise, then all motorists were potential victims. The media reported that fear was widespread, that some motorists were buying bulletproof windshields or arming themselves to fight back, and that there had been a "courtesy surge by drivers fearful of reprisals" (Gest 1987; Dean 1987).

In short, the media described freeway shootings as a crime wave, a growing problem, characterized by random violence and widespread fear. Without official statistics or public-opinion polls bearing on the topic, reporters relied on interviews with their sources to support these claims. Thus, the eleven televised network news stories on the topic used thirty-eight clips from interviews: eleven of these were with law-enforcement officials promising to take action or advising caution; thir-teen were with victims describing their experiences; ten were person-in-the-street interviews revealing public concern; and four were with experts offering explanations.

Explaining the Problem

Having discovered and described freeway violence, the press sought to explain this new crime problem. These explanations came from inter-views with experts, mostly psychiatrists and social scientists who offered some version of frustration-aggression theory (cf. Dollard et al. 1939):

> Maybe you have a short fuse. Maybe you have a gun in a car. You're wrapped in steel armor, plenty of power under your foot, but constantly boxed in by traffic. A feeling of impotence and anger, and then someone cuts you off. That, authorities say, is how the shootings began. Then perhaps some people began firing for fun. (NBC, August 3)

In this view, driving in congested "creep-hour traffic" produced stress and frustration that, in turn, led to anger and escalated into shootings and other violent acts (Lobue 1987).[8] Almost all press reports offered some version of this explanation; some added secondary accounts. Several stories suggested that a car's anonymity made aggression less risky ("It's the private bubble that brings out Mr. Hyde" [L. Johnston 1987]); others implied that media coverage encouraged copycat crimes. Still others alluded to the effects of summer heat, "increased levels of violent crime in general, the prevalence of violence on television, drug and alcohol abuse, and even the breakdown of the family" (Armstrong 1987:4).

Interpreting the Problem

If freeway violence was a social problem, what sort of problem was it? The media offered several answers to this question, examples of what William Gamson and Andre Modigliani (1989) call "interpretive packages":

> A package has an internal structure. At its core is a central organizing idea, or *frame*, for making sense of relevant events, suggesting what is at issue. . . . Finally, a package offers a number of different condensing symbols that suggest the core frame and positions in shorthand, making it possible to display the package as a whole with a deft metaphor, catch-phrase, or other symbolic device.
> (W. Gamson and Modigliani 1989:3; emphasis in original)

Different interpretations presented distinctive orientations to under-standing freeway violence and had different implications for social policy.

Perhaps the most straightforward interpretation treated freeway shootings as a *crime problem*. Government and law-enforcement officials emphasized this theme. One California Highway Patrol officer declared: "These are difficult crimes to try to stop for law enforcement. . . . These are crimes of passion which are akin to the types of crime that occur . . . between family members" (NBC, August 3). If freeway vio-lence was a crime problem, then its solution lay in increased patrols, better investigations, more effective prosecution, and so on. The three 1987 freeway-violence bills passed by California's legislature fit this model: A.B. 2416 added officers to the state Highway Patrol; A.B. 2142 forbade probation for convicted offenders; and S.B. 117 created an ad-ditional five-year penalty for persons convicted in freeway shootings (Gillam 1987).

Other analysts portrayed freeway violence as a *traffic problem*, a product of congested highways. In an op-ed piece in the *Los Angeles Times*, Los Angeles Police Chief Daryl Gates (1987), while warning of a "breakdown in self-discipline," concentrated on ways to improve traf-fic flow—for example, closing rush-hour freeways to single-occupant cars. Interpreting freeway violence as a traffic problem implied a need for new freeways, mass transportation, or other means of reducing congestion, although such long-term solutions rarely received detailed discussion.

Still others treated freeway violence as a *gun problem*, one more con-sequence of the ready availability of firearms. Newspaper editorial pages favored this interpretation; the *Los Angeles Times* (1987a, 1987b) and *San Francisco Chronicle* (1987) editorials on freeway shootings advocated gun control, and the *Washington Post* (1987) ran a Herblock cartoon show-ing a roadside gun stand with signs reading "Last Chance to Reload be-fore Freeway" and "NRA Freeway Special."

Several commentators spoke of a *courtesy problem*; they viewed the vi-olence as a product of aggressive, hurried, self-centered driving habits.

One "recovering Type A" urged people to change their habits: "It takes self-confidence to be a freeway wimp" (Brenner 1987). The CDC researchers offered a *medical* interpretation: "The full public health impact of roadway violence has never been investigated. Roadway assaults could have an enormous emotional impact on drivers in Los Angeles County as well as throughout the United States" (Onwuachi-Saunders et al. 1989:2264). Finally, there were suggestions that freeway shootings were really a *media problem*, "a combination of coincidence and media hype" (Royko 1987). But even these critics seemed to agree that more than hype was at work; after describing the "media circus," *Newsweek* went on to discuss traffic congestion—"the real cause of L.A.'s sudden evolution from 'Have a Nice Day' to 'Make My Day'" (Kaus 1987).

In covering freeway violence, then, the press concentrated on description, explanation, and interpretation. These are, of course, standard elements of stories about social problems; they form a template for social-problems coverage. Because the press places a premium on the novel and the exotic, description is central to the construction of new social problems. Explanation and interpretation offer accounts for these problems. Some analysts argue that although the American press is overtly nonideological, its underlying message is hegemonic (Gitlin 1980). In this view, freeway violence was an attractive candidate for press coverage because it could be explained as a problem caused by the flawed characters of deviant individuals rather than by flawed social institutions.

The only unusual feature of the press coverage was the diversity of interpretive schemes presented. Robert A. Stallings (1990:90) argues that the media prefer monocausal explanations; though early press coverage of a social problem may offer competing interpretations, "later accounts tend to converge on a single factor." This failed to happen in the case of freeway violence and, as noted earlier, in the case of wilding. In each case, the new crime became the subject of widespread—but brief—attention.

This attention faded because no one had reason to keep talking about

these new crimes. Take gun-control advocates' interpretations of freeway violence. People who already favored tighter restrictions on firearms found it easy to point to freeway shootings as further evidence of
the violence caused by readily accessible guns. Statistics about the thousands of shooting deaths each year have long been the centerpiece of
gun-control rhetoric, and news reports of motorists being fatally shot
offered a newsworthy example of the problem, a timely hook for re-
peating warnings about the dangers of guns. But freeway shootings were
too unusual to be of any lasting rhetorical use to gun-control activists;
the handful of people who died in freeway shootings in Los Angeles in
1987 added far less than one-tenth of one percent to the total number
of firearm homicides that year. Pointing to freeway shootings might add
something to gun-control advocates' claims, but it didn't add much. Similarly, freeway violence could be used to remind the public that Los Angeles's transportation system was inadequate—and advocates of both
mass transportation and additional freeways issued such reminders—but
a few freeway homicides hardly made much difference in the debate
over the city's transportation policy. The various commentaries about
wilding faced the same problems. Critics who linked violent crime to
pornography (or rap music or television violence and so on) might point
to wilding as one more product of these influences, but the presence or
absence of wilding really made no difference in the persuasive power of
their arguments.

Freeway violence and wilding could be understood or interpreted
from multiple perspectives. But no group of advocates adopted either
problem, made it their own, assumed ownership (Gusfield 1981). There
were no new social movements dedicated to stamping out these new
crimes, no Mothers Against Freeway Violence (or Wilding). Nor did
any of the existing movements favoring gun control or opposed to pornography or taking some other stand find a way to make these new
crimes central to their programs. Freeway violence and wilding might
play a minor rhetorical role as part of some litany of social ills caused

by guns or pornography, but neither retained a featured place in movements' claims once the initial interest in the new crime died down.

SHORT-LIVED SOCIAL PROBLEMS

To be considered social problems, both wilding and freeway violence, then, depended upon media coverage. The media discovered them, named them, brought them to wide attention, and soon dropped them. Media attention is, of course, notoriously short-lived. The very term "news" reminds us that the press trades in the new, in what seems novel and surprising. Unusual outrages against the social order—leading both to accounts of especially terrible criminal acts and to warnings about new forms of crime—make good news stories.[9] But press attention inevitably shifts (A. Downs 1972). Every news story runs its course: when there are no remaining facts to uncover or angles to explore, once there is nothing left to say, interest in the topic seems to die down; what once seemed novel becomes "old news," boring; and coverage shifts to a different topic. By themselves, the media cannot and will not remain focused on a particular crime problem.

Maintaining media interest in a crime wave requires one of two things. As long as the problem can be presented as increasingly serious, as getting worse, the press will cover it. For a few days in the summer of 1987, the dozens of reporters covering the freeway-violence crisis found ways to claim that incidents were increasing; with more people watching for reported incidents, with the public conscious of the problem and quicker to make reports, and with the definition of freeway violence becoming broader, reports increased—for a couple of weeks. But there was a limit. Even by the most generous definition, there were only a few dozen incidents in L.A. that summer; the perception that freeway violence was increasing could not be maintained for long. Similarly, claims about wilding depended upon the horrified reaction to the attack on the Central Park jogger; there were few reports of other wilding incidents. In both cases, the press soon found itself without enough material to justify further coverage.

The second possibility of maintaining media interest is for someone outside the media to "assume ownership" of the new crime problem, to make it a central focus for concern. This did not happen in the case of either wilding or freeway violence; although advocates of many causes used these crimes to promote their own agendas (e.g., gun control, opposition to pornography, etc.), no one made eliminating freeway violence or wilding *the* cause: no one focused attention on a single interpretation of either crime; no one promoted a program to halt the crime; no one printed the brochures, held the rallies, or organized the press conferences needed to keep the issue alive. In contrast, consider the familiar story of Mothers Against Drunk Driving. Following the death of her daughter, Candy Lightner created MADD, which offered a single, soon-to-be-dominant interpretation of the drunk-driving problem— that society was failing to control "killer drunks."[10] MADD courted the press, solicited members for a nationwide network of chapters, promoted new legislation, and generally kept the issue alive for years. One reason crime waves, such as freeway violence and wilding, fade is because no one does for them what MADD did for drunk driving: no one takes over the issue and makes it their own.

Studies of the emergence of social problems often assume that claims originate with activists, and that the media transform and translate those claims for a mass audience (Best 1990). The examples of freeway violence and wilding remind us that some social problems originate in press coverage; the media make the primary claims. But, although the news media have the capacity to create a social problem—to define it and bring it to wide public attention—they are not well suited to keeping a problem alive, at the forefront of concern. Someone else needs to assume ownership.

Still, however rapidly a problem may fade, it takes longer before it is forgotten. As noted above, both wilding and freeway violence have become part of our cultural repertoire. These terms are now part of our language; we continue to hear and understand references to them. When a best-selling book says that "cancer behaves like a gang of perpetually wilding adolescents" (Sherwin Nuland's *How We Die*, quoted in Elson 1994), or when *Doonesbury* (May 10, 1989) implies that shootings are routine on L.A. freeways, we know what is meant. Even after the news media stop covering a new crime, it can live on in popular culture. In this way, the most transitory crime waves can endure, even though other crimes may become the focus of more serious, more lasting attention.

CHAPTER 3

Beyond Instances

*Institutionalizing Stalking
and Hate Crimes*

Claims calling attention to new crimes are bids for public attention. They must compete with other social-problems claims; there are always many causes clamoring for the sort of public recognition and concern that only a few can receive (Best 1990; Hilgartner and Bosk 1988). When news about freeway shootings fills networks' news broadcasts and newspapers' front pages, other crime news inevitably gets less coverage. But, as noted in the previous chapter, even crimes that do receive intense press coverage eventually slip out of the media's focus, and, when that happens, all the coverage devoted to the crime wave may not have produced lasting changes. After their brief moments in the limelight, wilding and freeway violence virtually disappeared as social issues. In contrast, other new crime problems become institutionalized, enduring parts of the criminal justice landscape: the new crime becomes the focus of legislative hearings and new laws; the criminal justice system changes to address the new crime, keeping track of reported incidents or devising programs to deal with the problem; researchers begin studying the new crime; and so on. This chapter begins by examining two recent examples of this process of institutionalization: stalking, and hate crimes.

THE DISCOVERY OF STALKING

Stalking—an activity in which "men and women . . . are repeatedly followed, harassed, or physically threatened by other persons" (Gilligan 1992:285)—officially became a crime when California passed the first antistalking law in 1990.[1] Three years later, forty-eight states and the District of Columbia had such laws, and several states were considering further legislation to expand or toughen their statutes. As one legislator put it:

> Michigan and its sister States are creating a new crime. We are defining it, essentially, one unknown to the common law. We are making conduct illegal which has been legal up until now, and we are using the most serious proscription our society can devise, the deprivation of liberty, through a felony penalty. This is experimental legislation. (Perry Bullard in U.S. Senate 1992:64)

The federal government also responded: the U.S. Senate (1992, 1993) held hearings, and the National Institute of Justice (1993) developed a Model Anti-Stalking Code for States. By late 1993, claims about stalking had become familiar, and initial reports of strangers attacking women (e.g., the kidnap/murder of Polly Klaas, or the assault on figure skater Nancy Kerrigan) often assumed that stalkers committed the crimes (Toobin 1994; Ingrassia 1994). Less than five years after the term emerged, stalking had gained widespread recognition as a crime problem.

Stalking became a prominent issue in 1989, following the sensational murder of the television actress Rebecca Schaeffer, killed by a fan, Robert Bardo—a stranger who became obsessed with her, attempted to contact her, then shot her (Axthelm 1989). Schaeffer's murder became the typifying example for what the media now termed "star-stalking" (Cosgrove 1990; "Geraldo" 1990).[2] The victims of star-stalking were celebrities—actors and actresses, television personalities, and political figures—whereas star-stalkers were mentally disturbed, inappropriately obsessed:

> On a scale of zero to 10, among schizophrenics, [Bardo's] a 10—one of the sicker people I've seen. . . . With Rebecca Schaeffer, he found a—an obsession. She was the answer to his lonely, depressed, miserable life. (Psychiatrist John Stalberg in *48 Hours* 1992:3–4)

Some discussions of star-stalking referred to the psychiatric disorder "erotomania" (Cosgrove 1990). First described in 1921, erotomania entered the American Psychiatric Association's *DSM-III-R* as "delusional (paranoid) disorder, erotomanic type":

> The central theme of an erotic delusion is that one is loved by another. . . . The person about whom this conviction is held is usually of higher status, such as a famous person or a superior at work, and may even be a complete stranger. Efforts to contact the object of the delusion, through telephone calls, letters, gifts, visits, and even surveillance and stalking are common. (American Psychiatric Association 1987:199)

Erotomania usually affects women (Segal 1989), and discussions of star-stalking often mentioned women who had harassed David Letterman and other celebrities. The star-stalker's behavior, which might be threatening or merely inappropriate, needed to be seen as potentially violent (Dietz et al., "Letters to Congress," 1991; Dietz et al., "Letters to Celebrities," 1991). Unpredictable and possibly lethal, stalking was a form of random violence.

Concern over star-stalking led to California's antistalking law; its advocates linked Schaeffer's murder, the 1982 stabbing of the actress Theresa Saldana (in the news because her attacker was about to be paroled), and the deaths of four Orange County women within a six-week period (each killed by a man against whom she had a restraining order) (Morville 1993). These cases became typifying examples, evidence of the need for an antistalking law. Supported by peace officers' associations and the Screen Actors Guild (SAG), the bill passed in 1990 (*Pacific Law Journal* 1990:500). When it took effect, the Los Angeles Police Department established a six-person Threat Management Unit (TMU) to investigate stalking cases. Both SAG's lobbying and the creation of the TMU in Los Angeles (with its many show-business celebrities) reveal that concern over star-stalking inspired the first antistalking law.

But other states soon began following California's example. Often, a highly publicized local attack on a noncelebrity inspired lawmakers: "Behind almost every state stalking bill has been at least one local tragedy" (Morville 1993:929 n. 47). Twenty-nine states passed antistalking laws (many modeled on California's law) in 1992; eighteen other states and the District of Columbia followed suit in 1993 (National Institute of Justice 1993:12). In 1992, Senator William Cohen (Republican from Maine) began calling for federal action, and the national media dramatically increased their coverage of stalking. Some cases achieved high visibility: a *Washington Post* reporter, George Lardner (1992), received a Pulitzer Prize for a story about his daughter's murder by a stalker, and the award triggered additional press coverage; in 1993, Kathleen Krueger, the wife of U.S. Senator Bob Krueger (Democrat from Texas), used her own experiences as a stalking victim to campaign for a federal antistalking law (D. Ellis 1993; U.S. Senate 1993).

These new claims reframed stalking as a women's issue, a widespread precursor to serious violence, typically committed by men against former spouses or lovers. The term "stalking"—now the consensus replacement for such earlier labels as "psychological rape," "star-stalking," and "erotomania"—implied deliberate intent to harm the victim:

> The verb "stalk" is defined as: (1) "to move threateningly or menacingly"; (2) "to pursue by tracking"; and (3) to go stealthily towards

an animal "for the purpose of killing or capturing it." These definitions say much about the crime of stalking, suggesting that a stalker
is a hunter, is dangerous, and thus should be avoided if at all possible. (Perez 1993:265)

Advocates insisted that stalking was a common problem. An often-
repeated estimate suggested there were 200,000 stalkers in the United
States. This statistic first appeared in *U.S. News & World Report*'s issue
of February 17, 1992: "Researchers suggest that up to 200,000 people
exhibit a stalker's traits" (Tharp 1992:28). Like other statistical estimates of social-problem magnitude, this number soon took on a life of
its own; it was often repeated, but never examined or explained (Best
1990). Other claims suggested that 200,000 was an underestimate:

> There are an estimated 200,000 stalkers in the United States, and
> those are only the ones that we have track of. (Sally Jessy Raphael
> in *Sally Jessy Raphael* 1994:3)

> Some two hundred thousand people in the U.S. pursue the famous.
> No one knows how many people stalk the rest of us, but the figure
> is probably higher. (Sherman 1994:198)

> Four million women that we know about—know about each year
> are beaten and terrorized and stalked by somebody they know.
> (Oprah Winfrey in *Oprah* 1994:12)

There were various estimates that lifetime victimization by stalkers
would affect one American in forty (Safran 1992), or thirty (Tharp
1992), or twenty (*CNN Prime News* 1993). The numbers varied, but
there was agreement that stalking was increasing, was in fact "a national epidemic" (Gilligan 1992:337).[3]

Advocates also agreed that stalking was a form of domestic violence
against women. To be sure, occasional claims asserted that "the violent
ending is actually very rare" (psychologist Daniel Martell in *Maury Povich Show* 1992:8), that "men are stalked just as many times as women"
(former victim Kathleen Baty in *Donahue* 1992:5), or that the stalker

was "often a total stranger" (Safran 1992:266). But most claims typified stalking as "almost exclusive to women" (*John and Leeza* 1993), and "often preceding violent acts, from assault to rape, child molestation, and murder" (Beck 1992:60). In this view, stalkers were not strangers ("as many as 75 or 80 percent of cases involve people who were once married [to each other] or dating" [Ingrassia 1993:28]), and their victims were not celebrities ("38 percent . . . are ordinary Americans" [Goodwin 1993:50]).[4]

This redefinition linked stalking to a well-established social problem—domestic battering: "'The majority of battered women experience stalking in some form,' says Vickie Smith, head of the Illinois Coalition Against Domestic Violence" (Miller 1993:18). The battered women's movement had long complained that the criminal justice system failed to protect women trying to escape abusive partners, that restraining orders were ineffective (Loseke 1992). By reframing these women's problems as stalking, a suddenly prominent issue with connotations of extreme violence, battered women's advocates could move their concerns to the top of the policy agenda. In spite of the intense interest in stalking, as late as 1993 there were only two published scholarly studies of stalkers: an examination of LAPD TMU files (Zona et al. 1993); and a typology of "criminal stalkers" (Holmes 1993). Neither offered much original data, so antistalking crusaders routinely borrowed data from research on domestic violence to characterize stalking:

> Approximately 50 percent of all females who leave their husbands for reasons of physical abuse are followed, harassed, or further attacked by their former spouses. This phenomenon is known as "separation assault." . . . The broader concept is called "stalking." (Bradburn 1992:271)

> Studies in Detroit and Kansas City reveal that 90 percent of those murdered by their intimate partners called police at least once. (Senator William Cohen in *Congressional Record* 1992:S9527)

> Nearly one third of all women killed in America are murdered by their husbands or boyfriends, and, says Ruth Micklem, codirector

of Virginians Against Domestic Violence, as many as 90 percent of them have been stalked. (Beck 1992:61)

The juxtaposition of the latter two quotes reveals how evidence used to define new crimes evolves: Senator Cohen cited a finding that 90 percent of women killed by husbands or lovers had previously called the police; when later advocates repeated that statistic, they equated having called the police with being stalked, ignoring the likelihood that many women called to complain about abuse by partners living in the same residence (and therefore not stalkers). Presumably, similar assumptions lay behind the claim of U.S. Representative Joseph Kennedy (Democrat from Massachusetts) that "nine women a day are killed by stalkers in our country" (*Larry King Live* 1994:3). Advocates described antistalking laws as "an effective deterrent to domestic abuse" (Furio 1993:90); West Virginia's original law narrowly defined victims as "those who either cohabitated or had intimate relationships with their stalkers" (Perez 1993:267).

Claims that many stalkers were former husbands or boyfriends cast virtually all women as potential victims: "We're not idiots up here that asked to be victims. This happens to anybody, period" (former victim Stephanie in *Sally Jessy Raphael* 1993a:7). Here, as in earlier claims about star-stalking, victims bore no responsibility; advocates emphasized that few victims did anything to encourage their stalkers. (One exception was a talk show devoted to women harassing former boyfriends; the host repeatedly suggested that the men encouraged stalking [*Sally Jessy Raphael* 1993b].) In most ways, stalking's typification resembled that of domestic violence: "Wife abuse is a label for severe, frequent, and continuing violence that escalates over time and is unstoppable. Such violence is that in which unrepentant men intentionally harm women and where women are not the authors of their own experiences which they find terrifying" (Loseke 1992:20). Once they linked stalking to battering, advocates had little difficulty attributing the same characteristics to both crimes. Stalkers were "essentially evil" (psychologist Rick Shuman in *Oprah* 1992:13) men trying to dominate women:

They're not so much crazy men as slightly exaggerated men. They
have a view that women should be controlled. . . . They tend to view
women as property. . . . They target women because women are targets of opportunity in our society. (Psychiatrist Peter Breggin in
Larry King Live 1990:5)

The link between stalking and domestic violence became apparent in
state legislative proceedings. Illinois lawmakers, for example, justified
antistalking legislation by pointing to four recent cases of victims
murdered by former husbands or boyfriends in Chicago suburbs. The
Chicago Tribune's editorial (1991) endorsing an antistalking law noted:
"Hundreds of women are threatened and harassed and intimidated by
ex-boyfriends or ex-husbands. . . . [An antistalking law has] the potential to be a helpful weapon against domestic violence." Supported by
the Illinois Coalition Against Domestic Violence, the bill received unan-
imous support in both legislative houses; mothers of two of the dead
victims were on hand when the bill was signed into law. Both state and
national branches of the battered women's movement and the victims'
rights movement supported antistalking bills (Jenness and Broad 1997).
The National Victim Center lobbied in more than a dozen states, and
Theresa Saldana (a former stalking victim and the founder of Victims
for Victims) campaigned in behalf of the laws. In Nebraska, for instance, both the Nebraska Coalition for Victims of Crime and the
Nebraska Domestic Violence–Sexual Assault Coalition supported antistalking legislation. Stalking was now a form of both violent crime and
domestic violence.

Clearly, stalking took a different trajectory than such short-lived
crime problems as wilding and freeway violence. Whereas all three
crimes came to public attention through media coverage of sensational
crimes, stalking attracted influential sponsors—advocates who not only
kept the issue alive, but extended its boundaries. Initially, these were
celebrities (who saw themselves as victims or potential victims) and
those responsible for protecting celebrities (such as the Screen Actors
Guild, the LAPD, and individuals who provided security services for

celebrities [e.g., Gavin de Becker]) (Bacon 1990; de Becker 1997; *Geraldo* 1990); the media's eagerness to cover stories about celebrities undoubtedly helped make star-stalking a visible issue. But by 1991, new sponsors assumed ownership of what now was redefined as the broader problem of stalking. The crime victims' movement and the battered women's movement characterized stalking as a common problem, a form of domestic violence, that threatened ordinary people—particularly women.

Linking its cause with the visible problem of stalking gave the battered women's movement a fresh look. Coupling long-standing complaints about ineffective restraining orders to the lethal menace of stalking turned a tired topic into a hot issue. Antistalking laws put reform of the restraining-order process on the public agenda, promising to give an established system of control new teeth. Media coverage of stalking increasingly cited experts from such organizations as Virginians Against Domestic Violence (Beck 1992). These statewide groups had links to the National Victim Center, Victims for Victims, and other victims' rights organizations. In addition, new social movements and support groups devoted to stalking emerged—for example, Citizens Against Stalking, and Survivors of Stalking (Schaum and Parrish 1995).

At the same time, antistalking programs and legislation gave government agencies a way to earn credit with the victims' rights and battered women's movements by being responsive. The antistalking campaign faced little opposition; violent, even murderous crimes by vengeful ex-husbands or mentally disturbed fans had few defenders. Though civil libertarians questioned the laws' constitutionality, the public consensus deplored stalking. The result was the institutionalization of stalking as a crime problem: passage of state antistalking laws; federal efforts to coordinate responses to the stalking problem (Bureau of Justice Assistance 1996); generous funding for research on stalking—a range of measures that instantly established stalking as an enduring crime problem rather than simply another focus of short-lived media attention.

THE POLITICS OF HATE CRIMES

Like stalking, hate crimes emerged as a new crime problem in the 1980s, and soon became the subject of criminal statutes in many states. Most generally, hate crimes are crimes motivated by prejudice against some social category to which the victim belongs. Hate crimes usually are typified as violent assaults—for example, attacks on blacks, Asians, Jews, or gays and lesbians. Of course, violence against ethnic and religious minorities runs throughout American history, and it has inspired social movements opposed to such violence—for example, the lengthy campaign by the National Association for the Advancement of Colored People (NAACP) against lynching (Zangrando 1980). In the late 1980s, opposition to violent attacks on minorities coalesced in campaigns to criminalize "hate crimes."

"Hate crime" is a umbrella term, invented to cover crimes against various minorities, and thereby establish a common cause among a diverse set of activists. Originally, this alliance was between well-established groups dedicated to protecting the interests of African-Americans (e.g., the NAACP and the Anti-Klan Network), other racial minorities (e.g., the Japanese American Citizen League), and Jews (e.g., the Anti-Defamation League of B'nai B'rith [ADL] and the International Network of Children of Jewish Holocaust Survivors) (U.S. House 1985). These groups typified hate crimes by referring to acts of extreme racial violence or blatant antisemitic vandalism. Their narrow focus on ethnic and religious prejudice can be seen in a 1984 *Washington Post* op-ed piece's reference to "what are called 'hate crimes'—violence against racial or religious minorities" (C. McCarthy 1984).[5] Soon thereafter, however, gay and lesbian activists joined the coalition, expanding the category of hate crimes to include violent attacks against homosexuals.

The campaign against hate crimes became especially important to gay and lesbian organizations, and they began to play increasingly prominent roles in the movement. Homosexuals have long been targets of violent assaults (Harry 1982). Beginning in the early 1980s, the National Gay and Lesbian Task Force (NGLTF) and many local gay and lesbian organizations began "antiviolence" projects (Jenness 1995a, 1995b; Jenness and Broad 1997). These involved a range of services for gays and lesbians, including victim assistance, public education, and street patrols, but the antiviolence projects became especially known for collecting information about violent incidents and releasing statistical reports on the level of local violence against gays and lesbians. Both gay and mainstream press covered the reports' release.[6] These statistical reports proved to be rhetorically powerful. They often coupled horror stories—typifying examples of especially brutal assaults or murders—with statistics on the frequency of victimization, suggesting that terrible crimes were common. But, more important, these reports documented clear-cut victimization. Even conservatives with strong moral reservations about homosexuality could hardly endorse unprovoked criminal assaults against gays and lesbians: the sexual orientation of the victims was irrelevant; these were simply crimes. Perhaps more than any other gay-rights issue, opposition to violence against gays and lesbians could generate broad-based support. Movements for gay and lesbian rights relied on an analogy between homosexuals and racial and religious minorities: if blacks or Jews merited equal rights, and government action to protect those rights, so did gays and lesbians. This argument faced considerable resistance—not everyone accepted the claim that homosexuals were simply another minority deserving equal protection—but the issue of hate crimes had the potential to overcome that resistance. The movement against hate crimes made a powerful claim: minorities, including gays and lesbians, were subject to frequent criminal attacks; and the criminal justice system often failed to give those attacks the serious attention they deserved.

Opponents of hate crimes argued that attacks on gays and lesbians were no different than assaults on members of ethnic and religious minorities: they were all forms of violence motivated by bias against or hatred of a minority. This meant that gay and lesbian organizations, such as the NGLTF, were now allied with such older, politically influential groups as the NAACP and the ADL. These were valuable allies, respected by both politicians and the major media; if they argued that hate crimes were a major problem, the issue was likely to be treated seriously. The evolution of this alliance can be traced in the transcripts of congressional hearings. In 1985, the first hearing on hate crimes focused solely on crimes inspired by ethnic or religious prejudice (U.S. House 1985). The following year, the same House subcommittee held a hearing devoted to "anti-gay violence," but the participants in this hearing made little attempt to draw parallels between attacks on gays and lesbians and violence against other minorities (U.S. House 1986). But by 1988, an NGLTF representative was part of a broad coalition of witnesses testifying before a Senate hearing in support of a federal Hate Crimes Statistics Act (U.S. Senate 1988). While acknowledging that violence against gays and lesbians was part of the broader problem of hate crimes, gay and lesbian activists emphasized that it was an especially important part:

> Lesbians and gay men are principal targets of hate crimes. . . . A report to the National Institute of Justice . . . observed that "homosexuals are probably the most frequent victims" of hate violence. (Herek 1989:948)

Advocates described hate crimes as a widespread and growing problem (Jacobs and Henry 1996). They documented the increase with statistics based on data they had collected, and they insisted that, whatever the methodological limitations of their research, the increase in hate crimes was real. They pointed to heavily publicized incidents, such as the Howard Beach and Bensonhurst killings in greater New York (both involved blacks killed by groups of whites), as examples of the problem's seriousness. They offered various explanations for the wave of hate crimes: assaults on Asians were reactions to economic competition with Japan; increased gaybashing reflected anxiety over AIDS; and so on. Some blamed the increased violence on skinheads or other organized "hate groups"; others argued that violence was a product of widespread prejudicial attitudes, such as racism and homophobia. These claims received general acceptance; newspaper editorials on the subject routinely described hate crimes as getting worse.

At the state and local levels, advocates called for new laws and ordinances banning hate-motivated acts, or increasing the legal penalties for crimes motivated by bias. Some laws required state officials to collect data on the incidence of hate crimes. The need for more authoritative national statistics became the focus for efforts to pass a federal bill. The proposed Hate Crimes Statistics Act did not make hate crimes federal offenses, but it promised to commit the federal government to monitoring the incidence of hate crimes. Although representatives of the FBI and the Bureau of Justice Statistics testified in opposition, on the grounds that it would be difficult to develop a valid and reliable scheme for classifying and counting hate crimes (U.S. House 1985; U.S. Senate 1988), Congress passed the Hate Crimes Statistics Act and President Bush signed it in 1990. For gay and lesbian activists, the bill marked a major milestone: by including crimes motivated by prejudice based on sexual orientation, as well as ethnicity and religion, the act became the first federal legislation to, in effect, accept the analogy between homosexuals and other minorities. Gay activists were invited to the White House for the signing. The new law seemed to be a vital first step in gaining federal protection for gay and lesbian rights. In addition, some state laws also prohibited crimes motivated by bias against a sexual orientation.[7]

Although hate crime had achieved official recognition—become institutionalized—as a new category of crime, its boundaries and ownership remained in dispute. Criminal justice agencies charged with enforcing the new laws had to find ways to operationalize the category. Collecting federal data on hate crimes became the FBI's responsibility; the bureau added hate crimes to its Uniform Crime Reporting program, stating: "Hate crimes are not separate, distinct crimes, but rather tradi-

tional offenses motivated by the offender's bias." Determining motivation obviously involved more than simply establishing that a crime had
occurred. The bureau's initial classification guidelines noted: "While
no single fact may be conclusive, facts such as the following, particularly when combined, are supportive of a finding of bias"; there followed
a list of fourteen hypothetical "facts" (Federal Bureau of Investigation
1990). And, although most advocates had presumed that hate crimes involved, by definition, attacks on members of minority groups, that presumption was lost as bureaucracies created operational definitions for
hate crimes: the FBI guidelines ignored the question of minority status,
inviting listings for a wide range of offenses, including antiwhite, anti-
Protestant, anti-atheist/agnostic, and antiheterosexual crimes.[8] The program required that thousands of local, state, and federal law-enforcement
agencies report cases to the FBI. Participation grew, from reporting by
2,771 agencies in 1991 to 6,840 agencies (covering 56 percent of the
U.S. population) in 1993, but the reported data were obviously incomplete (e.g., eight of the twenty largest cities participating reported no
incidents in 1992) (U.S. Senate 1994:20, 49). Producing meaningful
data would take time.

At the same time, activists campaigned to expand the category's
boundaries. Hate crimes had been typified using incidents of extreme
violence, but some advocates began promoting a much broader range
of activities (e.g., "hate speech") as equivalent to assault:

> Aggression and violence against gays and lesbians take many forms
> from the obvious, such as physical attacks, insults, and vicious jokes,
> to the subtle but equally pernicious, such as the refusal to recognize
> the existence and legitimacy of the gay community and gay culture,
> the re-writing of verse by famous poets to obscure references to
> same-sex love, and the genocidal failure by the American govern-
> ment to fund AIDS prevention efforts at an adequate level. (Nardi
> and Bolton 1991:351)[9]

Such claims justifying broader definitions of hate crime were met by
arguments from civil libertarians and legal theorists questioning the

constitutionality of some hate-crime laws, as well as the wisdom of too readily interpreting crime as rooted in prejudice (e.g., Gellman 1991; Jacobs 1993; Jacobs and Potter 1997).

In the early 1990s, gay and lesbian advocates remained especially active in promoting hate crimes as a new crime problem. In some cases, they seemed almost to equate the general category with attacks on homosexuals; a book titled *Hate Crimes*, for example, had the subtitle *Confronting Violence against Lesbians and Gay Men* (Herek and Berrill 1992). But other groups also sought recognition as targets of hate crimes. Feminists, in particular, argued that the definition of hate crime ought to be extended to include rape, domestic battering, and other violence against women:

> When rapes *are* reported and counted, at no point is the phenomenon of rape interpreted as a hate crime against a gender category of people. . . . Counting hate crimes against [women] would reveal that half the population is, as a class, at serious risk of a hate crime. (Pellegrini 1990; emphasis in original)

> Let's get it straight: Sexual assault is mainly about gender. It is about how some men feel about women. . . . This is our number one bias crime. (Quindlen 1990)

And parallel calls for expansion come from other groups:

> More recently, the rhetoric of bias crime victimization has expanded to include discussions of personal appearance/physical appearance, age, mental and physical handicap, and political affiliation. This type of legislative activity pointed to a trend: more and more constituencies are being defined as (potential) victims of bias-motivated violence. (Jenness 1995b:225)

At least immediately after its establishment, the category of hate crimes seemed likely to expand as other groups sought recognition as victims of bigotry.

Both stalking and hate crimes, then, became institutionalized relatively quickly. Both causes received plenty of media coverage—not unlike the media's treatment of wilding and freeway violence. But stalking and hate crimes became more than news stories; they were causes promoted by activists who pressed not only for media coverage, but for government action. In response, states passed laws against these new crimes, and the federal government lent its support to both causes. The result was institutionalization. Regardless of whether the media continued to focus on stalking and hate crimes, there were now laws on the books and bureaucrats keeping records. These new crimes had made a transition: they were now objects of social policy.

THE "IRON QUADRANGLE" OF INSTITUTIONALIZATION

Institutionalization depends upon amassing sufficient social support for claims about new problems. Four social sectors are central to this process: the media, activists, government, and experts. When these four work together to reinforce one another, their influence seems overpowering. They constitute an "Iron Quadrangle" for promoting and establishing new crime problems.

The Media

Media coverage is necessary to bring public attention to new crimes, but it is not sufficient for institutionalization. Typically, media coverage of new crimes follows a standard pattern: (1) it typifies the crime by offering detailed accounts of particular, usually dramatic, incidents, thereby giving shape to the problem; (2) it describes the crime in compelling terms—as a widespread, growing problem, a serious threat to a large share of the population; (3) it explains some of the crime's causes; (4) it offers interpretations of the crime's meaning and significance; and (5) coverage continues as long as the crime can be approached from fresh angles (e.g., reports of new, extraordinary incidents, new interpretations, etc.), or until some other story demands attention. This pattern is apparent in coverage of both short-lived crime waves, such as wilding and freeway violence, and new crimes that become institutionalized, such as stalking and hate crimes.

Activists

The key difference between short-lived and institutionalized crime problems is the involvement of activists. Recall that no one assumed ownership of either wilding or freeway violence; instead, each crime inspired multiple interpretations, mostly by people whose interest in those crimes was largely tangential to their other concerns. In contrast, stalking and hate crimes were adopted by existing social movements: the victims' rights and battered women's movements assumed ownership of stalking, while various movements representing ethnic, religious, and sexual minorities adopted hate crimes. Existing movements make efficient owners of new crime problems; they already have leaders, members, budgets, offices, contacts with reporters and legislators, and other resources needed to mount effective campaigns to change social policy. Importantly, they also have ideologies—interpretive frameworks for making sense of the new crimes. By assuming ownership of a new crime, a movement applies its ideology to establish an authoritative interpretation, reducing the cacophony of competing interpretations in favor of one dominant view promoted by the movement. Thus, once the battered women's movement defined stalking as crime rooted in gender, it could be understood as a form of male domination and violence against women; individuals concerned with those larger problems now recognized stalking's importance and their interest in doing something about stalking, while existing interpretations of those broader problems (e.g., studies of the nature and causes of domestic violence) could now be applied to stalking. Meanwhile, other potential interpretive slants not sponsored by the movements—say, claims that televised violence fos-

ters stalking or hate crimes—got shoved to the periphery. Once a social movement assumes ownership of a crime problem, media coverage
tends to adopt the movement's interpretation.

Unlike the media's perpetual quest for new stories, social movements
are prepared to wage prolonged campaigns, to return for the next legislative session, to assemble yet another annual report documenting
grievances, to continue to recruit new members, to organize yet another
protest, to search for additional allies, and, generally, to keep promoting
an issue for months, sometimes years, even decades. Existing resources,
the power to establish a dominant interpretation, and the ability to stick
with an issue are what makes a movement's ownership so important in
institutionalizing a new crime. At the same time, movements depend
on novelty to keep their causes alive. Social-movement leaders tend
to have a long-term commitment to the cause; members of this small
leadership cadre are often professionals, employed by movement organizations (J. McCarthy and Zald 1977). But the members of most
movements have much less involvement in and commitment to the
cause. In hopes of keeping these members interested, and perhaps of
attracting more new members, leaders continually look for ways to make
their movements seem fresh and vital. Assuming ownership of a new
crime problem is visible, dramatic evidence that a movement is doing
important work and deserves continued support. This may involve little
more than repackaging familiar concerns (e.g., the battered women's
movement's long-standing complaint about the ineffectiveness of restraining orders was easily reworked to fit the issue of stalking, just as
established minority-rights organizations like the NAACP, ADL, and
NGLTF had no trouble joining the coalition opposing hate crimes).
Finding new ways to present their causes makes it easier for activists
to get further coverage in the media, thereby making their movements
more visible. A movement's assuming ownership of a new crime problem markedly improves the chances of that crime being institutionalized, but it also enhances the movement's long-term prospects.

Government

Obviously, since crimes are violations of the criminal law, government's involvement in passing laws and establishing enforcement procedures is essential to institutionalizing a new crime. Far more than social movements, government has the resources to remain focused on a particular crime, keeping its control a priority. It is one thing for the NGLTF to commit itself to an annual report on antigay and antilesbian violence, organizing enough volunteers to collect and analyze data, and write and publish the report. It is quite another matter for Congress to assign the FBI to collect national hate-crime statistics; the FBI has a budget (and can request increases to fund the additional work), clerical employees, computers—all the resources necessary to collect and report annual hate-crime statistics until it is ordered to stop.

Contemporary U.S. politicians, particularly state and federal legislators, stand to gain a good deal by joining campaigns against new crime problems. Opposition to crime is uncontroversial; there are no organized lobbies of wilders or stalkers making competing demands that might make legislators hesitant to take a stand. Moreover, crime is an issue that is both of considerable concern to—and easily understood by—voters; holding hearings on new crimes and passing laws are visible ways for legislators to act in the public interest. And at least some new crimes of violence seem perfect for generating broad, bipartisan support. For liberal Democrats (who often find themselves accused of being "soft on crime"), stalking and hate crimes offered opportunities to take tough anticrime positions in support of claims by liberal allies in the women's, civil rights, and gay/lesbian movements. At the same time, conservative Republicans could assume their customary tough-on-crime stance while simultaneously reaching out to new constituencies (e.g., President Bush invited gay activists to witness him signing the Hate Crimes Statistics Act at the White House).

Once the law defines new crimes, the criminal justice system and other government bureaucracies must administer those laws. New crimes offer bureaucrats the same attractions as any other new responsibility; new duties justify additional resources, perhaps new agencies. The FBI lobbied against the Hate Crimes Statistics Act, saying the data would be difficult and costly to collect yet not useful. However, once the bill became law, the bureau accepted the responsibility—and the budget—required to administer the program.

New crimes offer government officials opportunities for media coverage; the press reports on hearings, interviews key legislators, and covers signing ceremonies—and even the news that reports on the crime have been issued. Since violent crime seems dramatic, these events make good news stories as far as the media are concerned, and the coverage usually casts officials in a favorable light, making them eager to cooperate. In some cases, officials promote new crime problems to the media; the extensive press coverage given serial murder during the mid-1980s, for example, was generated by an FBI campaign to draw attention to the menace posed by that crime and thereby justify the bureau's proposal to establish a National Center for the Analysis of Violent Crime (Jenkins 1994). Thus, campaigns against new crimes forge strong, usually cooperative links between the media and government. At the same time, new crimes also offer officials opportunities to create or reinforce ties with the social movements promoting these issues.

Experts

The fourth and least visible sector of the "Iron Quadrangle" consists of experts. A variety of professionals—representing law enforcement, law, medicine, social science, and so on—can play key roles in creating and maintaining institutionalized crimes. Theirs are authoritative voices; because their expertise is respected, their endorsement of particular policies or interpretations can be especially persuasive in supporting claims and overcoming opposition. Experts can conduct research on the nature of the crime, its causes, patterns, and consequences, and recommend solutions. Turning their attention to new crimes offers experts a number of benefits—a fresh, neglected topic for study, opportunities to receive research funding and publish results, the chance to exhibit one's knowledge regarding a visible issue. Experts who address new crimes find themselves interviewed by the press, courted by social movements, consulted—and supported—by government. Experts who have personal commitments to a cause, such as feminism or gay and lesbian rights, can find opportunities to combine their scholarship and activism on cutting-edge issues. Over the long run, experts become particularly important; they reaffirm the nature of the new crime, track the progress toward controlling it, and offer more refined ways to think about the issue (N. Gilbert 1997).

The Iron Quadrangle

Table 1 summarizes the connections among these four sectors, revealing how each is linked to the other three in such a way that these four sectors reinforce one another to institutionalize new crime problems. The mass media, activists, government officials, and experts all stand to benefit by promoting new crime problems. Obviously, not every potential new crime problem offers these benefits to all four sectors. As noted in chapter 2, wilding and freeway shootings made good news stories, but social movements did not assume ownership of either crime. But when social movements choose to make a new crime their own, the prospects for cooperation among the media, movements, government, and experts improve. Each sector has something to offer—and something to gain from—each of the others. As the examples of stalking and hate crimes suggest, the "Iron Quadrangle" can produce a powerful consensus regarding the importance of the new problem, its causes, and needed solutions. The result is institutionalization of the new crime.

TABLE I

THE "IRON QUADRANGLE" OF INSTITUTIONALIZATION:
CONNECTIONS AMONG KEY SECTORS

	MASS MEDIA	ACTIVISTS	GOVERNMENT	EXPERTS
NEW CRIMES offer	fresh stories to cover	fresh issues to maintain interest in social movements	opportunities to act on the public's behalf on visible issues	new topics on which to apply expertise
MASS MEDIA offer	—	publicity for social movements	publicity for politicians, agencies, and programs	publicity for professions and individual experts
ACTIVISTS offer	sources for stories and interpretations	—	political support for politicians, agencies, and programs	clientele and recognition for expertise
GOVERNMENT offers	sources for stories and interpretations	creation and maintenance of policies desired by movements	—	funding, forums, and opportunities to influence policy
EXPERTS offer	sources for stories and interpretations	authoritative support for movements' concerns	authoritative support for policies, agencies, and programs	—

OCCULT CRIMES AND THE LIMITS OF INSTITUTIONALIZATION

Institutionalized crime problems are not static or permanent. "Sexual psychopaths" emerged as a popular term used in describing a highly visible crime problem in the 1930s, a problem that became the subject of media coverage and more than two dozen state laws by 1955; but the term fell out of favor and now seems antiquated (Freedman 1987; Jenkins 1998). It is too soon to know whether stalking and hate crimes will suffer similar fates, whether the new laws will be actively enforced, whether these crimes will remain subjects of attention from the media, activists, government officials, and experts. Certainly the recent history of claims about occult crime is proof that a crime problem that seems on the verge of institutionalization can nevertheless fall out of favor.

The 1980s saw the rise of claims about "occult crimes"—"ceremonial actions and/or ritualistic acts, involving occult-related behavior patterns, and . . . motivated by a belief in some occult ideology" (California Office of Criminal Justice Planning 1989:25). The boundaries of this new crime category were broad, encompassing *santeria* and other Afro-Caribbean religions, the People's Temple and other cults, and satanism. The most extraordinary claims posited a conspiratorial million-member satanic blood cult, conducting tens of thousands of human sacrifices annually in the United States and overseeing the ritualized sexual abuse of countless children (Richardson et al. 1991). Advocates speculated that many serial murders and much sexual abuse had their roots in occult motivations.

By 1990, occult crime seemed to be becoming institutionalized. It received extensive media coverage, although this largely involved talk shows and other info-tainment rather than coverage by the mainstream press (Lowney 1994). Occult crime also had attracted government attention: there were "cult cops" who specialized in investigating satanic crimes (Crouch and Damphousse 1991). Officers could learn to recognize and investigate occult or ritual crimes by attending one of the numerous professional training seminars dedicated to the topic (Hicks 1991a, 1991b), or by reading textbooks on criminal investigation (Holmes 1989) or even materials produced under the auspices of state criminal justice agencies (California Office of Criminal Justice Planning 1989). Some states added statutes on occult or ritual crime to their criminal codes (Bromley 1991). Activists, particularly those associated with fundamentalist Christian ministries, campaigned against the satanist menace, and a growing body of expert literature, particularly by therapists who specialized in helping patients "recover memories" of childhood ritual abuse, began to appear (e.g., Noblitt and Perskin 1995).

However, as it became increasingly visible, occult crime became the target of counterclaims by investigative journalists, social scientists, and some law-enforcement authorities (Lanning 1989; Loftus and Ketcham 1994; Nathan and Snedeker 1995; Ofshe and Watters 1994; Richardson et al. 1991). They challenged the evidence that occult crimes posed a significant problem, questioning the authenticity of recovered memories and arguing that there was no convincing evidence for the existence of a vast satanic conspiracy. Whatever momentum the movement against occult crimes had gained rapidly dissipated. Concern with occult crime remained, but it was generally limited to some fundamentalist Christians, as well as a few feminists who credited the recovered memories of "occult survivors" regarding widespread ritual sexual abuse.

The example of occult crime demonstrates that institutionalizing new crimes is a process—one that can continue, stall, or even be reversed. In 1990, stalking, hate crimes, and occult crimes all received a good deal of media attention and all seemed to be moving toward institutionalization. But by 1995, interest in occult crimes had diminished. Nor is it certain that either stalking or hate crimes will remain high-visibility crime problems; laws against both offenses face resistance from opponents arguing that they are unreasonably broad, that they criminalize constitutionally protected behavior (e.g., does the guarantee of free speech cover nonviolent expressions of unreciprocated interest [in the case of stalking] or prejudice [in the case of hate crimes]?). Depending upon how the courts rule, how vigorously officials choose to enforce the new laws, and whether activists, the press, and experts remain interested in these issues, stalking and hate crimes may remain important, institutionalized crime problems, or they may fade from public attention, becoming something people used to consider serious crimes.

CHAPTER 4

Gangs, Conspiracies,
and Other Cultural Resources

In January 1996, 550 people attended a gang-awareness seminar in Marion, Illinois, led by a "certified gang crime specialist from the Illinois Department of Corrections." The local press covered the meeting; the *Southern Illinoisan*'s front-page headline announced, "It's War," and relayed such information as:

> Gangs come into a community for the money. . . . "There is no
> such thing as a wannabee. That's a copout. A wannabee will be." . . .
> When someone sees a second- or third-grade student draw little
> triangles, circles or pitchforks, that is the time to get involved. . . .
> Wearing the clothing of a sports team does not automatically signify
> a gang affiliation. . . . The No. 1 goal of gangs is to make money
> and gain power through criminal activities, and narcotics is the
> No. 1 source of income. (Rosenberry 1996:7-A)

Gangs, it seemed, had arrived in Marion, the county seat of Williamson County. Once nationally renowned as "Bloody Williamson" for its shootouts and other lethal violence involving labor strife, the Ku Klux Klan, and bootlegging (Angle 1952), the county now heard warnings about a seemingly larger impending threat. The signs of danger—children's doodles, graffiti, and youths wearing team jackets—needed to be understood and addressed.

Of course, Marion was not alone. Warnings about gangs proliferated during the late 1980s and early 1990s. Gang-awareness workshops and seminars for both professionals and ordinary citizens appeared in many communities, alongside handbooks, pamphlets, and stories in the local press. One local community after another learned that it had a gang problem (Marsteller 1996; Tindle 1996; Zevitz and Takata 1992). But these gangs were not described as local problems, responses by local youth to local conditions, but as having links to—being affiliates, even franchises, of—gangs in major cities. Gangs were an infestation, a plague spreading out of the West and into the heartland. As one handbook explained: "MOST MODERN GANGS HAD THEIR START IN LOS ANGELES" (Bart Larson and Amstutz 1995:5; emphasis in original).

LOS ANGELES AND THE DIFFUSION OF GANG IMAGERY

Gangs have been considered an urban crime problem in the United States since at least the 1840s (Asbury 1927; D. Johnson 1979), a subject of periodic waves of concern (cf. Pearson 1983). These "cycles of outrage" (J. Gilbert 1986) are reflected in press coverage, popular culture, and social science. The last major wave of concern during the 1950s produced the reporter Harrison Salisbury's *The Shook-Up Generation* (1958), *West Side Story* and *Blackboard Jungle*, and such influential sociological studies as *Delinquent Boys* (A. Cohen 1955) and *Delinquency and Opportunity* (Cloward and Ohlin 1960), just as the previous wave, in the 1920s and 1930s, inspired Frederic Thrasher's *The Gang* (1927) and other classic works of Chicago School sociology. Our contemporary fascination with gangs can be seen as the most recent wave in this pattern of periodic concern, but there are some differences.

In particular, it is striking how routinely contemporary concern associates gangs with Los Angeles. The journalism, popular culture, and social science produced in earlier waves of concern almost always typified the problem in terms of New York's or, less often, Chicago's gangs.[1] In contrast, the key images used to define the modern gang come from southern California. Claims about the rivalry between huge "supergang" alliances (e.g., the Crips and Bloods) symbolized by wearing or avoiding the colors red and blue, about the highly profitable drug traffic that gives gang members beepers and automatic weapons, about the elaborate vocabulary of gang signs (e.g., gestures, clothing, and graffiti), about violent gang initiation rites targeting non–gang members (e.g., the "Lights Out" story), and about drive-by shootings—all first came to public attention in discussions about Los Angeles's gang problem.

There is some evidence that gangs have emerged in a growing number of U.S. cities. The sociologist Malcolm Klein, a longtime observer of gangs, describes the complexity of "gang cycles"—oscillating patterns of gang activity that reflect seasonal changes, as well as shifting conditions in particular neighborhoods or cities. At the same time, he argues that, since 1960, "through all the periodic cycles, gangs and gang problems have grown. The cycles end at higher plateaus, on average, as if the pendulum seldom reverts to its original level" (Klein 1995b:233). Klein's research documents the spread of street gangs to a growing number of U.S. cities between 1960 and 1992 (Klein 1995a). It is difficult to assess these data; they are based on retrospective interviews, mostly done during the early 1990s, with representatives of police departments in 1,105 cities, including departments in all cities with populations over 100,000 as well as "a random sample of smaller departments" (Klein 1995a:18). Asked whether their cities have street gangs, and if so, when they first appeared, many respondents reported that their cities had moved through "a denial phase" to acknowledging the gangs' presence (p. 39). Klein views these reports as essentially accurate; nationally, gang activity "amounts to a seriously accelerating problem: increases of 74 percent by 1970, 83 percent by 1980, and 345 percent by 1992" (p. 90);

"we can now estimate the number of gang-involved cities and towns in America to be close to 800 and perhaps as high as 1,100" (p. 18). Although Klein discounts claims that this expansion reflects a conspiratorial expansion of Crips and Bloods franchises, his respondents also reported that "gang migration"—"the movement of gang members from one city to another"—was widespread, although the evidence suggests that most gang members "migrate" because their families move (often in attempts to get away from gangs—what John A. Laskey [1996] calls the "familial gang transplant phenomenon") (cf. Maxson 1993; Maxson, Woods, and Klein 1996; Waldorf 1993; Zevitz and Takata 1992).

Klein's relatively measured interpretation can be contrasted with dramatic claims that gangs are intentionally infiltrating communities. Such claims appear in various print media:

In academic works:

Black Los Angeles cultural street gangs seem increasingly to look like gangs designed for the sale of drugs. . . . Los Angeles gangs are expanding their marketing throughout the western United States. (Skolnick et al. 1990:38)

In the press:

There are also signs that gangs are deliberately targeting smaller places. Although academics argue that the notion of well-heeled criminal gangs franchising their business to smaller towns is severely overplayed, the evidence flows in. . . . Chicago-based gang members have been stopped, searched or pulled over for one reason or another in virtually every county of [Illinois]. (*Economist* 1996:29)

In popular handbooks:

Due primarily to the influence of the Bloods and Crips, most new or existing gangs have now chosen to form affiliations and alliances with other gangs. There are now eight major umbrella groups in the United States . . . with hundreds of sub-sets under these classifications, plus numerous non-affiliated miscellaneous gangs. (Bart Larson and Amstutz 1995: 6)

In official documents:

Individuals associated with California's urban street gangs are traveling into other states to sell cocaine. Their presence has been documented as far north as Fairbanks, Alaska, and as far east as New Orleans, Louisiana. (California Council on Criminal Justice 1989:3)

Such warnings encourage local communities to expect ties between their gangs and the L.A. supergangs.

The discovery of local gangs fits the familiar—but routinely misunderstood—dynamics of the moral panic (Jackson 1993; Zatz 1987). Often, a terrible local crime is labeled a "gang crime," and attention then focuses on the city's "gang problem" as though it were a new and especially threatening phenomenon. This is a "moral panic," not because there really are no gangs, but because gangs suddenly become a focus of intense, frightened speculation. What were previously considered "crimes" become "gang crimes," what was once "delinquency" becomes "gang activity," just as offenders and victims begin to be identified as "gang members" or "associates" or "wannabes." The point is not that gangs are an imaginary threat, but that people now have a new framework within which they can interpret what is wrong. If a Chicago "gang member" is pulled over in a downstate traffic stop, or if an individual "associated" with a Los Angeles gang is found selling drugs in Alaska or Louisiana, this now becomes evidence of a nationwide problem of supergang infiltration and expansion.

Such interpretations became easier with the diffusion of gang imagery from Los Angeles. Beginning in the mid-1980s, news reports about Crips and Bloods redefined the gang problem with a set of fresh images. The press also carried stories about California's attempts to crack down on gangs with new laws, criminal justice task forces, and the like. These reports were reaffirmed in popular cultural depictions of

L.A. gangs—in gangsta rap (e.g., *Straight Out of Compton*) and movies (e.g., *Colors* [which opens with a printed explanation that, although Los Angeles County has 250 law-enforcement officers specializing in gangs, "in the greater Los Angeles area there are over 600 street gangs with almost 70,000 members"], *Boyz 'N the Hood*, and *Menace II Society*). As Klein suggests, the result is a widely available repertoire of gang imagery, accessible to both youth (who may adopt these images for their own uses) and adults (who can now search for evidence of gang contamination):

> Gang "style" has been diffused to youth across the country. Millions of youngsters now learn how to dress, talk, act, and even feel like gang members. It doesn't take a big city ghetto to teach about gang life; our media carry it to every vulnerable corner. . . . Even our police and research experts, funded at times by federal and state agencies, contribute to this cultural diffusion through lectures, demonstrations, seminars and workshops on gang behavior, given to other officials, schoolteachers, and parent groups. The depiction of gang life is a commodity, volunteered and marketed to every at-risk and gang-involved sector of our society. (Klein 1995b:230)

It is, then, no wonder that Klein's survey of police departments found reports of gang involvement in a growing number of cities. As youths became better informed about gangs, and with more authorities alerted to the danger of spreading gangs and increasingly knowledgeable about signs of gang activity, the chances that local crime and violence could be interpreted in terms of gangs continued to rise.

This diffusion of gang imagery from Los Angeles to the rest of the country is not unique. During the 1980s, events in Los Angeles brought national attention to and helped define other new crime problems, including freeway violence (1987) and stalking (when claims linked the 1989 murders of Rebecca Schaeffer and four Orange County women), just as the heavily publicized arrests of seven staff members at the McMartin Preschool in 1983 preceded charges of systematic sexual abuse at dozens of preschools and day-care centers around the country.

Why do new crimes often emerge in Los Angeles? Most obviously, Los Angeles is the country's second-largest city and its principal media center. Though New York remains the leading center for journalism (home to the *New York Times* and the *Wall Street Journal*, the major newsmagazines, and the networks' evening news broadcasts), Los Angeles also is a major press center; not only does it have its own influential newspaper (the *Los Angeles Times*), but all major national news media maintain bureaus or, in the case of the television networks, owned-and-operated affiliates in Los Angeles. Moreover, Los Angeles is the center for entertainment media—particularly the recording industry and movie and television production. This concentration of press and entertainment media gives stories set in Los Angeles an advantage: it is easier and cheaper for L.A.-based reporters to cover stories near where they are stationed than to have to travel, just as it is more convenient to stage films and television programs in southern California. This means that, because crime and violence are standard themes in contemporary popular culture, we are accustomed to fictional portrayals of a violent Los Angeles (e.g., the *Terminator* and *Lethal Weapon* movies).

In addition, Los Angeles occupies a special place in the national imagination. For much of this century, Los Angeles has been seen as a style leader. Trends, styles, and fads often seem to travel outward from Los Angeles, moving first to the East Coast, then inward toward the heartland. This pattern is less evident for high culture—New York remains the principal center of the art and fashion worlds—but much popular culture originates in southern California.[2] According to widely shared stereotypes, compared to that of the rest of the country, Los Angeles culture is freer, more diverse, less traditional, and therefore more open to experimentation and innovation. Or, less positively, southern Californians are stereotyped as "crazy," "nuts," and therefore more likely to slip the bonds of convention. This reputation doubtless encourages some innovators to move to L.A., in hopes that their idiosyncrasies may be tolerated, their innovations appreciated, or their influence enhanced.

Combined, these elements help explain why new social phenomena—including new crimes—often become associated with southern California. The notion that social changes begin there has wide acceptance, and the Los Angeles–based media—like news media everywhere, ever alert for whatever seems new and novel—find it easy to identify, package, and promote such news, generating self-fulfilling prophecies about changing social conditions. What might simply seem aberrant elsewhere is easily interpreted as an emerging trend when it occurs in L.A.

The diffusion of new crime problems reflects the competition among social-problems claims to attract the attention of the press, the public, and policymakers (Best 1990; Hilgartner and Bosk 1988). A new social problem must gain recognition, generate concern, and mobilize action; some claims succeed, while others get ignored. This, of course, raises a question: how and why do particular claims succeed? Clearly, geography plays a role. If one hopes to reach a national audience, it helps to be in one of the Big Three media centers: New York, Washington, D.C., or Los Angeles. New York and Los Angeles are the nation's two largest cities, and the national centers for journalism and entertainment media, respectively; and, as the national's capital, Washington is home base for the huge corps of journalists covering the federal government. The Big Three are, at least for social-problems claims, the center ring, where it is easiest to draw and hold the crowd's attention. Obviously, claims can be launched from other cities (e.g., major cities such as Chicago and Atlanta [CNN's home base], or state capitals—particularly in the largest states), and a dramatic incident may draw the media to a distant, relatively unpopulated location, but it is nevertheless relatively difficult to gain—and much more difficult to maintain—attention for social problems that emerge outside the major media centers. The Big Three constitute a geographic "core" from which information about social problems radiates outward, via the media, to the rest of the nation. News of social problems spreads from the core to the periphery, just as policy solutions, once debated in Washington, become subjects of hearings in state capitals.[3] Like the "trickle-down" model of fashion, in which styles originate in expensive goods marketed to an elite and then gradually disseminate in ever cheaper copies sold to those of lesser status who hope to emulate their betters (cf., e.g., Fallers 1954), claims about crime and other social problems trickle down—or, at least, outward—from the Big Three core to the rest of the country.

CONSPIRACIES OF DEVIANTS

Just as contemporary concern about gangs draws upon our belief that new crime problems often start in and spread outward from Los Angeles, today's gang imagery also taps into fears of deviant conspiracies. The notion that deviants—those who break society's rules—conspire against the social order is a standard way of thinking about crime and other evils. There is, of course, a conspiratorial element in many crimes: if two men decide to rob a store together, they agree to cooperate in breaking the law and keep their illegal plan secret from others; we might think of this as a miniconspiracy, involving only two people and lasting perhaps no more than a few moments. In contrast, our fears of supergangs and other conspiracies of deviants involve much grander alliances of evil.

What are the elements that make conspiracies of deviants so frightening? First, such conspiracies are *secretive;* they are hidden, underground arrangements. We don't know much about them, because their members don't want us to know. Second, though we can't be sure just how many belong to a conspiracy, we imagine that there are *large* numbers involved—hundreds, thousands, even millions of conspirators. Third, the conspiracy is *deviant,* dedicated to rule breaking, illegality, disorder, and other evil purposes. Fourth, the conspiracy is purposeful because its leadership is *centralized;* there are leaders giving orders. Fifth, those orders are obeyed because the conspiracy is *hierarchical,* with members who respect a chain of command. Sixth, such conspiracies are *powerful;* they have the ability to do terrible damage, not only because they have many dedicated members, but also because the conspiracy may have infiltrated many of society's vital institutions—police forces, courts, churches, schools, and the like. Seventh, the conspirators are *committed,* bound to the conspiracy through fervor, true believing, oaths, initiation rites, and other emotional ties:

> Conspiracy implies that members of a confession, party, or ethnicity (Jews, Freemasons, communists, pacifists, etc.) are united by an indissoluble secret bond. The object of such an alliance is to foment upheaval in society, pervert societal values, aggravate crises, promote defeat, and so on. The conspiracy mentality divides people, things, and actions into two classes. One is pure, the other impure. These classes are not only distinct, but antagonistic. They are polar opposites: everything social, national, and so forth, versus what is antisocial or antinational, as the case may be. On the one hand, everything normal, lawful, that is, native; on the other hand, everything abnormal, unlawful, and hence, alien. The opposing groups belong to two distinct universes: a region of daylight and clarity versus an opaque and nocturnal milieu. (Moscovici 1987:154)

These are striking, frightening images: they portray society pitted against a most dangerous opponent, a huge, powerful, secretive enemy, an army dedicated to evil, with strong leaders and dedicated, obedient followers.

Warnings about conspiracies of deviants often seek to expose these elements. They present organization charts and histories, glossaries of the conspirators' vocabularies, testimonies of defectors, inventories of signs of involvement, and other evidence suggesting the conspiracy's scope and power. Typifying examples of conspirators' crimes let us infer the conspirators' dedication to the cause, the degree to which the conspiracy has penetrated respectable society, and the like. Ours is a society characterized by bureaucratic institutions. When we envision evil, it, too, has an almost bureaucratic face.

We describe modern gangs in these terms: gangs are secretive; they are large (and spreading); their business is calculated, deliberate, and structured; dealing in drugs, violence, and other crime, they form great, powerful hierarchies through supergang alliances; and their members have a rich, secretive culture of colors, gang signs, and initiation rites. No wonder we worry about the gang menace.

It is striking how often the image of conspiracy appears in American history. At one time or another, Americans have denounced and warned against the dangers posed by conspiracies of witches, Catholics, slaves, Jews, abolitionists, Freemasons, carpetbaggers, the Ku Klux Klan, capitalists, workers, racketeers, white slavers, drug smugglers, Communists, outside agitators, and on and on. As the historian Richard Hofstadter (1966) argued, there is a "paranoid style" that runs through American politics.[4] This theme is apparent not only in political debates, but often in the ways we talk about crime; in contemporary fears about gangs, but also in recent discussions of satanism (as a million-member blood cult annually conducting tens of thousands of human sacrifices), organized crime (as a confederation of Mafia families not just controlling organized crime, but spreading its influence into government and legitimate business), and the market for illicit drugs (as controlled by the cartels of Colombian drug lords). Claims about conspiracies of deviants may appear in the mainstream media (e.g., press coverage of gangs and organized crime), in more specialized media (e.g., books from Christian publishing houses warning about the threat posed by satanists [J. Johnston 1989; Bob Larson 1989]), and even in everyday conversation (e.g., some African-Americans' claims that conspiracies of government or business elites are to blame for street crime, crack, AIDS, and other problems in black ghettos [Sasson 1995b; P. Turner 1993]).

Our emphasis on the conspiratorial qualities of gangs helps explain much of the contemporary reaction to gang problems: police departments' decisions to form "gang intelligence units"; the dissemination of workshops and educational materials designed to help adults recognize and interpret the gestures, clothing, graffiti, and other secret symbols of gang involvement; and the ubiquity of "the gang initiation rite" as an explanation for criminal activity.

Journalists, social workers, and sociologists who have observed gangs firsthand regularly report that gangs sometimes initiate new members. Gangs want prospective members to prove their toughness and commitment to the gang before they join; most often, the initiation requires that the newcomers physically fight other members of the gang for a minute or so. This "jumping in" demonstrates the initiates' willingness to defend themselves and the gang's territory. This sort of initiation has been documented in a wide variety of gangs over a period of decades (Best and Hutchinson 1996; Vigil 1996).

However, the public image of gang initiations is very different, involving random, often lethal violence against strangers rather than ritualized fighting among the gangs' members. Contemporary legends, such as the "Lights Out" and ankle-grabbing stories discussed in chapter 1, warn of gangs requiring new members to commit murder or rape. In addition, news reports regularly attribute particular crimes—or types of crimes—to gang initiations:

> Police assume Adams [shot in a drive-by] was victim of a gang initiation rite. . . . Adams, the father of two young sons, said he is not considering moving to the suburbs. (Such random violence can happen anywhere in America.) Instead, he and his wife, Carol, are seriously thinking about moving to the southwest coast of Ireland. (Saporta 1994)

> The FOLKS, the Crips and La Raza in Chamblee have made auto theft an initiation rite, police said. Those gangs, police say, have targeted suburban malls. (McDonald 1994)

Notice that both stories cite police claims that unsolved crimes were committed as part of gang initiations. For the victims, the police, and the press, gang initiations seem to offer a way of making sense of otherwise senseless crimes. We don't need to puzzle over why a respectable citizen is shot or has a car stolen from a mall; such hard-to-explain crimes can be attributed to gang initiation rites, to criminal conspiracies requiring initiates to commit terrible, otherwise senseless crimes. Moreover, the initiation rite is the entryway into gang membership. Presumably, gangs that require terrible crimes of their initiates do so because they are conspiracies dedicated to disorder. Having passed the initiation test, gang members will no doubt be willing and ready to commit other acts of random violence. Thus, if crime and victimization seem pointless, it is only because their true meaning is hidden, concealed behind the secrecy of a deviant conspiracy. In this way, any crime, no matter how mundane it may seem, can be seen as evidence of a major threat to society. Innocent people are injured because initiation rites require gang members to injure the innocent. That's just the kind of thing they do—and will continue to do.

The very term "initiation rite" has anthropological connotations; it suggests scientific objectivity, but it has other connotations as well. It hints that gang members might be characterized by various invidious terms for the anthropologist's subjects—"primitives," "savages," and the like. In these ways, claims about gang initiations borrow from what we know—or think we know—about initiation rituals. As Georg Simmel (1950:360) suggested: "Through the symbolism of the ritual, which excites a whole range of vaguely delimited feelings beyond all particular, rational interests, the secret society synthesizes those interests into a total claim upon the individual." According to legends and press reports about gang initiations, the rituals require prospective gang members to commit serious crimes; in doing so, the initiates both demonstrate their capacity for and commitment to the gang's criminality, and take an irrevocable step into deviance. Thus, descriptions of initiation rites for deviant conspirators serve to emphasize the gulf between deviance and respectability. Initiation makes the transformation from respectability to deviance manifest; requiring the initiate to commit some awful crime demonstrates a commitment to deviance and binds the new member to the deviant group.

Ethnographers and historians often dispute conspiratorial interpretations of deviance. In retrospect, witches, Reds, mafiosi, dope peddlers, and white slavers often appear less organized, less powerful, and less threatening than once claimed, just as the last great juvenile-gang menace of the 1950s became the stuff of nostalgic movies and musicals. Thus, researchers studying organized crime criticize descriptions of a nationally coordinated Mafia for exaggerating of the bureaucratization, centralization, and power of organized-crime families (Haller 1990; Ianni 1972; Reuter 1983), just as ethnographies of satanists find no evidence of a powerful, conspiratorial blood cult (Bainbridge 1991; B. Ellis 1991; Lowney 1995). Similarly, students of contemporary gangs detail the analytic problems that call most claims about gangs into question: defining gangs and distinguishing among various types of gangs; assessing the degree to which gangs have hierarchies of authority, centralized decision making, and other features of formal organizations; determining the nature and strengths of ties among gangs; and deciding which deviant acts committed by gang members should be designated "gang related." In general, careful research tends to find gang activities less structured, rationalized, and centralized than descriptions in the press or popular discourse would lead one to believe (Jackson 1993, Klein 1995a). But proponents of conspiracy claims do not consider such findings compelling: after all, a successful conspiracy can surely conceal its true workings from naive researchers, or even enlist researchers as coconspirators.

Studies of criminal violence commonly reveal that homicide, rape, and robbery emerge in relatively mundane interactions; the offenders' motives hardly seem to measure up to the awful consequences of their acts. One way we can rectify this discrepancy is by blaming terrible actions on terrible motivations. Explaining a killing as a product of gang culture, and therefore as part of the workings of a deviant conspiracy, in some ways both reduces and increases our fears. It comforts us by making sense of the world, explaining the inexplicable. But it also frightens us by characterizing the world as a most dangerous place, the scene of a titanic battle between the forces of good and a conspiracy of evil.

Of course, we don't imagine that all deviants belong to conspiracies. There are other, equally familiar ways of envisioning criminals and other deviants: as rational calculators, balancing the potential costs of being caught against the prospective benefits of getting away with it; as amoral offenders, lacking any standards for decency; or as irrational actors, whose offenses can be neither understood nor predicted. Each of these models is widely understood; each is readily available to be invoked as a framework for understanding new crimes: thus, wilding could be depicted as the actions of amoral offenders, stalking as a form of irrational behavior, and so on. When we discover a new crime problem, the particulars of the offense—shooting at other drivers on a freeway, say—may be considered new, but the offense is likely to be interpreted and understood in familiar terms, as belonging to some well-established category or type of deviance—conspiracy, irrationality, and so on.

CULTURAL RESOURCES

Thus we see that contemporary concerns about gangs, concerns that focus on specific, up-to-date details about supergangs, drive-bys, and other apparently new threats posed by gangs, combine those elements with existing—in some cases, centuries-old—ideas and images. Today's gang imagery cobbles together a diverse set of ideas, including notions about Los Angeles's place on the cutting edge of contemporary crimi- nality, fears about powerful conspiracies of deviants, and even images from earlier waves of concern about gangs.[5] In this way, we assemble new crime problems, building new fears by combining reports of cur- rent events (e.g., drive-by shootings) with older, familiar images (e.g., the threat of deviant conspiracies).

Our fears about new crime problems, then, draw upon an inventory of available cultural resources. Earlier generations of sociologists often spoke of culture as a unified whole, a coherent, consistent body of knowledge and rules that governed individuals' every action. But most modern sociologists have a looser vision of culture; they prefer Ann Swidler's metaphor (1986), viewing culture as a "tool kit"—a large collection of ideas that can be invoked by individuals when it seems appropriate. These ideas do not form a coherent whole; people use whichever pieces strike them as suitable and convenient at the time, and their choices may strike others as inconsistent. In this looser vision of culture, we draw upon what we know to create new knowledge, so that what we know about, say, Los Angeles and deviant conspiracies helps us make sense of contemporary gangs.

Sociologists of social movements argue that successful movements are those able to mobilize key resources, such as leaders able to lead and members willing to invest their time, energy, and money in the cause (McCarthy and Zald 1977). Rhys Williams (1995:125) argues that culture also serves as a resource for social movements: "Movement rhetoric and ideology can be thought of as 'cultural resources' and analyzed in many of the same ways as are the more conventional 'structural' resources of money, members, and organizations." That is, movements need powerful, compelling ideas in order to change society.

Just as social movements inevitably mobilize cultural resources in their efforts to advance change, advocates who hope to draw attention to social problems must find ways to make their claims persuasive. Because claims compete for public attention, they must adopt effective rhetoric. This means tapping into the broader culture, presenting an issue in ways that evoke "deep mythic themes or broad cultural preoccupations" (Hilgartner and Bosk 1988:71), that have "cultural resonance" (W. Gamson and Modigliani 1989:5–6), or that serve as "moral vocabularies, providing participants with sets or clusters of themes or 'sacred' symbols capable of endowing claims with significance" (Ibarra and Kitsuse 1993:35–36). Or, put differently, it means that claims about new crimes and other social problems draw upon cultural resources.

There are many ways to analyze the cultural meanings of social-problems claims. Various studies recommend using such concepts as "templates" (Best 1991), "idioms" (Ibarra and Kitsuse 1993), "motifs"

(Best and Hutchinson 1996), "styles" (Ibarra and Kitsuse 1993), "models" (R. Williams 1995), and "frames" (W. Gamson and Modigliani 1989). But, whichever concepts seem most useful in analyzing a particular case, all of these elements can be seen as cultural resources, borrowed to give shape to some social problem. Whenever someone says that X is a problem that deserves our attention, that claim invokes bits of cultural knowledge about the sort of problem X is, the reasons we ought to worry about X, the sorts of policies we ought to adopt to address X, and so on.

Of course, not all cultural resources are equally compelling or equally available. Rhetoric that may seem overwhelmingly powerful at one time or place can lose its punch in a different setting. As the language used to describe social problems changes, older terms become unfashionable, then embarrassing, and finally ridiculous. Terms like "pauper" and "drunkard," once signs of the most advanced thinking, drop out of use, while other words remain but change their meaning (e.g., in the nineteenth century, "prostitution" might refer to any act of nonmarital sex). One hundred years ago, it was routine for public figures to couch claims about social problems in terms of sin, redemption, and other religious language, for religious leaders to be among the most visible and vocal advocates of social change, and for the press and government officials to acknowledge social policy as a religious obligation. Today, although religion has not completely vanished from discussions of social problems, it has been pushed aside in favor of more secular language. The cultural resources chosen for talk about social problems, then, constantly change, as advocates look for ways to make their claims seem compelling to a contemporary audience.

Similarly, not all cultural resources are accessible to all advocates (R. Williams 1995). Every cause places constraints upon its advocates: it is easy to make some arguments, harder to make others, and virtually impossible to say yet other things without losing credibility. For example, if we describe a crime as a form of clear-cut exploitation, it becomes easy to talk about innocent victims, but much harder to discuss victims who may be viewed as less than perfectly innocent. Whenever we declare a principle—a reverence for life, say, or equal justice under the law—it becomes easier to make some sorts of claims than others. The process is circular: who we think we are shapes the cultural resources we choose, and those choices in turn affect how we look at ourselves.

What does all this have to do with gangs and other new crime problems? When advocates bring a new crime to our attention, they package it as a set of claims: there is a crime (say, stalking); it should be understood in particular terms (e.g., it is serious, a form of domestic violence, very common, on the rise, etc.); the offenders have particular motivations (e.g., obsession, hatred of women, etc.), engage in particular behaviors (e.g., following and harassing), and will probably engage in others (e.g., becoming violent); the victims have particular qualities (e.g., innocence and vulnerability); and this crime should be addressed in particular ways (e.g., passing and strictly enforcing antistalking laws). Each element in such claims can be seen as a cultural resource; the words we choose, and the meanings they have, depend upon our larger cultural framework (e.g., our understanding of violence against women).

Claims about new crimes lean heavily upon melodramatic imagery (Nelson-Rowe 1995). The key figures in melodrama are the victim and the villain. In melodrama, the victim is good, innocent, vulnerable, powerless (for a more detailed discussion of contemporary views of victims, see chapter 5). Most claims about crimes typify victims as respectable citizens, particularly people who are both respectable and vulnerable—children, women, the elderly. In contrast, melodrama's villains are not just bad, but threatening: they are evil, depraved, cruel, powerful, vicious predators. The crime involves the intersection of these two characters: the villain attacks the victim, inflicting terrible harm. Warnings about new crimes tell us about these offenses; they describe outrages and enlist our concern against the villains and on behalf of the victims and the well-being of the larger society. Thus, we learn about wilding and freeway violence, stalking and hate crimes, conspiratorial gangs, and other new crimes as forms of random violence. We react with fear and outrage. Something, we say, must be done.

This melodramatic formula can be recycled endlessly. Thus, U.S. history features recurring drug scares (Reinarman 1994). Periodically, someone—perhaps a politician or a criminal justice official, perhaps an investigative journalist, perhaps an antidrug activist—draws attention to a "new" drug problem. During the twentieth century, Americans have worried periodically about the dangers posed by opium, cocaine, morphine, bootleg alcohol, heroin, moonshine, marijuana, LSD, speed, crack, ice, and on and on. Although some new drugs have been discovered during the twentieth century, most drug problems involve existing drugs. There are cycles in concern about particular drugs; the press reports that some once-familiar drug (heroin or marijuana or LSD) is "making a comeback," spreading through a new generation of users. The dynamics of these drug scares are well known: a drug is brought to public attention; we are warned that it poses particularly severe dangers (this threat is always much greater than ever before) and that the drug's use is spreading (always much more widely than ever before); new antidrug policies are promoted (naturally, they must be much tougher than ever before); and then, after a while, the drug begins to drift out of the public's notice. Essentially the same cycle appears in the periodic concern over other social problems, including gangs.

The appeals of melodramatic claims are obvious. Melodrama is vivid; it presents social issues in black and white, in terms of evil villains and innocent victims. It is the foundation for most popular entertainment—an easily understood, endlessly popular formula. But the formula for fictional melodrama can be adapted to serious talk about social issues. This was a central discovery of the early penny press: a good ax murder makes a great news story (Tucher 1994). Contemporary journalists know this, too—and not just the tabloids; even relatively serious programs such as *60 Minutes* depend on their ability to dramatize social issues in terms of innocents harmed by callous predators. And crime stories, which inevitably feature someone breaking the law, can be presented effortlessly in melodramatic terms. Melodrama itself, then, is a major cultural resource, readily available to anyone hoping to draw attention to some new crime problem.

Moreover, alternative ways of depicting crime are much less satisfying. Criminologists know that most crime—even most violent crime—is mundane, inspired by base, but not especially dramatic, motives. People hurt other people because they are angry or jealous, or they don't want to look weak, or for other reasons equally ordinary. It is hard to get the press to cover the mundane, the public to worry about it, or policymakers to do something about it. The basic crime story is too familiar; we already know that things get stolen and people get hurt. Mundane crimes seem routine, boring, unworthy of our attention. Reporters ignore or pay minimal attention to violence and theft among the poor. Killing a spouse is news when it involves the rich or the famous, but not when it happens in a housing project. Mundane problems, by definition, don't grab our attention. Arousing concern about a new crime demands that advocates choose compelling cultural resources. No wonder we prefer melodrama.

THE APPEAL OF NEW CRIMES

Novelty is a central theme in our culture. Advertisers consider "new" a powerful word. The assertion that ours is a "rapidly changing" society may be our most common sociological cliché. The ever-expanding news and entertainment media watch for "news" to report. We love novelty, we celebrate it, even when we talk about our afflictions. New problems are more interesting than old problems; new problems command media attention, inspire advocates to rally around the new cause, and become the topics of everyday conversations.

The history of gang concerns displays this love of novelty. Gangs have long been with us, yet we periodically contrive to rediscover them. And we inevitably find that today's gangs are somehow worse than their predecessors—bigger, badder, harder to fight. Such warnings, packaged in ways that speak to our fears, seem necessary to arouse concern and induce us to act. But the price of this action is fear, the taken-for-granted pessimism that things are bad and getting worse, that our glass is half-empty—and probably leaking.

As lovers of novelty, we demand new crimes. But our efforts to discover and understand new forms of crime extend beyond our images of criminality and offenders. Just as we search for new crimes and new kinds of criminals, so too are we alert for new forms of suffering at those criminals' hands.

CHAPTER 5

The New Victims

By the mid-1990s, the shelves of every shopping-mall bookstore revealed a wide-ranging fascination with—and ambivalence toward—victims and victimization. The "True Crime" section featured book-length accounts of grisly homicides, especially within well-to-do families. The "Recovery" or "Self-Improvement" section contained guidebooks for victims of crime, abuse, addictions, and other disorders (the appeal of books about recovery was very broad; some of the same titles stocked in chain bookstores could also be found in women's bookstores operated by radical feminists and Christian bookstores run by conservative evangelicals, as well as in the emerging specialty shops that sold only recovery books). Meanwhile, the "Current Events" section displayed *I'm Dysfunctional, You're Dysfunctional* (Kaminer 1992), *A Nation of Victims* (Sykes 1992), *Culture of Complaint* (Hughes 1993), *The Abuse Excuse* (Dershowitz 1994), and other titles criticizing a culture that seemed to celebrate victimization.

The rise of victims to public prominence parallels the way we learn about new crime problems. The media not only bring new crimes to public attention; they also discover and describe new categories of people—stalkers and hackers and slackers and soccer moms. With new categories emerging and old ones fading from use, our sense of the

composition of our social world continually shifts. Changing historical circumstances cause new categories of actors—carpetbaggers and
consumptives, flappers and beatniks—to appear on society's stage at
particular historical moments, only to exit as events change and other
new figures enter. This shifting cast of characters, these social types, reflect changes in culture and social structure (Hacking 1986; Klapp
1962; Loseke 1993).

By and large, we take the changing categories used to classify people
for granted; we rarely ask why new categories appear, or how they
arise. Even most sociologists ignore the social arrangements that generate new social types.[1] One exception is research on the "manufacture" or "mass production" of deviants, focused on social control campaigns such as witch-hunts and political purges that lead to large
numbers of people being labeled deviant (e.g., Ben-Yehuda 1980; Connor 1972; Currie 1968; Greenblatt 1977). Viewing these episodes as
extraordinary, analysts try to understand the social arrangements—the
ideologies and institutions—that make it possible to identify thousands
of witches or traitors. What we fail to notice is that even the most in-
nocuous new social category involves labeling people, and there are
ideologies and institutions that make that labeling possible.

This chapter and the one that follows examine how new categories
of victims emerge in contemporary America. Their focus is on what we
might call the "new victims," forms of victimization that achieved high
visibility during the past twenty or twenty-five years.[2] Like new crimes,
new victims must be brought to public attention by advocates who tap
into cultural resources to make compelling claims about a particular
form of victimization. In the contemporary United States, there is a
readiness to accept such claims at face value: "Conventional victimology . . . *presupposes* that some persons or groups are objectively 'victims' without explicitly considering the interpretive definitional processes implicated in assignment of victim status" (Holstein and Miller
1990:104; emphasis in original). In contrast, these chapters will focus

on the emergence of victimization, on the processes of devising, publicizing, and gaining acceptance for new categories of victims.

What are the new victims? They are categories or social types describing people whose sufferings came to widespread public attention sometime around or after 1975. In most cases, these new victims do not experience brand-new varieties of suffering; their advocates usually argue that these forms of victimization have long histories, but that they have been systematically ignored, neglected, or hidden from view. What is new is that they finally are receiving the recognition, sympathy, and support they deserve, that Americans now recognize these new categories.

"New victims" is a general label for a broad range of categories. Advocates do not speak for new victims in general; rather, they make claims about particular categories or types of victimization. Many categories involve direct exploitation by a victimizer, such as marital rape, acquaintance rape, date rape, elder abuse, sibling abuse, peer abuse, work abuse, emotional abuse, telephone abuse, verbal abuse, clergy abuse, satanic ritual abuse, sexual abuse, sexual harassment, hate crimes, serial murder, freeway violence, bullying, stalking, drunk driving, and UFO abductions. Other forms of victimization are associated with psychological problems such as sexual addiction, love addiction, food addiction, eating disorders, post-traumatic stress disorder (PTSD), multiple-personality disorder (MPD), false-memory syndrome, credit-card dependency, and codependency. Although these psychological problems may not involve direct exploitation, they often are considered maladaptive responses to abusive or dysfunctional family relationships—in effect, indirect products of victimization.[3]

Obviously, this is a diverse list. It includes categories, such as sexual abuse, that have gained universal acceptance, as well as others, such as UFO abductions, that continue to face considerable skepticism.[4] The advocates for different categories of new victims have varied credentials and backgrounds: several campaigns began within the women's movement, but others emerged within various therapeutic or helping professions, conservative Christianity, the recovery movement, and elsewhere. Grouping them into the general category of new victims emphasizes what they have in common rather than their obvious differences. What they share is the process by which they come to public attention. The new victims are new not because their sufferings are unprecedented, but because the combination of ideas and social arrangements that bring them to public prominence is new. After roughly 1975, Americans established new ways to talk about and act toward victims. Just as we worry about new crimes, we now have sympathy for new victims.

Exploring this process requires first examining recent historical developments that prepared the way for claims about new victims, and then examining the resulting ideology of victimization. These are the tasks of this chapter. Chapter 6 continues the argument by first identifying the ideology's institutional supports, and then describing how these social arrangements create a "victim industry"—an apparatus capable of identifying and labeling large numbers of victims.

HISTORICAL CONTEXT: DRAWING ATTENTION TO VICTIMS, 1960–1975

All claims about social problems belong to particular historical periods; they have roots in the culture and social structure of their time. Because the interconnections among ideas are so complex, we can never trace the entire social context for a set of claims; we can identify only some of the most important links. Thus, we can note several historical developments, particularly between 1960 and 1975, that reshaped attitudes toward victims and victimization. Obviously, the idea of victimization did not originate in 1960; calling attention to victims has long been a staple of social-problems rhetoric. Still, during these years a diverse set of claims by social activists, political conservatives and liberals, and medical, scientific, and legal authorities promoted increased aware-

ness of and concern for victims. Together, these developments drew attention to the plight of victims, laying a foundation for claims about the
new victims.

Social Movements for Equal Rights

The visibility of the black civil rights movement during the early
1960s inspired other social movements demanding equal rights for
women, homosexuals, the disabled, the elderly, children, and others.
Later movements borrowed tactics, rhetoric, and sometimes personnel
from their predecessors. The Great Society programs of the 1960s af-
firmed already expanding notions of entitlement—of what society owes
its members—and expectations for fair treatment spread. The rhetoric
of rights proved to be exceptionally malleable in the hands of different advocates: if feminists argued that pregnant women had abortion
rights, the religiously devout could insist that the endangered fetus had
a right to life; fathers, as well as mothers, could claim rights to their
children; and movements arose to expand the rights of prisoners, mental patients, and even animals.

Calls for equal rights portrayed particular groups as systematically
disadvantaged—as victimized by a society that gave the groups' members less than their due. These movements complained that their constituents faced prejudice and discrimination, and demanded that they
receive equal rights. Radicals in some movements used more extreme
rhetoric, speaking of oppression or exploitation. However advocates
characterized these problems, equal-rights movements defined large seg-
ments of society—totaling well over half its population—as victims,
described the processes of their victimization, and advocated reforms
to correct these inequities (Bumiller 1988).

The Victims' Rights Movement

Rulings by the Supreme Court of the 1960s under Earl Warren extended the rights of criminal suspects and restricted police powers to

search, arrest, and interrogate. Many political conservatives deplored these decisions: the Court, they argued, was protecting the rights of criminals while ignoring the rights of the criminals' victims. By the late 1960s, many Republican political campaigns featured rhetoric about the need to support victims' rights.

At roughly the same time, the emerging women's movement drew attention to women's victimization, particularly through rape and domestic battering. Feminists called for tougher laws and stricter enforcement, for more sensitive, supportive treatment of victims by the authorities, for the establishment of shelters and counseling services. Like conservatives, feminists began referring to victims' rights.

A new victims' rights movement developed where conservatives' and feminists' concerns overlapped (Weed 1995).[5] Victim advocacy organizations emerged and began campaigning for victims' rights legislation—such as state laws permitting victim compensation, victim impact statements, and victim allocution at sentencing and parole hearings—and the addition of a "victims' bill of rights" to state constitutions. Although some critics (Elias 1986, 1993) argue that these laws did little to improve victims' lives, "victims' rights" had become a symbolically important slogan.

The campaign for victims' rights shifted attention away from the police practices criticized by the Supreme Court, and onto the suffering inflicted by criminals. Victims' rights advocates blamed the villains. Unlike early studies of "victimology," victims' rights crusaders did not speak of victim precipitation or provocation; their rhetoric typified "ideal victims"—vulnerable, respectable innocents, exploited by more powerful, deviant strangers (Christie 1986). Crime victims were sympathetic figures who needed the state's help to rectify the unequal conflict between innocent victims and evil criminals.

By the late 1970s, several social movements operated under the broad banner of victims' rights. Not all focused on criminal violence. Denouncing the notion that abortion was a "victimless crime," antiabortion crusaders made the "murdered" fetus the centerpiece of their movement, insisting that abortion had a victim, and that that victim should have the right to life. Other movements to protect children, less clearly linked to political conservatives, also spoke of the rights of victims, including Mothers Against Drunk Driving, Parents of Murdered Children, the missing-children movement, and the child-pornography movement (Best 1990). Like equal-rights movements, victims' rights crusaders argued that society was neglecting millions of victims.

Blaming the Victim

The political left also adopted victim imagery during this period. William Ryan (1971), a psychologist and civil rights activist, published a well-received book, *Blaming the Victim*, focusing on the problems of what would later be called the black underclass—children who did poorly in school, unwed adolescent mothers, drug addicts, street criminals, rioters, and so on. Ryan argued that this underclass, too often seen as villains in middle-class eyes, were the products—or victims—of racial and class oppression, and that criticizing their behavior amounted to blaming powerless people for their own victimization. The notion was not new; earlier generations of psychiatrists and social workers had argued that delinquents were "victims of society," but Ryan's rephrasing caught on. Part of its appeal may have been its ambiguity; it let one identify victims without necessarily naming the villains.

A catchy expression, "blaming the victim" quickly took on a life of its own; Ryan's original focus on the underclass was soon lost as the phrase became applied to a broad range of victims. Feminists, for instance, attacked institutional arrangements for blaming female victims—the rape investigation that amounted to a second assault, psychiatrists who characterized battered women as masochists, and so on. Within universities, victim blaming assumed the status of a logical fallacy, an unacceptable line of reasoning that, once identified, seemed to discredit any argument (Wright 1993). The term became a rhetorical trump card, playable in almost any political contest.

Just as the slogan "victims' rights" shifted attention away from police practices and onto criminal offenders, "blaming the victim" redirected critiques away from the actions of individuals and toward the structure of the social system. Both the right and the left now portrayed the victim as a sympathetic figure, using victim imagery to promote crackdowns on crime or calls for social reform, respectively. Both conservatives and liberals treated victims as powerless unfortunates, blameless for their circumstances and suffering at the hands of powerful exploiters. Of course, the street criminal who functioned as the exploitative villain in the right's imagery might be considered a blamed victim in the left's, but identifying villains was usually less important than labeling their victims. Thus, victim imagery became central to a broad range of positions on many political and social issues.

Expanding Therapists' Influence

After 1960, the ranks of mental-health professionals grew more rapidly than the general population. Public and private medical-insurance plans spread, and their coverage for mental-health services (e.g., substance-abuse programs and personal counseling) expanded. These benefits fostered a growing number of therapeutic professionals—clinical psychologists, licensed clinical social workers, family counselors, and so on—whose eligibility to receive compensation from insurers was established in new state and federal legislation (Dorken 1986; McGuire 1980). There was a parallel proliferation of specialists outside the therapeutic mainstream, in alternative therapies associated with health foods, the New Age movement, evangelical Christianity, women's healing, and so on. These therapists routinely medicalized family dynamics and other aspects of their patients' lives. The medical model's authority, and its natural focus on the afflictions experienced by patients, made it easy to describe individuals' troubled behaviors as "disorders" or "syndromes" that, often, were products of victimization (Conrad 1992).

Therapists could apply a growing number of diagnoses; within the professional mainstream, the American Psychiatric Association's *Diagnostic and Statistical Manual* (the official catalog of diagnostic categories) grew with each new edition and revision (Kirk and Kutchins 1992). The domains of individual diagnoses also expanded. Thus, when Vietnam veterans lobbied to have combat-induced disorders included in the *DSM*, the APA listed post-traumatic stress disorder as a diagnosis (Scott 1993). The label PTSD could be—and soon was—extended in ways a more directly combat-linked term might not have been, as therapists argued that PTSD's symptoms were exhibited by victims of many different forms of "traumatic stress" (Herman 1992). More therapists, armed with more diagnoses, could identify far more victims.

The Rejection of Risk

Science, too, assumed growing authority in interpreting social problems. Following the 1964 U.S. surgeon general's report ratifying scientific research on the dangers of smoking, research-based warnings proliferated about a wide range of risks associated with various products, foods, and activities. Claims about risk were central to the emerging health and consumer movements. News stories about risks became common, and debates raged over causality, evidence, and interpretations, with advocates denouncing various risks and their critics insisting that the claims exaggerated or distorted the hazards. Contemporary culture's dependence on—and suspicion of—technology provided a background for these debates over risk (Douglas and Wildavsky 1982).

Claims about risks often held those who developed, distributed, or regulated technology accountable to those who suffered harm (Stone 1989). Increasingly, government agencies sought to regulate risks, while hazard victims turned to the civil courts, demanding compensation for their suffering (Priest 1990). Procedural reforms and new legal theories increased both would-be litigants' access to the courts and defendants' vulnerability to lawsuits, providing the basis for precedent-setting court decisions (Olson 1991). Both the new regulations and the court cases attracted further news coverage, contributing to the awareness of risk.

There was a growing presumption that the causes of social problems could be understood, and therefore that risks could be known and should be prevented. Those who suffered were not merely unfortunate pawns of random fate; rather, they were victims, harmed by callous social arrangements.[6] The sense that risks were widespread and unacceptable had corollaries: victimization from hazards was common; and victimizers should be held accountable. Thus, like medicine, science and the law became increasingly involved in identifying victims.

The Visibility of Victims

This list of developments between 1960 and 1975 is obviously incomplete. Other changes drew attention to victimization during the same period: critical social scientists increasingly defined their task as exposing powerful institutional arrangements while defending society's most vulnerable members; victimology emerged as a specialty within criminology; social-service programs expanded; and so on. But the general point should be clear: a broad range of authorities—including social-movement activists, political conservatives and liberals, therapists, scientists, and lawyers—became more likely to talk about victimization in society. The effect was cumulative: early claims often served as reference points for those that followed. Between 1960 and 1975, victims became far more visible, an increasingly common focus for social-problems claims.

THE CONTEMPORARY IDEOLOGY
OF VICTIMIZATION

These earlier developments drew attention to issues of victimization and laid the foundation for talking about the new victims. Increasingly, advocates insisted that victims' problems needed to be recognized and addressed. Claims about different kinds of victims were mutually reinforcing; advocates borrowed language, orientations, explanations, tactics, and solutions from one another. That is, the elements in particular claims became cultural resources, capable of being adapted to characterize a broad range of victims. Thus, how people talked about forms of victimization that emerged in the mid-1970s, such as sexual abuse, shaped claims about problems that only later gained attention, such as stalking. This cross-fertilization was ongoing. Borrowing among campaigns was not just taken for granted; it was desirable—a way to keep up, to stay current. Advocates published newsletters and organized conferences that emphasized parallels among forms of victimization. Gradually, a coherent, albeit implicit, ideology evolved. Seven ideas seem central to discussions about the various new victims. Combined, these ideas form the contemporary ideology of victimization, a powerful set of ideas that made it easy to identify and label individuals as victims. Each of these ideas deserves close consideration.

1. *Victimization is widespread.* Advocates almost always argue that victimization is very common. Claims about social problems often emphasize the large numbers of people affected. Big numbers imply a big problem, one that demands attention (Best 1990). Such statistics suggest that the suffering experienced by the new victims is widespread, even ubiquitous: "'What we're hearing from experts,' John Bradshaw confidently told an interviewer not long ago, 'is that approximately 96 percent of the families in this country are dysfunctional to one degree or another'" (Rieff 1991:51). Similarly, 96 percent of the population is reported to be codependent (Kaminer 1992:10). Although these claims

of near-universality are atypical, estimates that particular forms of victimization affect a substantial fraction of the population are common:

> Something's wrong in a society where 60 million are seriously affected by alcoholism; 60 million are sex abuse victims; 60% of women and 50% of men have eating disorders; one out of eight is a battered woman; . . . and there is massive child abuse. (Bradshaw 1988:172)

> One of every 50 American adults—some 3.7 million people—indicate they may have had an abduction experience with an unidentified flying object, according to Roper Organization polls sponsored by the Intruders Foundation and the Fund for UFO Research. (Jefferson 1992:1)

In order to justify these estimates, advocates promote broad definitions of victimization. Frequently, their initial campaigns focus attention on clear-cut, especially severe examples of social problems, while later claims seek to expand the problem's domain (Best 1990). Thus, the modern campaign against child abuse first addressed the "battered-child syndrome" (typified by severe beatings of very young children); the acceptance of child abuse as a social problem then laid a foundation for expanding the domain to include neglect, sexual abuse, emotional abuse, and so on. Claims about the new victims often feature this sort of domain expansion. For instance, the evolution of feminist thought on rape has led to increasingly broad standards for redefining the domain of sexual assault, including arguments that "no means no," that anything short of an explicit "yes" means no, and even that "women in our patriarchal culture can never freely consent to sex" (Muehlenhard et al. 1992:34). Post-traumatic stress disorder originated as a diagnosis for combat-related psychiatric problems of Vietnam veterans, but later claims applied the PTSD label to victims of a broad array of traumatic stresses, ranging from battering and incest (Herman 1992) to receiving contaminated fast food (Cowell 1992). Early examples of sexual harassment involved male supervisors extorting sex from their vulnerable female subordinates—only a small sector of what, by the 1990s, would become the problem's domain, encompassing anything that individuals experienced as an intimidating, hostile, or otherwise adverse environment (Patai 1997; Weeks et al. 1986). In each case, these redefinitions markedly expanded the problem's domain.

Advocates often bolstered their claims with research designed to produce big numbers (DeKeseredy 1995; M. Smith 1994). Any attempt to measure a social problem requires operational definitions—defining what does or doesn't count—and every definition runs the risk of making two potential errors. On the one hand, an overly narrow definition might lead researchers to exclude from analysis serious cases that should be considered (in effect, labeling false negatives). On the other hand, an excessively broad definition might cause them to include minor, marginal cases that perhaps ought not be considered (in effect, identifying false positives). Convinced that victimization was widespread and too often ignored and neglected, advocates for the new victims considered false negatives far more troubling than false positives (N. Gilbert 1997). They did not want their research to repeat society's error by overlooking victims. Therefore, they designed research using broad, inclusive definitions and multiple measures of victimization, research unlikely to exclude any serious incidents (but thereby almost certain to count large numbers of what might be considered less troubling events): "Feminist surveys . . . that define violence on the basis of women's subjective experiences of violence, including noncriminal and marginally criminal acts, uncover very high levels of violence" (M. Smith 1994:111).[7]

Obviously, big numbers, broad definitions, and inclusive research reinforce one another. Defining victimization broadly fosters higher estimates for its incidence. If the domain of "sexual violence" includes flashing and "touching assaults by relatively young boys," then the proportion of women who have been victims of sexual violence will be far greater than if some narrower definition is applied (Kelly 1988:68). Documenting this level of victimization requires inclusive research that measures victimization's full range, while the big numbers produced by this research encourage us to think about the problem in expansive terms. Together, these elements support claims that victimization is surprisingly common—an idea that in turn justifies the ideology's remaining claims.

2. *Victimization is consequential.* Even a single, brief episode of victimization can have consequences that extend throughout the victim's life—and beyond (Best 1990). Claims about sexual abuse, for instance, suggest that one childhood experience of being flashed or fondled "can have profound and long-term consequences" (Kelly 1988:69). The theme of lasting consequences is central to claims about intergenerational victimization—for example, claims about a cycle of child abuse in which abused children become abusive parents—and to the movements of adult children (and grandchildren) of alcoholics, abuse, or divorce (Rudy 1991; A. Smith 1988).

In most cases, advocates assume that victimization's consequences are fundamentally psychological, that the victim experiences anxiety, doubt, fear, or other negative psychological reactions.[8] Although the victim may have impaired social relationships, the root cause of these problems is not social forces but some psychological disturbance, and the legacy of victimization can be lasting psychological damage. This characterization invites the medicalization of victimization, since it is therapists who presumably have the appropriate knowledge and skills for diagnosing and treating such psychological problems. This causes therapists to become the leading advocates in many new-victim campaigns; they define victimization in medical, particularly psychological, language, speaking of "syndromes," "disorders," "trauma," "symptoms," "treatment," and the like. Other institutional arenas, such as legislatures, courts, academia, and the media, often acknowledge therapists' expertise by discussing victimization in these terms.

Claims about victimization's serious consequences are linked to the ideology's other ideas; in particular, talking about consequences helps justify activists' broad definitions. If even apparently minor incidents can be consequential, no incident should be considered insignificant;

the full range of victimization demands society's attention: "With the ever-widening definition of abuse, the milder end of the continuum can begin with a look and the harder end culminate with ritual murder" (Furendi 1997:83). In turn, claims that victimization is common alert us to the possibility that there are many people suffering its consequences.

3. *Victimization is relatively straightforward and unambiguous.* According to James A. Holstein and Gale Miller (1990:106): "Calling someone a victim encourages others to see how the labelled person has been harmed by forces beyond his or her control, simultaneously establishing the 'fact' of injury and locating responsibility for the damage outside the 'victim.'" Advocates characterize victimization as an exploitative encounter between two actors: the victimizer takes advantage, and the victim suffers. These claims usually portray the victimizer as more powerful than the victim, more aware of the exploitative nature of their relationship, and more responsible for the victimization. For example, "most claimsmakers construct wife abuse as a phenomenon crossing all demographic lines which involves men as offenders who intend to do harm and women as victims who do not create their victimization" (Loseke 1992:16). Because "any approach that focuses on social interaction 'muddies the water' in terms of blame, rendering the offender less evil and the victim less virtuous" (Felson 1991:16), advocates avoid examining interactional processes, except in typifying examples that seem straightforward. Thus, victimization becomes unambiguous: the victimizer is exploitative, the victim innocent.

In practice, persons identified as victimizers—and even some victims—may dispute that characterization. Holstein and Miller (1990) describe *victim contests* in which both parties claim to have been exploited by the other. But advocates usually discount any counterclaims by those they have designated victimizers as disingenuous, self-serving rationalizations. Similarly, if the person labeled the victim is unsure whether an offense "really" occurred, advocates define this confusion as part of the pattern of victimization. Where actors may consider their situations ambiguous, victim advocates seem not just confident in their interpretations, but outraged by counterclaims of ambiguity (cf. Pollitt 1993 and other critical reactions to Roiphe 1993).

The readiness to view victims as powerless innocents is consistent with the injunction against blaming the victim.[9] More problematic is the tendency to blame victimizers. After all, can't arguments be made that many victimizers have themselves suffered? They may, for example, come from dysfunctional or abusive families. As one psychologist warns:

> The current overemphasis on victimization and the concomitant overpurification of victims have actually been helpful to perpetrators looking to escape responsibility. Through the all-embracing victims' rights movement, where victims can be rendered into passive, incapacitated shells of people whose acts are seen not as emanating from any self within, but as mere reactions to the abuse and victimization suffered, perpetrators who once were victims themselves can now escape blame. (Lamb 1996:8)

For the most part, advocates resolve this dilemma by focusing intently on victims and their plight, while paying far less attention to the victimizers. Glossing over the victimizer's circumstances lets advocates avoid confronting ambiguity, while maintaining the understanding that victimization is clear-cut.

By adopting broad definitions of victimization and arguing that victimization is both consequential and unambiguous, advocates blur distinctions among different forms of victimization. Seeking to avoid anything resembling false negatives, they are reluctant to label some sufferings worse than others, to delegitimize any claim to sympathy that victims might deserve. Thus, within categories, they draw few distinctions: a single episode of fondling and repeated rapes are both "sexual abuse"; being forced to have sex with your boss and overhearing an offensive joke are both "sexual harassment"; and so on. And the label— and the attendant moral innocence—of "victim" is easily assigned to a broad range of other categories:

> What's remarkable about our notion of victimhood today is its
> inclusiveness. . . . Smokers are the victims of tobacco companies,
> troubled teenagers are the victims of rock and roll . . . and a sup-
> port group for the "Victims of Plastic Surgery" claims 3,500
> members. . . . The men's consciousness movement . . . celebrates
> the victimization of middle-class males. (Kaminer 1992:154–55)

Thus, claiming that victimization is clear-cut stakes out the moral high
ground; it lets advocates defend good victims beset by evil victimizers.

4. *Victimization often goes unrecognized.*   If victimization is common,
consequential, and clear-cut, we might imagine that it would be a visible, prominent aspect of social life. However, advocates argue that victimization often goes unrecognized and unacknowledged, not only by
the larger society, but even by the victims themselves.

Society may fail to recognize victimization for several reasons, including simple lack of awareness. Advocates often claim to be calling
attention to a social condition that has been ignored. Thanks to new
ways of looking at the subject or new evidence or a new willingness
on the part of victims to speak up, a social problem that has been neglected becomes visible. In this view, identifying new types of victims
is simply a form of social progress in which a more enlightened society finally awards victimization the attention it deserves.

Other advocates offer more critical interpretations of victims' social
invisibility; they denounce institutional arrangements that function to
obscure victims' suffering. Thus, feminists may argue that a patriarchal
social structure discounts the significance of women's victimization, or
gay-rights activists warn that homophobic police fail to treat assaults
on gays seriously. In these claims, not only do social institutions fail to
respond properly to victims' complaints, but, more fundamentally, language and culture may pose constraints, making it difficult to identify
and articulate claims of victimization.

Finally, victimization may be concealed from society through secrecy. This secrecy may be the work of powerful conspiracies, such as
a million-member satanic blood cult that holds tens of thousands of

undetected human sacrifices annually, or UFOs that use superior alien technology to abduct and conduct experiments on thousands of victims. But secrecy need not involve large-scale conspiracies. Individual offenders may convince their victims (e.g., sexually abused children) to keep the experience a secret; if such secrets are widespread, their sum may be collective invisibility.

Beyond society's failure to recognize victims, advocates point to some victims' failure or inability to recognize victimization for what it is. This may be due to victims mistakenly defining victimization too narrowly. The title of an influential book on date and acquaintance rape suggests the nature of the problem: *I Never Called It Rape* (Warshaw 1988). Precisely because advocates believe that many victims fail to recognize their victimization for what it is, advocates' inclusive research measuring the incidence of victimization may apply their own operational definitions to identify victims, rather than simply asking respondents whether they have been victimized. Thus, studies of date rape may count incidents that the women involved say were not rapes (N. Gilbert 1994), and estimates of UFO abductions count people who report sleeping disorders and other abduction symptoms, regardless of whether they recall being abducted (Sagan 1996).

Still other individuals may indeed define themselves as victims, yet be ashamed, unwilling, or unable to reveal their victimization to others. Although ambiguity and shame figure into discussions of the new victims' failure to grasp the meaning of their experiences, repression and denial are more central concepts in some new-victim campaigns (Loftus and Ketcham 1994; Ofshe and Watters 1994). Here, advocates argue that victims often respond to the trauma of victimization by repressing their memories of the experience. They neither recall nor acknowledge being victimized. They are "in denial." Once again, victimization is medicalized. Repression and denial are psychological mechanisms that require treatment by therapists using a medical model.

Taken together, ignorance, social structure, secrecy, and denial ac-

count for society's failure to acknowledge the full extent of victimization: "The very fact that a problem is not visible invites us to speculate
about its intensity" (Furedi 1997:39). Because the ideology of victimization insists that victimization is also widespread, consequential, and
clear-cut, advocates consider this failure to recognize victims and their
plight as a serious social problem, one that demands correction.

   *5. Individuals must be taught to recognize others' and their own victim-
ization.* Because victimization often goes unrecognized by both victims and the larger society, advocates call for extensive victim-education
programs. Potential victims may need preventive education, such as the
"stranger danger" and "good touch–bad touch" programs designed to
warn preschoolers about abduction and sexual abuse, or campus workshops intended to make entering college students aware of—and help
them avoid—date rape. Other educational efforts seek to inform the
larger society about the nature of particular forms of victimization.
Newspaper and magazine feature stories, talk shows, made-for-TV
movies, and other press and entertainment genres regularly present information about victims; this media coverage routinely incorporates
the advocates' perspectives, relaying both substantive claims about particular forms of victimization and instruction in the ideology of victimization (Lowney 1994).

   In addition to championing educational programs aimed at potential victims or the general public, advocates seek to teach individuals to
recognize, acknowledge, and address their own victimization. This may
require breaking through the individual's psychological defense of denial. Self-help books and support groups offer readily accessible ways of
learning to deal with one's victimization—once one acknowledges that
victimization has occurred.

   But what of those victims said to be in denial, unaware that some
prior, now-forgotten victimization continues to trouble them? Advocates argue that these victims must be helped to recognize and identify the victimization at the root of their problems. Typically, although

these individuals do not recall their victimization, they are aware that something is amiss. Some advocates, in order to help individuals diagnose their own or others' problems, present checklists of symptoms that may indicate prior victimization. Thus, adult children of alcoholics may "have difficulty following a project through from beginning to end," "feel they are different from other people," and be "either super responsible or super irresponsible" (Woititz 1983:28, 46–47); codependents may "come from troubled, repressed, or dysfunctional families," "deny their family was troubled, repressed, or dysfunctional," "[not] take themselves seriously," "take themselves too seriously," "try to say what they think will please people," "try to say what they think will provoke people," "say everything is their fault," "say nothing is their fault," "be extremely responsible," or "be extremely irresponsible" (Beattie 1987:38–44); child victims of ritual abuse may destroy toys, be preoccupied with urine, feces, and flatulence, be clingy, or have nightmares (Jenkins 1992:159). These lists of indicators may be lengthy; Beattie's inventory of codependency characteristics (1987) features more than 230 items. Sometimes advocates offer alternative lists that specify different, even contradictory, symptoms. For instance, one review of various guidelines for identifying sexually abused children notes: "Some believe . . . that a reluctance to disclose [sexual abuse] is characteristic of a true allegation, while others look for spontaneity in the child's disclosure as an index of veracity" (Faller 1994:10).[10]

Of course, many—probably almost all—people display at least some of the symptoms on these lists, yet most deny having been victimized. In the advocates' view, an individual's denial of prior victimization may be nothing more than another symptom. Regarding her recently recovered memories of childhood sexual abuse, the television comedienne Roseanne Barr announced: "When someone asks you, 'Were you sexually abused as a child,' there's only two answers. One of them is, 'Yes,' and one of them is, 'I don't know.' You can't say no" (*Oprah* 1991: 6). Similarly, a failure to display any symptoms need not be significant: "The absence of positive indicators does not mean the child hasn't

been sexually abused" (Faller 1994:10). Within such diagnostic frameworks, claims of victimization are easily made but difficult to disconfirm.
Coupled with the claims that victimization is widespread yet largely
hidden, these frameworks justify the suspicion that virtually anyone
might be a victim.

Of course, checklists of symptoms merely raise the possibility that
someone is a victim; confirming this possibility requires additional investigation, often by therapeutic specialists. The therapist's task may be
defined as helping the victim "recover the memories" of victimization.
Critics note that transcripts of therapists' conversations with patients
reveal a variety of leading questions and other linguistic devices that encourage patients to acknowledge their victimization (Lloyd 1992). Here
too, therapists adopt special techniques to elicit memories of victimization, including hypnosis, guided imagery, play with dolls or puppets,
massage, fantasizing, and "facilitated communication" (for the mentally
impaired) (Mulhern 1991, Showalter 1997). These are often successful. As one best-selling guidebook for survivors of child sexual abuse
advises:

> Assume your feelings are valid. So far, no one we've talked to
> thought she might have been abused, and then later discovered that
> she hadn't been. The progression always goes the other way, from
> suspicion to confirmation. If you think you were abused and your
> life shows the symptoms, then you were. (Bass and Davis 1988:22)

The authors offer parallel advice to therapists:

> You must believe that your client was sexually abused, even if she
> sometimes doubts it herself. . . . So far, among the hundreds of
> women we've talked to and the hundreds more we've heard about,
> not one has suspected she might have been abused, explored it, and
> determined that she wasn't. (Bass and Davis 1988:347)

Viewing victimization as widespread yet hidden—recognizing that it
has many common, and even contradictory, symptoms, while discount-
ing denial and uncertainty—makes it easy for advocates to use—and

justify—methods that identify large numbers of victims. (It is, of course, precisely the ease with which victims can be identified that causes critics to question the advocates' methods [Furedi 1997].)

In sum, the ideology of victimization justifies raising the general public's awareness of victims and, perhaps more important, encouraging individuals to break through denial and recognize their own victimization. Not surprisingly, these methods succeed in identifying and labeling many victims. In turn, discovering these victims confirms the ideology's other claims: that victimization is common, that victims suffer terrible consequences, and that victimization will be hidden from view unless advocates take the heroic step of exposing it.

6. Claims of victimization must be respected. Once individuals learn, via education or therapeutic intervention, to recognize their victimization, their claims to the status of victim must not be challenged. Victim advocates declare that it takes great courage to step forward and acknowledge one's victimization, that such individuals take a precarious stand against both their victimizers and the institutional forces that promote and conceal widespread victimization. Injunctions against challenging claims of victimization warn against "blaming the victim"; victims have already suffered, and calling their claims into question can only constitute further victimization. Thus, advocates denounce as a second stage in rape or abuse those courtroom proceedings in which victims face skeptical questioning. They charge the critics and skeptics of various new-victim campaigns with mobilizing a "backlash" that, at best, plays into the victimizers' hands and may, at worst, represent something more sinister: "Their work aids and abets perpetrators in the excuses they make for their behavior. . . . They reflect deep fears of the public, fears grounded in the protection of men and male dominance" (Lamb 1996:113).[11]

Some advocates insist that victims' claims are always legitimate (Furedi 1997). They may argue that some claims of victimization are by definition true (e.g., that children never lie about being sexually abused, or that "no one fantasizes abuse" [Bass and Davis 1988:347]), or they may suggest that there is no reason for individuals to make false claims about being victimized. Or they may argue that similarities in the stories of many victims (e.g., parallel accounts of satanic ritual abuse or UFO abduction) constitute strong evidence for the stories' truth. Memories of victimization that have been recovered through hypnosis or other therapeutic techniques sometimes receive validation from therapists who insist that the techniques elicit reliable information about past suffering (Loftus and Ketcham 1994; Mulhern 1991; Ofshe and Watters 1994).

For all these reasons, advocates charge, claims about victimization must not be questioned. Obviously, any labeling process that stands above criticism is potentially powerful. But the ideology justifies validating victim claims: because victimization is common, consequential, and morally unambiguous, because it remains concealed and must be revealed, the resulting revelations represent something too important to challenge. There is no middle ground; calls for narrower definitions of victimization or more rigorous screening of labeling practices run the unacceptable risk of classifying false negatives, of failing to recognize some people's victimization. That is, skepticism threatens to become part of the problem that victim advocates are trying to address: if skepticism causes even one victim to go unrecognized, it contributes to the broader social tendency to conceal victimization.

The fact that the interpretation of victimization is considered therapists' turf reinforces the advocates' arguments. Therapists may insist that their principal responsibility is to heal their patients, and that expressing any doubts or reservations might disrupt the patients' recovery. Further, therapists understand that victimization is common yet hidden, and can be ferreted out only through the determined application of a broad range of methods; this turns therapy into a heroic enterprise. When a patient finally acknowledges victimization, a great thing has been accomplished, but if patients deny victimization, therapists may feel frustrated—not because they have mistakenly assumed that a patient was a victim, but because they have failed to apply the proper therapeutic methods to help the patient recover.

Precisely because the ideology of victimization has broad acceptance, its critics sometimes turn it to their own uses. Thus, the leading social-movement organization challenging recovered-memory therapies, the False Memory Syndrome Foundation (FMSF), argues that patients who recover memories have been victimized by their therapists, and suffer from "false memory syndrome." (This term enrages victim advocates, who charge that the FMSF has illegitimately seized medical language to make a political argument: "No such syndrome or diagnosis has been proposed formally in writing by the American Psychological or Psychiatric Associations" [Lamb 1996:100].) Similarly, a leading organization denouncing the authority of child-welfare workers calls itself Victims of Child Abuse Laws (VOCAL). In both these debates, opponents both claim the mantle of the victim, reaffirming that this label offers a moral advantage. As powerless innocents, self-designated victims cry out for social support.

7. *The term "victim" has undesirable connotations.* Although the status of victim may confer advantages, the label itself seems problematic. Some advocates reject the term "victim" on the grounds that it has negative connotations of being damaged, passive, and powerless.[12] They prefer more positive, "empowering" terms, such as "survivor," "adult child," "recovering," or even "person" (e.g., "persons with AIDS").

These terms reinforce the ideology of victimization. "Survivor"—favored by feminists and other progressive advocates (see, e.g., Alcoff and Gray 1993; Furedi 1997)—gained its contemporary currency as a label for those who lived through the Holocaust. Thus, "survivor" reaffirms the ideological claim that victimization is consequential, on a par with the worst history has to offer: "The Holocaust gave us as heroes 'survivors,' victims who endured the worst and emerged with immeasurable moral authority, for which many compete today" (Kaminer

1992:157). "Recovering" also reflects the enduring impact of victimization: one can never fully recover from the consequences of victimization; at best, one can be "in recovery." Similarly, "adult child" reminds us that victimization is clear-cut, that victims share children's innocence and vulnerability. This renaming affirms that victimization has occurred, yet serves to reduce individuals' reluctance to define themselves or others as victims. In addition, to the degree that these category names derive from therapeutic discourse, the terms may lend another degree of medicalized or scientific legitimacy to claims of victim status.

THE IDEOLOGY'S POWER

These seven ideological propositions routinely appear in claims about the new victims. Taken together, they form a virtually incontrovertible ideology that encourages identifying and labeling victims: it defines victimization as common, consequential, and clear-cut, yet unrecognized; it justifies helping individuals identify themselves as victims; it delegitimizes doubts about victims' claims; and it provides new, nonstigmatizing labels for those who have suffered. It is, in short, a set of beliefs that makes it easy to label victims, and very difficult to dispute those labels.

It is important to recall that claims about the new victims are not made as generalizations regarding all victims. There is no overarching new-victims movement. Rather, the ideology of victimization is applied piecemeal, to specific forms of victimization. No one makes the general argument that *all* victimization is common or consequential. Instead, each form of victimization has its own advocates, who argue that that form of victimization is surprisingly common, and consequential, and so on. Yet the fact that parallel claims have been made about other types of victims makes an advocate's case seem more plausible. In effect, the contemporary ideology of victimization offers a formula—a familiar set of claims—that can be adapted by would-be advocates of new forms of victimization. Because we have heard similar claims regarding other forms of victimization, we tend to be receptive when we hear these claims about some new type of victim. It has become relatively easy to draw attention to victimization. Of course, attracting attention is not enough; victim claims must gain acceptance from those in authority.

CHAPTER 6

The Victim Industry

Because it simplifies labeling victims and makes it hard to challenge those labels, the contemporary ideology of victimization is a *potentially* powerful set of ideas. Of course, these ideas have no intrinsic power; for them to become powerful, they must be adopted and applied by powerful people. Much of the power in our society resides in institutions. Recall that, in chapter 3, we found that new crime problems must become institutionalized if they are to endure; in particular, the mass media, government officials, activists, and experts must cooperate to transform claims about a new crime into lasting concern about that problem. In much the same way, claims about the new victims depend upon institutional ratification. The contemporary ideology of victimization has become powerful precisely because it has found support in a broad range of institutional sectors. After examining the nature of this support, we will consider how this institutional base, combined with an incontrovertible ideology of victimization, fosters a victim industry—a set of social arrangements capable of labeling large numbers of victims.

INSTITUTIONAL RESPONSES
TO VICTIMIZATION CLAIMS

Commitment to ideologies varies: at one extreme, true believers fervently accept an ideology and faithfully follow its tenets; at the other, an ideology may encounter lip service, cynicism, or outright skepticism. Any ideology exists within an institutional context, receiving varying degrees of ratification and validation within different institutions. Ideological commitment need not be universal within an institution for an ideology to have institutional power; when an ideology's adherents are vocal and committed, when they hold positions of power and leadership within an institution, or when doubters see little to be gained or much to be lost by challenging the ideology, that ideology can develop great influence within the institution.

Again, there is no general ideology of victimization. As noted in chapter 5, advocates make piecemeal claims about particular sorts of victims. They describe the nature of date rape or ritual abuse or stalking as it is experienced by its victims. There is no general claim that all forms of victimization are common; rather, advocates confront particular institutions with specific claims—that date rape is common, that ritual abuse is consequential, and so on. Institutions address these new-victim campaigns one by one, although advocates for later causes no doubt find that an institution's earlier acceptance of preceding claims makes their job easier. Still, some advocates have great difficulty in receiving respectful hearings for their claims within key institutions, while others achieve widespread institutional acceptance (Hilgartner and Bosk 1988).

Campaigns to draw attention to new forms of victimization often take time to unfold. Typically, advocates' initial appeals are *sensitizing;* they seek to draw an institution's attention to victims who have been neglected or ignored. Once an institution acknowledges the plight of these victims, advocates usually call for measures of *accommodation,* ways of integrating the victims' needs within the existing institutional structure. Later, defining such accommodation as insufficient, advocates may call for *institutional changes*—significant alterations to meet the victims' needs. For example, early claims denounced the criminal justice system's insensitive treatment of victims of rape and child sexual abuse (e.g., not responding to all complaints, investigating cases with skepticism, and subjecting complainants to humiliating courtroom interrogations) as amounting to a "second stage" of rape or abuse. Such claims sought to sensitize the law to the ways in which it discouraged victims, blamed them for their suffering, publicly humiliated them, and then failed to deliver justice. In turn, acknowledging these deficiencies produced calls for changes in the procedures for investigations and trials designed to make the legal system more accessible to and protective of victims. The resulting reforms ranged from what were initially relatively minor accommodative arrangements (e.g., letting victims of child sexual abuse testify while seated in child-size chairs) to later, more substantial institutional changes (e.g., prohibiting or limiting the cross-examination of child victims giving testimony).

Thus, claims about particular types of new victims inspire specific reforms intended to sensitize, accommodate, and produce change within different social institutions. These responses emerge one by one, as advocates seek particular reforms to protect particular types of victims from particular abuses. Thus, a state might pass a law to extend the period within which a victim of sexual abuse can sue for damages, so that adults who recover memories of childhood abuse can bring charges against their abusers, or a university might require all faculty to attend workshops on sexual harassment. Although many of these developments might seem to be modest reforms, taken together they represent considerable institutional support for victims and, in many cases, for the ideology of victimization. This support extends across several major institutional sectors, including law, medicine, education, and the mass media, as well as the recovery movement.

Law

Many claims depict victimization as a form of interpersonal exploitation, in which an individual victimizer takes direct advantage of a victim. Because much of the law concerns protecting individuals against various forms of exploitation, the law becomes a central institutional arena for making claims about victimization. The contemporary ideology of victimization has influenced several of the law's various facets, including legislation, the criminal justice and court systems, and legal scholarship.

Advocates often successfully call for new laws prohibiting the exploitation of victims or requiring reporting of victimization. We have already examined the rapid spread of federal and state legislation against stalking and hate crimes in chapter 3; other examples include the widespread adoption of tougher rape statutes that make prosecution easier and reduce the indignities the law inflicts on rape victims, stricter laws against various forms of family violence, and legislatures' attempts to crack down on drunk driving. The Violence Against Women Act promoted by feminists became part of the 1994 federal crime bill signed into law, and, though proposals for a federal constitutional amendment continue to be debated, several states have added a "victims' bill of rights" to their constitutions (Weed 1995). Victim advocates, then, find a receptive audience in legislators. Lawmakers stand to gain by taking what are often highly visible, symbolic stands in favor of protecting innocent, vulnerable victims. Such laws have bipartisan appeal: Republicans like the opportunity to "get tough on crime," while Democrats can emphasize their commitment to protecting women, children, ethnic minorities, and others vulnerable to victimization. Framed as a clear-cut issue of moral principle, standing up for victims runs politicians little risk. After all, there is rarely vocal opposition; there are no organized lobbies of victimizers campaigning against most of these bills.

In addition to calling for new laws, victim advocates criticize the legal system's failure to protect individuals from victimization, as well as its further failure to give victims appropriate treatment once they bring their victimization before the law, as in the complaints about the criminal justice system's insensitive treatment of victims of rape and child sexual abuse. This has led to both formal and informal procedural reforms: using female officers to interview victims, conducting interviews in comfortable surroundings, offering victims counseling services, and so on. Here, too, advocates may find a supportive audience within the criminal justice system, if only because helping victims in these ways is thought to improve the chances of successful prosecutions (Elias 1993). Still, because the criminal justice system retains relatively elaborate arrangements for preserving the rights of defendants (viewed as victimizers by victim advocates), there has been growing interest in the use of the less restrictive civil courts to permit victims to recover damages. The difficulties of winning criminal prosecutions based on recovered memories of childhood sexual abuse have led some therapists to advise their patients to file civil suits against their victimizers. At the same time, courts confront victimization as a defense; advocates argue that women suffering from battered-woman syndrome and other syndromes caused by victimization may not be responsible for their own violent actions (D. Downs 1996; Gagne 1996).

Many of these legislative and procedural reforms find support in law schools and academic law reviews. New claims about victimization often receive sympathetic treatment, as legal scholars recommend ways to modify the law to redress victims' grievances. Scholars do not agree on all these issues (e.g., there has been considerable debate about the need to balance the rights of complainants and defendants in sexual-abuse trials, the constitutionality of antistalking and hate-crime statutes, the evidentiary value of recovered memories, etc.). This is to be expected; legal scholarship thrives on controversy. But it also provides an important forum for all sorts of novel views. Through law-review articles, law students and law-school professors can achieve prominence by promoting the cause of new victims, and often influence legislative deliberations and court decisions.

Of course, the various new-victim campaigns have not achieved universal acceptance within the law. There are legislators and prosecutors and legal scholars who continue to resist—or are indifferent to—various claims. Yet these claims have had an effect; they have in many—often apparently minor—ways changed how laws affecting victims are written and applied.

Medicine and Other Therapies

Many claims about new victims medicalize their problems, defining treatment as the appropriate response and giving assorted therapeutic professionals ownership of these social problems. Medicalization carries scientific authority; in the late twentieth century, claims couched in medical language seem almost beyond questioning or criticism (Conrad 1992). As a result, a surprisingly diverse set of advocates claims this medical/scientific imprimatur.

The medical model—the language of disease/symptom/diagnosis/treatment, usually associated with physicians, psychiatrists, and perhaps clinical psychologists—has spread throughout what are sometimes called the "helping professions." Whereas modern medicine defines itself as a scientific enterprise, grounded in empirical research based on scientific methods, medical language, with its overtones of science, has been adopted by a broad range of therapists whose training is in less scientific disciplines, including clinical social work, family counseling, education, health science, and theology. Although these practitioners may use the language of medicine to describe their work with the new victims in terms of symptoms, diagnosis, and therapy, their treatment practices often are guided less by scientific principles than by various other ideologies, ranging from fundamentalist Christianity to feminism. In many cases, these therapists are "professional ex-s," individuals with little formal training who, having recovered from victimization, have now begun careers helping others into recovery (Brown 1991a, 1991b). In other words, my definition of medicine as an institution is very broad—

including conventional scientific medicine, but extending well beyond it to encompass all therapies that invoke the medical model to treat the new victims. The professional backgrounds and credentials of therapists using medical language and claiming medical authority vary wildly.

Many therapists who work with new victims insist that their principal responsibility is to their patients rather than to abstract principles of inquiry. This rationale justifies therapeutic practices that some critics argue are inconsistent with the rigorous standards of proof demanded by scientific inquiry or criminal investigations. For example, therapists interviewing children thought to have been sexually abused may use leading questions to elicit acknowledgment of abuse, and justify this practice as a necessary therapeutic step (Lloyd 1992). Therapists may urge patients to ignore doubts and ambiguity when acknowledging their victimization. Some therapists encourage victims to share their experiences with one another in group therapy, on panels at conferences, or in informal conversations; critics argue that such contacts contaminate the evidence, so that it becomes impossible to gather independent reports, thereby accounting for the "astonishing," "inexplicable" parallels in the accounts of victims of UFO abduction and satanic ritual abuse (Mulhern 1991; Sagan 1996). Such practices of bringing victims into contact with one another, justified as therapeutically beneficial, distinguish much of the treatment of new victims from more traditional medical-scientific inquiry.[1]

Medicalized discussions of the new victims usually focus on the harms experienced by the victims, while largely ignoring their victimizers. Where earlier generations of psychiatric claims medicalized deviants (e.g., sexual psychopaths), contemporary claims often medicalize the victims of deviance (e.g., survivors of sexual abuse) or else redefine deviants as victims (e.g., recovering alcoholics, codependents, and so on). When deviance is deemed extraordinary, we search for explanations—including medical explanations—in the peculiarities of offenders. But when victimization is seen as commonplace, victimizers no longer seem remarkable; they merely become the embodiment of an oppressive social system. To be sure, some advocates also medicalize victimizers when they refer to cycles of abuse (e.g., arguments that sexual abusers were themselves sexually abused children, and that those experiences led them to become abusive). But most claims pay little attention to victimizers, focusing instead on the new victims, and limiting the use of medical language to describing their problems.

As in the law, there is no overarching medical response to the new victims. Different therapeutic professions tend to focus on different forms of victimization, and individual therapists usually specialize in identifying and helping particular types of victims, so that one therapist may have success in recovering patients' memories of satanic ritual abuse, another specializes in recovering memories of child sexual abuse, and so on. Nor do all therapeutic professionals credit all claims about victimization. There is, for example, a bitter debate within academic psychology around the rival claims about recovered memories and false memories (cf. Pezdek and Banks 1996). Still, every medical profession—including those with the highest prestige and strongest claims to scientific authority—has at least some representatives who endorse some new-victim claims, and thereby add their authority to the contemporary ideology of victimization. In particular, physicians and psychiatrists often serve as especially visible advocates. For example, John E. Mack, a psychiatrist on the Harvard Medical School faculty, emerged as a leader in the campaign to call attention to UFO abductions—presumably because his professional credentials gave him much greater authority than most other UFO advocates. Thus, even the most prestigious therapeutic professions are represented in the ranks of new-victim crusaders.

Education and Academia

The ideology of victimization also has made significant inroads among educators. The need to educate victims, potential victims, and society at large is central to the ideology, and many educators believe they can play a vital role in this process. Because children make especially vulnerable victims, and because teachers are the non–family members most often charged with the day-to-day supervision of children, teachers can both detect some child victims and teach other children how to avoid victimization. Teachers from preschool to high school can attend victimization workshops to learn how to recognize the signs of victimization, as well as how to present age-appropriate information on preventing victimization to their students (Berrick and Gilbert 1991). Similarly, colleges and universities offer programs to teach their students about the risks of—and methods for avoiding or dealing with—date rape, sexual harassment, and other forms of victimization. Defining themselves as progressive, enlightened institutions, colleges are often leaders in establishing policies to protect from victimization not only their students, but also their employees (Patai 1997).

Within higher education, enthusiasm for the ideology of victimization seems greatest in the applied disciplines, the helping professions—such as social work, health education, educational counseling, and family relations—and the areas of criminal justice and child development. Students trained in these fields learn to identify and respond to a range of human problems, and their course work presents claims about the new victims as up-to-date knowledge that has useful applications. Concern about the new victims also appears in the traditional arts and sciences, especially in feminist writings, and women's studies programs often provide leadership for on-campus victim advocacy (Patai and Koertge 1994). The new victims become the subjects of lectures, classes, term papers, theses, and dissertations.

Further, victimization is a focus for scholarship. In universities, as well as law schools, medical schools, and other professional schools, victimization has become an attractive, visible research topic. Arguing that most victims are overlooked, researchers devise inclusive studies designed to explore the full range of victimization. Scholars personally concerned with the plight of victims may see such research as an opportunity to serve as scholar-activists; as experts, they can forge ties

with the mass media, social movements, and government agencies (recall the discussion of these interlocking sectors in chapter 3). Studying victims thus becomes a means of advancing social progress. Moreover, researchers may find foundations and government agencies eager
to fund research on victimization. Specialized conferences and professional associations emerge as forums for inquiry, and the proliferation of scholarly publishing has produced numerous scholarly journals
devoted to studying the new victims, including the *Journal of Family
Violence* (which began publishing in 1986), the *Journal of Interpersonal
Violence* (1986), *Violence and Victims* (1986), the *Journal of Child Sexual
Abuse* (1992), and *Violence against Women* (1995). Some of these associations and journals are narrowly focused; for example, the journal *Dis-
sociation* publishes only studies of multiple personality disorder.

As studies of victimization become increasingly specialized, scholarly
discussions of victims tend to become confined to advocates committed
to the ideology of victimization. With the notable exceptions of satanic
ritual abuse and UFO abduction, most new-victim campaigns inspire
little skepticism, let alone opposition, from academics. In most cases,
the vast majority of scholars who care about a form of victimization
accept the ideology's claims. They encounter one another at workshops
and conferences, read and review one another's research, and otherwise
form a scholarly community that usually endorses advocates' claims.
Their insulation from skepticism increases as the number of scholar-
advocates rises; once they attain the critical mass to support their own
professional associations and journals, they can communicate largely
among themselves (cf. Felson 1991; N. Gilbert 1997). Their few vocal
critics encounter harsh, discrediting reactions: they are blaming the victims; they are part of the problem, not the solution; they represent a
backlash of traditional, oppressive values; by calling victims' claims into
question, they have allied themselves with the victimizers (a choice that
suggests questionable motives); and so on. As a consequence, victim
studies tend to flourish within sequestered pockets of academia, shel-
tered from skepticism and criticism.[2]

Like medicalization, academics' support gives authority to claims about the new victims. Their work becomes particularly important when their research produces evidence to support advocates' claims; scholar-activists soon become the source for claims about the extent of victimization, its consequences, and so on. Over time, their work buttresses the ideology of victimization.

Mass Media

Most contemporary advocates depend upon the mass media to disseminate their claims to the larger public. In general, claims about the new victims receive sympathetic coverage in the press, in popular culture, and most especially in made-for-TV movies, talk shows, "reality shows," tabloid television, and the other genres that combine news and entertainment. Claims about the new victims tend to fit the media's template for social-problems coverage: they can be typified in dramatic terms (an innocent victim beset by an exploitative villain); they are relevant (if victimization is widespread, then many people are, might become, or at least have ties to victims); they are upbeat (the intervention of sympathetic authority figures from law, medicine, or academia offers new hope for victims); and they can be portrayed with few unacceptable political overtones (as long as media coverage blames individual victimizers rather than the social system [e.g., capitalism, the class system, or patriarchy] for the victimization) (Gitlin 1980). Moreover, because most campaigns to draw attention to new victims depict victimization as straightforward exploitation, and because most advocates face little organized opposition, the media typically feel no obligation to "balance" their coverage by presenting "both sides" of the issue. In most cases, advocates frame the issue, and the media's coverage retains that frame.

Recent changes in the mass media's structure also have worked to the advocates' advantage. Cable and satellite delivery have expanded the

number of television channels, thereby creating vast blocks of broadcasting time that need to be filled with programming. Broadcasters need
relatively inexpensive, relatively popular offerings, and newsmagazine
shows, talk shows, and "reality shows" (e.g., *America's Most Wanted*)
meet these requirements. These genres frequently cover claims about
the new victims (Lowney 1994). Though political radicals may complain of being ignored by the media, advocates promoting the new victims find few obstacles to getting national television coverage. Even
claims that encounter considerable skepticism, such as reports by survivors of satanic ritual abuse and UFO abductions, have received sympathetic treatment on major television talk shows. Similarly, the rise of
the Internet makes it possible to circulate claims of all sorts, and many
advocates have created Web sites to promote their claims.

Media coverage rarely criticizes claims about new victims. Typically,
coverage focuses on one or two individual victims—sometimes cases
taken from the current headlines, sometimes individuals selected by advocates to exemplify a form of victimization. These typifying examples
tend to be dramatic, featuring terrible suffering by attractive, innocent,
vulnerable victims. These become the examples used not just to demonstrate that a problem exists, but to typify its qualities. But, advocates
argue, these cases are just the tip of the iceberg—examples of a common, consequential, hidden problem—and the advocates usually can refer to legal, medical, or academic authorities who endorse these claims.
The story, in short, reaches the media prepackaged. Shaped by the ideology of victimization, its form resembles those of other stories about
other types of victimization; as a result, it is easy for the media to pre-
sume that the new story ought to be treated just as earlier victim stories
were covered. Usually there is no organized opposition for the media
to seek out and quote. No wonder new victims usually receive sympathetic treatment in the media; the ideology of victimization presents
them as sympathetic figures with a new—yet fundamentally familiar—
problem.

Other Institutional Supports

Law, medicine, academia, and the mass media all serve as influential authorities in our culture. Theirs are key voices in identifying new social problems and devising appropriate social policies to address those problems, and the acceptance of the ideology of victimization within these institutions gives that ideology the weight of authority. There are, of course, other influential social institutions, and the ideology receives support within many of these as well. Virtually all religious bodies, from traditional mainline denominations to new religions, from radical women's spirituality groups to conservative fundamentalists, have found occasion to express sympathy with and concern for at least some sorts of new victims. Within the private sector, firms increasingly devise formal policies to protect employees from and help them deal with victimization (e.g., sexual harassment policies, employee assistance programs, and benefits packages that offer expanded coverage for mental-health treatments). State and federal government agencies increasingly ratify concerns about victimization, sponsoring research on victimization, using their influence to educate the public about victimization, and so on. The overall pattern is clear: people within several major institutions have responded sympathetically to claims about the new victims. As a result, social arrangements have changed in many ways that support the ideology of victimization.

THE RECOVERY MOVEMENT

Observers have long noted American culture's fascination with self-help. Historically, the celebration of independence, individualism, and self-reliance has encouraged a variety of social movements based on individual self-improvement (A. Katz 1993). And although the contemporary self-help movement is not an institution in the sense that law, medicine, education, and the mass media are institutions, it has become a large, influential sector within American society.[3]

In recent years, the self-help movement—and Alcoholics Anonymous in particular—has inspired numerous campaigns to help new victims recover from their victimization. AA's twelve-step model for recovery has been adopted for an extraordinary array of individual problems: early offshoots, such as Gamblers Anonymous and Narcotics Anonymous (Sagarin 1969), presaged the 1980s explosion of twelve-step programs for cancer patients, schizophrenics, depressives, survivors of ritual abuse—"even trichotillomaniacs (people who pull their hair too much) have a twelve-step recovery group" (Reinarman 1995:96). In addition to these (usually noncommercial) support groups, there is the for-profit recovery business: weekend workshops and conferences, lecture tours, and the production and publication of books, pamphlets, magazines, bumper stickers, key chains, and audio- and videotapes filled with inspirational slogans and advice (Kaminer 1992). During the 1980s, most bookstores opened substantial sections labeled "Recovery" or "Self-Help." By 1990, nearly three hundred specialized bookstores sold nothing but movement literature (Rivkin 1990); the Recovery Room in St. Louis, for instance, had separate sections, each with one or more bookcases, devoted to alcoholism, adult children of alcoholics, codependency, and so on. The popularity of recovery-movement literature transcends otherwise important ideological divisions: recovery sections can be found in most women's bookstores—and most evangelical Christian bookshops.

The recovery movement often provides the grassroots embodiment of claims about the new victims. It offers continual socialization for neophytes and experienced members, links victims to experts (at least via lectures and books), and often serves as the inspiration for media coverage. Whereas AA traditionally emphasized anonymity and shunned celebrity, found practical authority in the experiences of others in the program and questioned the knowledge of experts, and turned for wisdom to the "Big Book" (first published in 1939, and only in its third edition in 1976), its more recent imitators tend to favor contemporary stylings. Many of these movements have stars—celebrities who travel the talk-show and lecture circuit, emphasizing their professional credentials at least as much as their in-recovery status and churning out the many little books that fill recovery-section bookshelves. With its medicalized rhetoric and media connections, the recovery movement has significant institutional ties.

To be sure, the movement has some academic critics. Sociological observers (Irvine 1995; Rice 1992; Reinarman 1995) argue that the movement medicalizes everyday troubles and encourages people to define contemporary life as requiring special coping methods. In particular, these analysts focus on codependency and dysfunctional families—problems said to affect virtually everyone. Here, the recovery movement and victim advocates make their most expansive claims. But it is the broad range of recoverable conditions—from codependency to hair pulling—that makes the recovery movement both a source of and a support for new-victim claims.

THE VICTIM INDUSTRY

The emergence of the contemporary ideology of victimization, coupled with widespread institutional support for that ideology, encourages identifying large numbers of victims. Studies of witch-hunts and political purges describe these social control arrangements as "industries" engaged in the "manufacturing" or "mass production" of deviants (Connor 1972; Currie 1968; Greenblatt 1977). Analogously, we can speak of a contemporary *victim industry*, producing large numbers of labeled victims.[4] The parallels between these apparently very different arrangements merit closer attention.

Characteristics of Social Control Industries

Elliott Currie (1968) contrasts witch-hunting in England, which he describes as a small-scale "racket," with the far more extensive inquisitions in Continental Europe, which he calls an "industry." He argues that the Continental witch-hunts—which ranged across much of Europe, recurred over centuries, involved more social control agents, and labeled many more witches—had three key characteristics: (1) they were relatively invulnerable to external restraints from other social institutions; (2) they had extraordinary powers for suppressing deviants, coupled with few internal restraints on the use of those powers; and (3) they had structured or vested interests in apprehending and processing deviants. Currie suggests that these features characterize systems of repressive—as opposed to restrained—social control. The term "repressive" suggests that social control agents are dedicated to identifying and sanctioning deviants and eradicating deviance, no matter what the costs. Analysts who have applied Currie's model have focused on other repressive systems of control, such as political purges under Stalin and Mao (see, e.g., Connor 1972; Greenblatt 1977).

Although Currie created his model of repressive control to explain the workings of inquisitions and secret police, it has much broader implications. When social control agents have few external restraints, few internal restraints, and vested interests in their work, they find it easy to label large numbers of deviants. But calling these arrangements repressive links them to punitive abuses of authority. This interpretation is too narrow; parallel arrangements can facilitate labeling other types of people for other reasons. The impulse to "manufacture" social types may be humanitarian, yet the degree to which any campaign succeeds in widespread labeling depends on the levels of external and internal restraints, and the labelers' interests. Thus, we are told, only by identifying the countless learning disabled, the children "at risk," or those with eating disorders can we help the individuals who need it. Such humanitarian concern is, of course, the impulse behind most campaigns to identify the new victims; it is the basis for the victim industry.

The victim industry is not repressive in Currie's sense, but it shares all three characteristics he found in Continental witch-hunting. Just as the absence of external and internal restraints and the presence of structured interests fostered Continental witch-hunters' efforts to label large numbers of deviants, parallel arrangements support the victim industry's campaigns to identify large numbers of new victims.

Absence of External Restraints

Because the contemporary ideology of victimization receives broad support from several major institutions, victim advocates encounter few external restraints. For instance, individuals receiving therapeutic treatment for some form of victimization may find that their claims—and the claims of their therapists—are protected by sympathetic laws, ratified by academics, depicted favorably in the mass media, and endorsed by the recovery movement. Although everyone in these institutions may not accept these claims about new victims, skeptics usually have little to gain by voicing their doubts. The ideological prohibition against challenging victims' claims discourages skepticism: doubters find themselves characterized as part of the problem: at best, they ignorantly interfere with social progress; at worst, they are allied with the victimizers. Moreover, because labeling victims is defined as beneficial, for both the individual being labeled and the society at large, there is no obvious basis for objecting to the labeling.

It is worth noting that most new-victim campaigns demand support without simultaneously insisting that the victimizers be sanctioned. In some cases, victimizers cannot be identified: the stranger-rapist who was never apprehended; the unfamiliar adult satanists who abused the victim as a child; or even extraterrestrial aliens. As long as advocates restrict themselves to labeling victims, they face little opposition. Only when victims or their advocates publicly identify particular people as victimizers and call for their sanctioning do many people have a vested interest in challenging the new victims' claims. Thus, claims about recovered memories of satanic ritual abuse encountered little opposition until victims began bringing suits against their relatives for childhood abuse. At that point, a countermovement, organized around the False

Memory Syndrome Foundation and enlisting its own lawyers, therapists, academics, and journalists, began to mobilize.

Extraordinary Powers Coupled with an Absence of Internal Restraints

The contemporary ideology of victimization offers many alternative means of identifying victims: long lists of symptoms indicative of victimization; rationales for doubting individuals' denials of victimization; prohibitions against doubting victims' claims; and so on. Moreover, this ideology has been adopted by people with various professional credentials, including therapists, lawyers, academics, and professional ex-victims. Defined as experts who are qualified to identify and label victims, these individuals have extraordinary influence on discussions of putative victimization. They often operate from a secure base: acknowledged as selflessly helping the damaged and the vulnerable, screened by favorable media coverage, reimbursed by insurance programs, occupying prestigious professional positions, and protected by tenure, they are able to make claims with little risk. Because victimization is often hidden, and because these experts have the means to discover and reveal victimization, their assessments become authoritative. Moreover, because they believe in the ideology of victimization, these advocates have the right— even the obligation—to label individuals as victims and guide them into acceptance of that label. They are doing good and have only the best motives. Since they are engaged in helping the victim understand the truth, there is no reason to question what they are doing, and their ideology offers little basis for doubt. Like all incontrovertible ideologies, the ideology of victimization provides few internal restraints on labeling victims.

Structured Interests

Currie notes that, because witches' property was confiscated and distributed among the inquisitors, Continental witch-hunters stood to benefit directly from labeling witches. Although the members of the victim industry may not have such a direct financial stake in the labeling process, they clearly have structured interests in the identification of victims. These include: enhanced prestige and influence for themselves and their professions; supportive validation from various key institutions within society; and, at least among those therapeutic professionals who label on a fee-for-service basis, increased income. We might also note that not only advocates, but some people identified as victims, benefit from this status: they become professional ex-victims, write books, travel on the lecture circuit, appear on talk shows, receive praise and favorable attention, and even get treated as experts in their own right.

Some of the most intriguing benefits accrue to those advocates or victims who achieve celebrity; they become widely known for their connection to the new victims. The media's fascination with celebrity, as manifested in *People* magazine, talk shows, and tabloid television, makes it easiest to package social problems in terms of one or two individuals whose experiences come to represent the larger issue.[5] Sometimes, these celebrities start as advocates; just as Jean-Martin Charcot brought hysteria to widespread attention in nineteenth-century France, Harvard's John Mack has achieved national notoriety for his claims about alien abductions. (Probably all new-victim campaigns feature advocates who become prominent figures within their movements, although most of these fail to achieve national celebrity among the general population.) Other are victims who become known for their victimization—victim-celebrities. Some of these have died—it is their memory that is celebrated—but others survived to tell their tales and speak on behalf of their fellow victims. But the most interesting figures are what we might call celebrity-victims: individuals already known for other accomplishments who reveal their victimization—the comedienne Roseanne Barr recovering memories of childhood abuse, Miss America reporting having been battered, a senator's wife describing being stalked, and so on.

Social movements can use celebrities as a resource to promote the cause (Meyer and Gamson 1995). Celebrity involvement in a movement draws media coverage, particularly in campaigns for the new victims. Celebrity-victims reinforce the ideology of victimization's claims that victimization is widespread yet hidden (although we might never suspect it, even celebrities have been victimized), and they can testify to the effectiveness of efforts to help victims. Such public revelations cause the celebrities' accomplishments to seem all the more extraordinary, making them even more sympathetic figures and enhancing their reputations. Obviously, celebrities who reveal their own victimization are involved in a complex process, one that helps reveal the many ways advocates and victims stand to benefit from labeling victims.

WHY VICTIMS?

Obviously, the analogy between Currie's repressive witch-hunts and the contemporary victim industry can be stretched too far. Though both are efficient arrangements for labeling large numbers of people and are characterized by few external restraints, few internal restraints, and structured interests in the process, there are clear differences in the motives for labeling, the consequences for those labeled, the meaning of labeling for the larger society, and so on. Still, the notion of a victim industry offers a useful way of addressing contemporary moral concerns about victims and their advocates.

The growing attention to victims has not gone unnoticed. Robert Hughes (1993:22) remarks: "As our 15th-century forebears were obsessed with the creation of saints and our 19th-century ancestors with the production of heroes . . . so are we with the recognition, praise, and, when necessary, manufacture of victims." Contemporary critics complain that our society fosters crybabies, complaints, excuses, pique, busybodies, meddlers, "the moral prestige and political spoils of victimhood [and] whining rights in the victimization bazaar" (Kinsley 1995:62); that "the route to moral superiority and premier griping rights can be gained most efficiently through being a victim" (Sykes 1992:12).

These popular critiques emphasize that victim claims abdicate responsibility: "Terms such as 'character,' 'weakness,' and 'individual responsibility' are no longer appropriate" (Rieff 1991:49); "we create an infantilized culture of complaint, in which Big Daddy is always to blame and the expansion of rights goes on without the other half of citizenship—attachment to duties and obligations" (Hughes 1993:16). Further, expansive claims about victimization blur key distinctions:

> Victimism reaps its advantage at the direct expense of those most deserving of compassion and support. *If everyone is a victim, then no one is.* . . . There is a victimist version of Gresham's Law: Bogus victims drive out genuine victims. (Sykes 1992:18–19; emphasis in original)

The critics blame lawyers, feminists, the recovery movement, and assorted other villains for promoting these morally faulty claims. Their critique is, at its core, a disagreement about moral philosophy; they largely ignore the cultural and structural context for contemporary claims about victims.

In contrast, these chapters have focused on social organization, on the ideological and institutional arrangements that, when combined, generate the contemporary victim industry. As sociologists—and as citizens—we tend to view the various claims about new victims separately. That is, we treat claims about sexual harassment as unrelated to the antisatanism movement. My point, of course, is that there are striking similarities among the different new-victim movements: they share historical roots, ideological justifications, and institutional supports, and they resemble one another in their efficient arrangements for labeling victims.

But how can we explain these similarities? Why do claims about victims strike a responsive chord in contemporary society? Why are various categories of victims being constructed at this time, and in this society? Here, I can only speculate: I believe that the new-victim movements offer a contemporary answer to fundamental, primal issues that every culture must address—issues of justice and evil. Social order is society's most basic accomplishment. But, in every society, order sometimes breaks down. Some people do the right thing, but they do not get their just deserts. Other people break the rules and get away with it. Social control mechanisms attempt to right these wrongs and return the social system to order, but they inevitably fall short of true justice.

In most societies during most of recorded history, punishment has been central to social control. Society roots out the rule breakers, the deviants, the evildoers, and dispenses justice by punishing them. But during the twentieth century we have become increasingly suspicious of these traditional practices. We favor a rational, scientific point of view, and we suspect that evil is a superstitious notion, and that punishment is a barbaric method of achieving justice.

The social sciences bear a good deal of responsibility here. We are in the business of explaining social patterns, of identifying causes and their effects. And we have been very diligent in trying to understand the causes of deviance. But the social-scientific perspective on deviance doesn't translate particularly well into social policy. The sticking point, of course, is the notion—fundamental to law—of responsibility. If we can point to the causes of deviant behavior, how can we hold the deviant responsible? Is it just to blame deviants for rule breaking when we believe that their deviance is caused by social conditions? Note the term "blame"; it is central to much social control, but largely foreign to social science (J. Wilson 1997). This issue—the degree to which deviants are and should be held responsible for their deviance—has been at the core of policy debates throughout the twentieth century.

All this helps us identify the attractions of talking about victims. Talking about victims avoids the conflicts between the social-scientific and social-policy perspectives raised when we talk about deviants. To social scientists, victims can be understood as effects of causal processes. But, as activists continually warn, social policy must sympathize with—support—victims, not blame them. As long as we remain focused on victims, disagreement vanishes. This helps explain why the new-victim movements tend to gloss over the victimizers. Once we start identifying victimizers, we are back in the messy, divisive business of trying to both understand and blame deviants. As long as we stay focused on the victims, we can hope to mobilize consensus.

This explanation suggests that the new-victim movements may have more in common with witch-hunting than simply organizational features. The victim plays a symbolic role in our society, not unlike the role played by witches during the witch-hunting craze. Both allow society to identify sources of evil and injustice. In societies that interpret events in religious terms, witches consorting with the demonic can explain all sorts of problems. Similarly, our contemporary society, which seeks to understand the world in rational, scientific terms, finds processes of victimization useful explanations for all sorts of contemporary ills. In this way, the new victims answer old questions.

CHAPTER 7

Declaring War
on Social Problems

Just as we create new crimes, new victims, and other social problems,
we create social policies to deal with them. Of course, we rarely talk
about "creating" social problems; we act as though our problems exist
independent of our actions, that social problems are simply objective
conditions. Instead of acknowledging that stalking or sexual harassment
are categories created and brought to public attention through advocates' claims, we speak of "discovering" or "recognizing" these problems, as though they have always existed and we have simply ignored
them up until now.

In contrast, we recognize that social policies are our creations, the
products of our choices.[1] We understand that there are many ways
in which society might respond to different problems, and we debate
these choices: should we emphasize punishment or rehabilitation for
criminals, promote curative or preventive medicine, try to eradicate or
regulate vice? Most social problems inspire debates along these lines.
Whatever we choose, the policies must be articulated and justified, and
this means that language is an inherent feature of social policy. How we
talk about policy shapes what we do, what we think we are doing, why
we think we are doing it, and so on. Policy talk has consequences—

often unintended, unexamined consequences. This chapter explores the consequences of one popular form of policy talk: "declaring war" on social problems.

THE WAR METAPHOR
AND SOCIAL POLICY

President Ronald Reagan's 1986 declaration of a "war on drugs" was preceded by several earlier presidential proclamations of drug wars, including one by Richard Nixon and an earlier declaration by Reagan himself in 1982. As a statement of drug policy, then, declaring war on drugs is somewhat trite. Nor is the metaphor of declaring war limited to drug policy or Republican rhetoric. Other twentieth-century presidents from both parties declared war on numerous social problems. The most familiar example is Lyndon Johnson's War on Poverty, but we may forget that Johnson also spoke of "the war against crime," or that Dwight Eisenhower called for "a new kind of war . . . upon the brute forces of poverty and need." Nixon declared wars on crime and cancer, Jimmy Carter called the energy crisis "the moral equivalent of war," Gerald Ford declared "an all-out war against inflation," Franklin Roosevelt's New Deal declared wars on the Depression, farm surpluses, rural poverty, and crime; and so on (Powers 1983; Sherry 1995).

Nor is the rhetorical power to declare war on social problems restricted to presidents. Throughout the twentieth century, other federal, state, and local officials have declared war on various social problems; academics often use the metaphor to characterize social policies; activists and the press regularly call for—or make their own—declarations of war (Bricklin 1993; Gorelick 1989; Sherry 1995); and even corporations present themselves as waging war against their customers' problems (Russell 1996). The columnist George Will (1992) deflates policymaking enthusiasms with his sarcastic acronym for the "moral equivalent of war"—MEOW—while policy critics invert the term for their own ironic purposes (e.g., at least three recent books have titles that are variants of "the war on the poor" [Albelda et al. 1996; Gans 1995; Sidel 1996], just as drug-war critics denounce "the war on our children" [Trebach and Ehlers 1996]). In short, declaring war on social problems is a familiar, commonplace way of talking about social policy.

Declaring war is simply one instance of a broader tendency to use militarized language to describe social problems and social policy. References to battles, campaigns, attacks, mobilizations, enlistments, recruits, arsenals, weapons, targets, enemies, fronts, strategies, tactics, and similar military terms regularly appear in the rhetoric of policymakers, advocates who hope to influence policy, and academics who analyze policymaking (Blain 1994; Sherry 1995). This fondness for military language reveals that declarations of war are part of a more general tendency to use war as a metaphor. Critics argue that the United States is a militaristic society—that militaristic values are deeply embedded in our culture, shaping the way we understand our world (cf. Englehardt 1995; J. Gibson 1994):

> [After 1945] war defined much of the American imagination, as the fear of war penetrated it and the achievements of war anchored it, to the point that Americans routinely declared "war" on all sorts of things that did not involve physical combat at all. . . . Militarization reshaped every realm of American life—politics and foreign policy, economics and technology, culture and social relations—making America a profoundly different nation. To varying degrees, almost all groups were invested in it and attracted to it—rich and poor, whites and nonwhites, conservatives and liberals. (Sherry 1995:x)[2]

In their most extreme form, social policies can be conducted in an overtly military manner; for instance, police paramilitary units, wearing military-style uniforms and equipped with assault weapons and other military gear, play an increasingly active role in policing some cities (Kraska and Kappeler 1997), while military units conduct missions against drug smugglers. Policymakers don't just declare war; they sometimes carry out military operations against social problems.

Although there are many analyses and critiques of the current war on drugs, the War on Poverty, and other specific "wars" against social problems, the frequency with which social policymakers adopt the metaphor of warfare and the implications of that metaphor have not received as much critical attention. This chapter begins by exploring why Americans are fond of declaring war on social problems, then examines the disadvantages of using this metaphor. It concludes by considering why we need to pay more attention to policy rhetoric.

THE ATTRACTIONS OF DECLARING WAR

All metaphors, including "declaring war," carry implications:

> Metaphors are important devices for strategic representation in policy analysis. On the surface, they simply draw a comparison between one thing and another, but in a more subtle way they usually imply a whole narrative story and a prescription for action. . . . Buried in every policy metaphor is an assumption that "if *a* is like *b*, then the way to solve *a* is to do what you would do with *b*." Because policy metaphors imply prescription, they are a form of advocacy. (Stone 1988:118; see also Edelman 1971:65–72)

What, then, are the implications of declaring war? What similarities between warfare and social policy do those adopting this metaphor mean to evoke? First, of course, warfare involves open conflict with an enemy, so the metaphor defines the social problem—drugs or poverty, cancer or crime—as an enemy to be fought:

> The "war on poverty" suggests massive mobilization against a universally hated enemy, and thereby helps win political support. It gives people the gratification of seeing themselves support a crusade against evil. (Edelman 1971:71)[3]

Wartime propaganda routinely transforms human enemies into evil, inhuman abstractions (Keen 1988). Because the enemy is evil, war is justified; this is what the sociologist James A. Aho (1994:11) calls the first paradox of the enemy: "My violation of you grows from my yearning to rectify the wrong I sense you have done me. Violence emerges from my quest for good and my experience of you as the opponent of good." Of course, this transformation requires little effort when the enemy is a social problem; in such cases, the enemy is already an inhuman abstraction, generally agreed to be evil. Declarations of war against social problems, then, invoke a sense of righteousness. Society can demand the support and sacrifice of its members only in pursuit of a just cause, so declarations of war must justify conflict in terms of the greater evil of allowing the problem to remain.

Of course, it can prove difficult to wage a prolonged war against an abstraction. Over time, a more specific enemies list often emerges. Official rhetoric in the current drug war, for instance, variously blames foreign farmers and domestic growers (for growing the crops from which drugs are manufactured), drug cartels and dealers, the media (for glamorizing drug use), drug users (particularly blacks living in urban ghettos), hopelessness, and "everyone who looks the other way" (President George Bush, quoted in Elwood 1994:34). Once one is committed to the war metaphor, it becomes easy to characterize all obstacles and opponents as enemies.

The opposition to and fight against these enemies is public; wars are not covert operations. Declaring war is dramatic, an uncommon step, a last resort, taken when nothing less will do. Wars therefore demand unity and commitment: "If our government is at war, be it against poverty or fraud or crime, then we are traitors if we do not support the cause. The symbol of war is an obvious tactic used by leaders to create support for their policies" (Stone 1988:121). Leaders invoke the war metaphor quite intentionally. Lyndon Johnson (1971:74) recalled that his advisers debated what to call their antipoverty policy, and he deliberately chose the "War on Poverty": "I wanted to rally the nation, to sound a call to arms which would stir people in the government, in private industry, and on the campuses to lend their talents to a massive effort to eliminate the evil." The language of unity and commitment runs throughout calls for wars against social problems: "Our country needs to swiftly launch a comprehensive war on breast cancer that attacks it on all fronts—basic research, education of the public and more innovative treatments" (Bricklin 1993:39).

Warfare presumes that fighting the enemy is a common cause of the entire society; individuals should set aside their doubts and reservations and join in the larger struggle. Society stands committed to the war effort, willing to make the sacrifices necessary to defeat the enemy: "War making is one of the few activities that people are not supposed to view 'realistically'; that is, with an eye to expense and practical outcome. In all-out war, expenditure is all-out, unprudent—war being defined as an emergency in which no sacrifice is excessive" (Sontag 1989:11). And uniting to make war strengthens a society; as Aho's second paradox (1994:15) notes: "There can be no harmony without chaos, no peace without war. While groups ostensibly fight only to secure their own short-term interests at the expense of others, the latent 'function' or unintended end of such fights is social solidarity."

Undoubtedly, these are the key elements policymakers mean to evoke when they declare war on social problems: the problem is an enemy of society at large; society is justified in fighting this enemy; society's members should rally to this cause; and they should be willing to make sacrifices for the war effort. Declaring war, then, is a call for a united, committed campaign against a social problem.

WHY WARS AGAINST SOCIAL PROBLEMS FAIL

But the war metaphor has other, more troubling implications. We need to begin by examining Americans' historical experience with war and their expectations for warfare. Beginning with the American Revolution, the United States has fought ten major wars (the Revolution, the War of 1812, the Mexican War, the Civil War, the Spanish-American War, World Wars I and II, and the Korean, Vietnam, and Gulf Wars).[4] In general, U.S. wars have been brief; aside from the Revolution and the Vietnam conflict, no U.S. war lasted much more than four years; our history does not feature "thirty years'" or "hundred years'" wars. And, in general, the United States has won—or at least not lost—its wars. Prior to Vietnam, it was common to hear that "we've never lost a war." Although Vietnam might seem to be an exception—a long conflict that ended in failure—it is important to recognize that at least a vocal segment of the public continues to insist that, had the government only been committed to the cause, willing to adopt different strategies and tactics, that war, too, might have been won in a short period of time. The Gulf War—a quick, decisive campaign with relatively few American casualties—is far more representative of the U.S. experience with war than is Vietnam.

In other words, declaring war on social problems enlists the U.S. public in a particular sort of enterprise. The metaphor invokes a complex set of meanings: a righteous cause, unity of purpose, commitment to the war's goals, and a clear-cut enemy, but also a concentrated yet relatively brief struggle, ending in ultimate victory. This is what war means to Americans; it is what we expect of war. Policymakers declare war on social problems precisely because they hope to invoke some of these expectations—commitment, unity against a common enemy. The problem is that social policies rarely live up to all that the metaphor promises.

In practice, declaring war against social problems is very different from waging international war. The war metaphor may be useful as a dramatic device for inaugurating policies: it highlights the new social policy, makes it a priority, and indicates official commitment to the cause. However, war rhetoric seems ill suited to the actual conduct of social policy.

The Problem of Complexity

Wars—at least in Americans' collective memory—usually are recalled as simple narratives: treachery by the enemy leads to a period of struggle as the nation mobilizes; then Americans begin a steady march toward victory. Of course, this simple story ignores a great deal: debates over strategies, setbacks and difficulties, complicated relationships with allies and enemies, and so on. But our underlying vision of warfare—at least from a distance—is fairly straightforward.

In contrast, social problems are not simple. Our *names* for our problems are simple—"poverty," "drugs"—but the problems those names describe are not. Social problems tend to be multifaceted. "Poverty" encompasses great diversity—poor people living in rural Appalachia and in urban ghettos, the elderly poor, the homeless, and so on. And social problems ordinarily have multiple, often hotly debated causes. Is there a culture of poverty? Is poverty an inevitable product of capitalism? Is it caused by structural shifts in the economy? How it is linked to racism and sexism? There are many competing explanations for most social problems, and probably most of them contain at least a grain of truth. The war metaphor depicts the social problem as a single enemy, but even a moment's thought reveals this view to be unrealistically simplistic.

Nixon's 1971 decision to wage war on cancer is a case in point. "Cancer" is a wishful oversimplification. Cancer is not one disease, but a broad category that includes many distinct diseases; although we speak of "breast cancer" or "stomach cancer," even these names are crude classifications encompassing varieties of malignancies affecting particular organs. In all likelihood, these diseases must be "fought" one by one as medical scientists seek to identify their causes and then search for particular therapies that are effective against particular diseases (usually at particular stages in their development). Although there might be progress in addressing particular diseases, there was, at least in 1971, no hope that a war on cancer could be won—that "cancer" could be cured or eliminated anytime in the foreseeable future. Declaring war—"the House of Representatives passed a bill mandating a cure for cancer by 1976, a present for the country's 200th birthday" (Culliton 1976:60)—created unrealistic expectations, and invited critics to quickly declare the war on cancer a failure (Beardsley 1994; Patterson 1987).

The Problem of Victory

Social policy, however warlike, is unlikely to result in clear-cut victory. In international wars, opponents suffer defeat: they sue for peace, accept terms, or surrender, publicly acknowledging their defeat and the other party's victory. Wars end—if only because the enemy can call a halt.

In contrast, social problems cannot surrender, and they rarely disappear. This raises an important question: how can we know when a war against a social problem has been won? Does victory mean that the problem has been reduced (and if so, how much of a reduction is involved? and of what sort? relative to projected increases? in absolute terms?)? Or must the problem be eradicated (what exactly does this mean? and how might it be demonstrated?)? The answers to such questions are not at all obvious.

Consider LBJ's War on Poverty. Perhaps the single most publicized war against a social problem, the War on Poverty became a target for a broad range of critics who insisted that the policy failed. Initially claims about the policy's defeat came from the left; liberal activists and social scientists were quick to announce the poverty war's failure in books such as *How We Lost the War on Poverty* (Pilisuk and Pilisuk 1973) and *Poverty: A History of the Richest Nation's Unwon War* (Lens 1969). Marc and Phyllis Pilisuk (1973:8) complained: "The war on poverty—never a real war at all—has been lost." Liberals' references to a lost war continue to appear:

The War on Poverty didn't fail. It was called off. . . . In effect, [in the late 1970s] state legislators called a truce, if not a full-scale retreat. Then, in 1980 [*sic*], President Reagan's inaugural speech rallied conservatives around a war on welfare. (Albelda et al. 1996:10)

Notice how the war metaphor contains its own vocabulary of failure, easily adopted by a policy's critics: wars are lost, are called off, or end in retreat.

The policy's more recent critics have been conservatives, who insist that the failure of the War on Poverty demonstrates the limitations of government-led social policies. Charles Murray's *Losing Ground* (1984) concludes that antipoverty programs actually made things worse:

Social programs in a democratic society tend to produce net harm in dealing with the most difficult problems. They will inherently tend to have enough of an inducement to produce bad behavior and not enough of a solution to stimulate good behavior; and the more difficult the problem is, the more likely that this relationship will prevail. (Murray 1984:218)

Or, as President Reagan liked to quip: "In the sixties we waged a war on poverty, and poverty won" (Lemann 1988:37).

It is possible to argue that the War on Poverty was a success. For example, Christopher Jencks (1992) insists that War on Poverty programs caused the material condition of the poor to improve and the proportion of the population living in poverty to fall. In other words, the policy worked to the degree that it reduced poverty; it made things better. But—and of course this is the critics' point—poverty did not disappear. Poor people remain: therefore, the War on Poverty failed; it ended in defeat.

Critics of the current war on drugs adopt much the same argument. They argue that the social organization of illicit markets makes it impossible to eradicate drug use, so drug wars are doomed from the start. Moreover, traffic in and use of illicit drugs continues—proof that the war on drugs has failed (see, e.g., McCoy and Block 1992; Johns 1992). Again, the rhetoric of warfare opens the door to partisan critiques. Democratic Senator Joseph Biden attacked George Bush's policy: "The President says he wants to wage war on drugs, but if that's true, what we need is another 'D Day,' not another Vietnam, not another limited war fought on the cheap and destined for stalemate and human tragedy" (quoted in Inciardi 1992:271), just as Republicans in the 1996 presidential campaign charged that President Clinton had been "AWOL in the war on drugs."

Thus drug warriors find themselves sandwiched between pessimists who insist that no punitive policy can succeed and antidrug enthusiasts arguing for escalation because the existing forces, tactics, and so on aren't enough to win. Even the drug war's defenders, such as the sociologist James Inciardi, find it necessary to redefine success in narrow, ambiguous ways:

> Is the war on drugs being won? Can the war on drugs be won? Should the war on drugs be fought? To these three questions, one could answer, respectively, "Yes, to some extent, at least in the middle class"; "Perhaps, to some degree at any rate"; and "Yes, why not?" (Inciardi 1992:267)

While drug warriors can point to reductions in drug use, the policy's critics charge that these declines are not evidence of success, that drug use began falling before the current drug war started. And, more important, decline is not enough; the critics define victory as the eradication of drug use, not merely its reduction. By this standard, the war on drugs has been lost.

Note that the wars on poverty and drugs show a neat reversal in their critics' ideological postures. As a policy promoted by a liberal president, the War on Poverty was called an inevitable failure by its conservative critics, while liberals insisted that the policy could have been successful if only the government had tried harder. In contrast, when a conservative president declared war on drugs, most of the critics predicting certain failure were liberals, while many conservatives claimed that greater commitment could produce victory. Clearly, partisan politics, not philosophical principles, determines critics' rhetorical postures in these debates.

In short, the war metaphor—at least in U.S. society—carries the implication that the enemy can be defeated. When the metaphor is applied to social problems, there is an implicit expectation that victory will be total, that the problem will be eliminated. But this is unrealistic. Most social problems are products of complex cultural and structural arrangements, and are unlikely to be completely eradicated, regardless of which social policies are chosen. Therefore, declaring war on social problems creates an unrealistic, unachievable expectation of total victory. And, when total victory fails to materialize—as it most surely will—the policy stands vulnerable to attack as a failure.

The Problem of Duration

A third issue concerns speed. Social change tends to occur over decades. The most effective social policies cannot produce overnight changes in social arrangements; it can take generations for policies' effects to permeate a social system. In contrast, because wars—at least in U.S. history—have tended to be concentrated, relatively brief experiences, the war metaphor invites expectations that the conflict will soon end, that the problem can be solved quickly.

Of course, enthusiasts can point to terrible problems that seem to have had quick solutions; the dramatic success of the polio vaccine became a touchstone for post–World War II believers in scientific progress. But to do so ignores the years of research required to develop the vaccine, as well as the people already affected by polio when the vaccine was released. Polio did not suddenly vanish.[5] And vaccines are preventive measures—they eradicate diseases by keeping them from spreading. The analogy doesn't fit most social problems; because social problems have complex causes, they are rarely amenable to "magic bullet" solutions, technological fixes. Most successful social policies produce modest improvements over time.

The expectation that wars don't take too long is related to the expectation that they end in victory. It is noteworthy how quickly critics assess wars on social problems as failures. The war on cancer, inaugurated in late 1971, was being attacked as a failure by 1975; criticisms of the War on Poverty and the current war on drugs came at least as quickly. It is as though the fact that U.S. involvement in major wars (e.g., the Civil War, World War II) tends to last about four years means that a social-policy "war" should produce total victory within that time. It is one thing to direct social policy toward a long-range goal of reducing or eliminating some socially problematic condition; it is quite another matter to expect cancer or poverty or drug use to disappear within five or ten years. Yet the war metaphor seems to encourage these short-range expectations.

The Problem of Unity

Declarations of war on social problems are dramatic events: they call for society to rally behind a single policy, against a common foe. Typically, the initial pronouncements receive favorable attention in the mass media; the press details the nature of the problem and outlines the efforts designed to wage war against it. Usually, the enemy—cancer or poverty—has no one speaking on its behalf. There is the sense that society is united behind the war effort. Declaring war seizes the moral high ground; at least at first, the policy seems above criticism.

But, as the war continues (for all the reasons noted above), this sense of moral purpose and unity is easily lost and the policy comes under attack. One set of critics affirms the war's goal—the eradication of the social problem—but argues that policymakers have adopted the wrong means, so that the war effort is half-hearted or wrong-headed. Officials ought to be doing more, or doing something different, if they really want to end the problem.

Other critics denounce the lack of unity in prosecuting the war. In practice, not everyone unites behind the war effort, and this dismays the policy's proponents. Because the war metaphor implies a united effort, the failure to achieve unity can be bitter. Thus, a drug-war official complains about defense lawyers accused of obstructing justice in drug cases: "I look upon these attorneys, if they're guilty, as traitors. Hell, are we in a war or not? Why aren't these guys being charged with treason?" (Dannen 1995:31–32).

Still other critics oppose the policy but not the metaphor; they argue that the war targets the wrong enemy. Some of the same liberals who criticized Reagan for pursuing a war on drugs were outraged by his failure to declare war on homelessness or AIDS: "Reagan recognized that war rhetoric sanctioned federal action on AIDS—by refusing to use it. . . . His choices about when to use and not use the war metaphor clearly reflected his priorities" (Sherry 1995:457).

Finally, critics may denounce war itself. This has been the stance adopted by critics of the current drug war, who argue that drug education coupled with legalization or decriminalization are more sensible goals for drug policy than eradication. Thus, the Drug Policy Foundation sells baseball caps with the slogan WAR IS NOT A DOMESTIC POLICY on the front. Although wars against social problems rarely inspire large antiwar movements, unity tends to dissolve over time.

Again, the expectation implicit in the war metaphor—that wars can be won quickly—gives the policy's critics the ammunition they need:

> The search for war's moral equivalent had invited government to
> pursue quick solutions to chronic problems resistant to speedy solu-
> tions. When the inevitable failure, waste, and repression surfaced,
> many Americans bewailed government's ineffectiveness, finding
> confirmation of the very weaknesses that had initially inspired their
> rhetoric. (Sherry 1995:460)

The Consequences of Choosing the War Metaphor

Choosing to declare war on social problems is consequential. It has obvious advantages. The metaphor is dramatic; it attracts favorable press attention, encourages everyone to move the issue higher on the policy agenda, and—at least temporarily—seems to silence critics. Undoubtedly, it is these obvious advantages that lead policymakers to continue to declare war on social problems.

At the same time, the very drama and visibility created by declarations of war make these social policies especially vulnerable to criticism:

> In the short run, the Johnson administration must be judged amazingly successful at its rhetorical task. Over a period of but a few months, strong support was obtained for measures for which there had been no public clamor or demand. Tragically, however, the very rhetorical choices which were so useful in gaining initial support proved to be dysfunctional in the long run. (Zarefsky 1986:xiv)

The war metaphor carries implications—of societal unity and speedy victory—that few social policies can fulfill. Within four or five years of declaring war on a social problem, we can expect to find, regardless of whether the policy has achieved some modest successes, the core problematic condition enduring, and critics denouncing the policy's failure. With each passing year, the sense that the policy has failed is likely to become more widespread.

At the same time, the melodrama of the war metaphor, its insistence that social problems can be understood as a straightforward struggle between good and evil, constrains discussion of alternative policies. If society is at war with drugs, if drugs are our common enemy, it is easy to respond to antidrug policy failures by escalating the war, by cracking down even harder. It is much more difficult to shift paradigms, to redefine drugs as, say, a public health problem that ought to be addressed with a very different set of policies (Bertram et al. 1996). The popularity of the war metaphor, the ease with which it portrays policy as melodrama, makes it harder to adopt alternative imagery. It is much easier for the policy's critics to turn the metaphor to their own uses (e.g., criticizing defeatism) than to reframe the issue in completely different terms, to think of drugs as a health problem rather than an enemy. Public health policies produce slow changes over the long term; they seem to admit compromise and moral ambiguity. No wonder waging war offers more popular imagery.

We live in a pessimistic age. As this century's end approaches, we are surrounded by evidence of social progress: longer life expectancy, a higher standard of living, a more educated population, greater social equality, and so on. One might write the history of the twentieth-century United States in terms of this social progress. But the idea of progress has fallen into disrepute. There is a widespread sense that our society is deteriorating. In particular, there is considerable doubt that social policies make things better.

In part, this doubt reflects a sense that recent social policies have failed. Although this assessment is not limited to the policies called wars against social problems, those policies, because they were dramatic efforts, highly publicized and designed to create high expectations for social progress, have been especially visible and easily defined as policy failures. The lesson seems clear: even when society dedicates itself to solving a particular social problem, it cannot succeed. Pessimism, then, is justified.

SOCIAL POLICY AS MELODRAMA

Declaring war on social problems is dramatic. It is a headline-grabbing move that tries to enlist everyone in a collective melodrama, uniting as good guys in a just, all-out struggle against evil. A similarly melodramatic vision runs through much contemporary talk about social problems. In earlier chapters, we examined how melodramatic imagery shapes

our understanding of wilding, stalking, and other new crimes of random violence, and how advocates use melodrama to typify the new victims as vulnerable innocents. Defining social problems in terms of villains and victims makes it easy to understand these issues: propelled by
evil motives in pursuit of evil goals, criminals become the equivalent of
the dark-cloaked, mustache-twirling villain of nineteenth-century melodrama, while the exploited new victims are like the fair-haired maiden
tied to the railroad track. Similarly, in declaring war on some social
problem, the state/society/everyone assumes the hero's role, dedicating
ourselves to protecting the innocent, righting wrongs, and stamping
out evil. No wonder we are so fond of melodramatic imagery; it simplifies complex issues, resolving the blurry grays into stark black and
white.

In contrast, effective social policy tends to be boring. It seems mundane, if only because we take what works for granted. But no high-tech
medical miracle has saved anything like the number of lives that have
been spared since people recognized the need and devised the means
to keep sewage separate from drinking water. The mundane social
changes that caused nineteenth-century crime rates to fall included industry's growing demand for workers, compulsory schooling, the spread
of street lights, and the presence of police on patrol (Tobias 1967). It
is the seemingly minor, taken-for-granted reforms, such as requiring
vaccinations and seat belts and smoke detectors, or establishing building codes and water treatment and Social Security, that eventually
change the social landscape.

We aren't much interested in these mundane policies, and we usually don't hear much about them. The mass media thrive on novelty,
drama, and excitement. All television formats for news and quasi news,
from talk shows and made-for-TV movies to regular news broadcasts,
depend on being interesting enough, dramatic enough, to hold the audience's attention. Newspapers are more likely to report on gradual
progress, but stories that lack drama don't make the front page. Politicians, depending on media coverage for visibility, learn to couch their

actions in new, dramatic terms. Even bureaucrats, hoping to enlist politicians' support, discover the need to make bureaucracy seem exciting. Thus, policymakers come to favor dramatic gestures, such as declaring war. Social policy, like social problems, attracts attention when it seems new and dramatic; otherwise it gets ignored.

No wonder those trying to define social issues favor melodramatic imagery. Both advocates promoting new social problems and policymakers introducing new policies recognize melodrama's advantages. By defining social issues as straightforward struggles between good and evil, melodrama compels our attention and enlists our emotions. It simplifies complexity, and reduces opposition to whatever is being proposed. Who, after all, opposes fighting against evil, protecting the vulnerable, and preserving innocence?

Melodrama's simplicity—and its costs—become apparent in hotly contested social issues. Consider the vivid rhetoric injected into the debate over social policies on guns. Opponents of gun controls envision jack-booted government thugs, intent on ravaging the Constitution, rendering citizens defenseless, and preparing the way for an authoritarian world government, while gun-control advocates portray guns, the irrationality of "gun nuts," and the evil influence of the National Rifle Association as being at the root of American violence and crime. Both visions are fundamentally melodramatic; both seek to enlist right-thinking people in a struggle against evil. Similarly, the rhetoric of both those attacking and those defending abortion can be melodramatic, as advocates mount crusades on behalf of murdered babies or oppressed women. By characterizing one's opponents as evil villains and one's cause as the protection of innocents, melodramatic rhetoric makes such debates that much more difficult to resolve.

Melodrama stands opposed to subtlety. In *Body Count*, their analysis of "how to win America's war against crime and drugs," former U.S. "drug czar" William Bennett and his colleagues blame "moral poverty" for "America's violent crime plague," warning that "thickening ranks of juvenile 'super-predators'" mean that "America is a ticking crime bomb"

(Bennett, DiIulio, and Walters 1996:13, 21, 27). Like other claims about callous criminals and deviant conspiracies, this portrayal stands opposed to the bulk of criminological knowledge that finds crime's motivations in relatively mundane, situationally specific thrills and fears (J. Katz 1988). Similarly, advocates present new victims as faultless, as pawns in the hands of their evil victimizers; in melodrama, victimization is the product of straightforward exploitation. And, of course, declarations of war identify social problems as enemies preying on society rather than the result of existing social arrangements. Melodrama's simplicity is appealing precisely because it makes complex issues so easy to understand.

But, of course, melodrama comes at a cost. Simplifying complexity inevitably distorts what we know, and melodrama lends itself to oversimplification and, therefore, serious distortion. In particular, by equating social problems with evil, melodramatic rhetoric discourages us from understanding their mundane roots. By exaggerating threats and arousing our fears, melodrama also raises the emotional stakes, making it harder to calmly consider policy options. Whenever we respond to social problems as emergencies, we lose sight of alternatives and sacrifice our ability to weigh costs, set priorities, and make reasoned choices (Lipsky and Smith 1989).

In part, such short-circuited reasoning is precisely why policymakers and other advocates favor melodramatic claims. In the competition for attention in the social-problems marketplace, dramatic, compelling claims have an advantage; unassuming, boring claims get overlooked. Therefore, advocates package their claims to attract attention, making new crimes seem especially threatening, new victims especially sympathetic, and proposed policies especially bright with promise. This need not be cynical or dishonest; caught up in their enthusiasm for the cause, advocates often believe their own rhetoric. But claims that define issues in melodramatic terms contain the seeds of their own destruction. This is apparent in declaring war on social problems. Declarations of war seem to offer—*do* offer—a means of rallying people around a common cause. But the war metaphor also encourages other expectations of quick, decisive victories, expectations that inevitably lead to disappointment and disillusionment. Similarly, denouncing random violence compels our attention, but it proves to be a singularly unmanageable, almost useless way to think about crime.

Although melodramatic rhetoric characterizes social issues in exaggerated, oversimplified ways, some distortion is inevitable in all claims about social problems. All claims carve off a slice of reality and give it a name, specify its causes, identify its consequences, and so on. Claims focus our attention on a particular social condition and encourage us to define it as a problem of a particular sort. In drawing our attention to some things, claims lead us to ignore others; inevitably, we see less than the whole. Every time we focus on some new social problem, we risk losing sight of its larger context.

CHAPTER 8

Connections among Claims
The Context for New Social Problems

When advocates call our attention to a particular social problem, they want us to concentrate on that problem's substance: perhaps it is a new sort of crime, involving a new type of criminal, injuring a new kind of victim, or demanding new social policies. They probably consider the words they use to describe the problem as relatively unimportant, just the necessary means by which they can raise concern. But those words are important; they make a difference. We cannot understand crime or other social problems except through language, so advocates' words give shape to what we believe.

In particular, the way in which we commonly talk about social problems encourages us to worry about one problem at a time. Like advocates, the media usually present problems in isolation, in a front-page story about freeway violence, a newsmagazine report on sexual predators, or a talk-show episode featuring survivors of satanic ritual abuse. Similarly, policymakers try to focus their deliberations, holding a legislative hearing on hate crimes or passing an antistalking law. We routinely separate topics, draw distinctions, try to avoid confusing the issue or muddying the water.

162

Sociological research also tends to be narrowly focused. Constructionists—sociologists who study how and why particular social problems emerge and evolve (i.e., how they are "socially constructed")— favor case studies, in which the researcher examines the development of a single social problem. There are good reasons for this preference. Like everyone else, sociologists are accustomed to thinking about one problem at a time; when the media suddenly begin covering freeway shootings, or antistalking activists start lobbying state legislatures, it becomes easy to imagine studying the rise of this newest problem. Moreover, the case study is a manageable piece of research, possible to complete in a reasonable amount of time with a reasonable amount of effort. Often, too, the researcher has a personal or ideological interest in the particular topic chosen for study; it is the specifics of this problem that interest the analyst. As a result, the case study has become the scholarly norm, and sociology journals have published dozens of articles titled "The Social Construction of [problem X]," examining the emergence of social problems one problem at a time.

Constructionists sometimes generalize beyond case studies, identifying patterned ways in which social problems emerge and evolve. Thus, *moral panics* (Cohen 1980; Goode and Ben-Yehuda 1994) feature exaggerated claims and intense concern about new threats to the social order; *drug scares* (Reinarman 1994) involve warnings about the hazards posed by particular drugs; while *medicalization* (Conrad 1992) occurs when medical authorities claim that some problem lies within their expertise. These categories have some analytic value—for example, researchers can classify claims about some new social problem as, say, an instance of medicalization—but they do not lead to a general theory of social problems, if only because these categories refer to different analytic dimensions: the nature of the public reaction (moral panics); the substantive focus of the claims (drug scares); and the advocates' perspective (medicalization). A social problem might fall within all three categories (e.g., early claims about crack babies), or apply to none.

But social-problems claims do not emerge in isolation, nor do they inevitably fall into one of three categories. How advocates describe a new social problem very much depends on how they (and their audiences—the public, the press, and policymakers) are used to talking about other, already familiar problems. Thus, when carjacking or stalking suddenly becomes the focus of public attention, advocates define the new crime in familiar terms, drawing upon what they already understand about random violence, victimization, and so on. That is, new social-problems claims are, in various ways, linked to familiar notions about other, well-established social problems. Yet case studies usually downplay these connections. This chapter explores these links, focusing on four sorts of connections among social-problems claims: those involving cultural resources, the new problem's scope, its advocates' orientations, and its historical context.

CULTURAL RESOURCES

Claims about different problems are connected through the great inventory of cultural resources available for talking about social problems. All manner of ideas and imagery can be borrowed by advocates trying to give shape to a new problem or policy. Thus, current concerns about gangs draw heavily from centuries-old fears of conspiracies of deviants; advocates depend on established understandings of the nature of victimization when bringing attention to new sorts of victims; and politicians seek to mobilize support by declaring war on yet another social problem. Conceptions of conspiracy, victimization, and warfare are part of the common culture; invoking such cultural resources lets us bring what we already know to our understanding of claims about new social problems.

In a sense, there is no such thing as a new social problem. To be sure, previously unknown phenomena (e.g., HIV infections) may emerge, be discovered, and become the subject of advocates' claims. But those claims inevitably borrow from other claims about other problems: they use familiar language (e.g., "infection," "epidemic," "plague") and rhetoric (e.g., presenting melodramatic examples to arouse fear and gain sympathy); their advocates adopt familiar orientations (e.g., medicalization) and choose familiar tactics (e.g., organizing protests to attract media coverage); and so on. Every time advocates borrow such cultural resources, they link their claims and the problems they describe to other claims and other problems.

The array of cultural resources from which advocates can choose elements to construct claims about a new social problem is vast, and the choices made should not be taken for granted. Advocates do not pick elements at random; a particular cultural resource may be selected and incorporated into advocates' claims for various reasons—because it is consistent with the advocates' ideology, because it seems likely to appeal to the claims' audience, because it reminds the audience of other problems or policies, and so on (Fine and Christoforides 1991; R. Williams 1995). Sometimes the choice of elements links problems in overt, obvious ways (e.g., claims that stalking is a form of domestic violence), but other connections are more oblique (e.g., claims about new forms of victimization that implicitly invoke the ideology of victimization). Still, the choice of resources is patterned, not random: particular advocates favor particular imagery at particular times and in particular places. Advocates, whether seventeenth-century New England Puritan preachers denouncing sin or contemporary feminists exposing sexism, emerge in specific historical and geographic contexts, and develop characteristic ways of thinking about new social problems.

In dozens of ways, then, claims about any given social problem have connections to other problems past and present. And it is precisely these connections that tend to vanish when sociological case studies examine one problem at a time, as though each social problem exists as an independent product of particular advocates responding to a particular social condition. The connections—the ways in which social-problems claims influence and are influenced by one another—get forgotten. Examining a new problem's scope, its advocates' orientations, and their claims' historical context can reveal important connections among claims.

THE SCOPE OF SOCIAL PROBLEMS

Every social problem must be recognized *as a problem* and defined as a distinct phenomenon. Particular incidents come to be seen as instances of the larger problem. This recognition is not automatic; it is an accomplishment. Someone—some advocate—must make the claims necessary to define the problem's scope. At first, this involves *classification*—specifying what the problem involves. However, the initial definition of a problem's scope tends to expand over time, through the processes of *domain expansion* and *diffusion*.

Classification

Naming is a key moment in the history of any social problem. Some advocate must set the problem apart from other social phenomena, point to it, and give it a name, as when reporters announced that the young men who attacked the Central Park jogger had been "wilding." Suddenly, acts with familiar names—rape, robbery, assault—were repackaged, so that what had happened became an instance of a new, even more terrible crime: it was not just rape, it was wilding. And the attack on the jogger became a focus of attention and concern not just because it was a serious crime, but because it now exemplified a new threat, perhaps a new sign of moral decay or societal collapse. Wilding—at least for a few weeks—became a new classification for criminality: the press watched for other instances to report; and commentators offered explanations for this new crime trend.

"Wilding" was never really defined. Certainly the name encompassed the assault on the Central Park jogger, but what else did it cover? Could one person go wilding, or did wilding require crimes committed by a group? What crimes could be involved (e.g., did wilding require serious violence, or could it involve vandalism or shoplifting)? Was it necessary that the victims and offenders be strangers? Was it necessary for the offenders to be young or, as some critics implied, black or Hispanic? Was it necessary that the offenders know or use the term "wilding" to describe their actions? No one bothered to ask or answer these questions. Wilding was a crime without a definition, a quality that no doubt helped it fade quickly from view.

Though wilding is an extreme case, it is remarkable how rarely public discussions of social problems invoke precise definitions (Best 1990). Most often, social-problems claims begin with a typifying example—usually a melodramatic example, a horror story, an atrocity tale. Although advocates explain that this incident (the attack on the Central Park jogger) is an instance of a larger problem (wilding), the problem often receives little or no definition. The scope, the exact domain of the problem, is never specified. But who cares? If the example is sufficiently frightening, it holds our attention. We readily agree that "things like that" are a shame, that they shouldn't be allowed, that somebody ought to do something.

Advocates tend to avoid precise definitions because they invite controversy and threaten the consensus of concerned attention that their claims aim to arouse. Typically, advocates prefer broad, expansive definitions; they see, and they want policymakers to address, the larger problem, the big picture. Advocates favor inclusiveness, and want to avoid denying the sufferings of any victim. Thus, advocates use the term "sexual abuse" to include children victimized by repeated incestuous rapes, but also the child who briefly sees a stranger expose himself. After all, they argue, a single experience of being flashed might have devastating psychological consequences. At the same time, advocates realize that it may be difficult to combine broad definitions with the moral outrage aroused by melodramatic examples. Everyone is deeply shocked and offended by tales of incestuous rape, but many will be less exercised by flashing. Moreover, other specifics may threaten the consensus of outrage; in particular, some victims may have done things that helped place them at risk, making them fall short of the standard for naive, powerless purity that melodrama assigns to victims—the sort of innocence featured in most typifying examples. Thus, advocates find it far easier to gloss over the matter of definition, to avoid specifying the problem's scope. At least in the early stages of bringing a problem to public attention, it is enough to provide troubling examples and name the problem.

Nor are there many pressures to force advocates into making precise, public definitions. In relaying advocates' claims to the public, the media often gloss over definitions. Pausing for an exact definition can disrupt the dramatic flow of a good story; the media seem more concerned with finding disturbing statistics (e.g., "there are 200,000 stalkers") and eliciting statements from experts (often scholar-activists who double as advocates) to document claims about a new problem. It usually falls on policymakers and the officials who implement policy to create operational definitions; after all, an antistalking law presumably must define what constitutes stalking. But these definitional details rarely receive close attention from the media, and therefore they remain out of sight. Unless advocates face overt opposition (e.g., the conflict between antiabortion and proabortion advocates fosters highly visible claims and counterclaims about the nature of abortion), definitions rarely become public issues.

Domain Expansion

Once a problem gains widespread recognition and acceptance, there is a tendency to piggyback new claims onto the old name, to expand the problem's domain (Best 1990). The initial claims become a foot in the door, an opening wedge for further advocacy. Thus, the diagnosis "posttraumatic stress disorder" originated as a classification for Vietnam veterans' delayed psychological reactions to combat, but therapists soon began applying it to other "traumatic stresses," including rape, sexual abuse, crime victimization, natural disasters, work-related stress, UFO abductions, and so on. Similarly, initial claims about sexual harassment focused on workplace supervisors extorting sexual favors from their subordinates, but the domain of sexual harassment gradually expanded to encompass jokes, innuendo, pin-ups, teasing, and anything else that might be seen as constituting a hostile environment, not only at work, but also in other settings, including elementary school playgrounds.

A related process—domain elaboration—involves the identification of new aspects of a problem (Stallings 1995). Here, advocates offer a fresh angle from which to view a problem—additional implications that demand attention. For example, child sexual abuse and other forms of victimization have many ramifications: sexual abuse can cause psychological and other medical problems; it can disrupt a student's educational progress; it may lead the child to run away, use drugs, or break other laws; and so on. Elaborating a problem's domain lets advocates make a problem relevant to—and enlist support from—additional audiences, such as physicians, teachers, school nurses, and the like.

Domain expansion and elaboration reflect advocates' preference for inclusive definitions. Many social-problems campaigns begin with activists calling attention to extreme typifying examples in order to mobilize societal consensus. From that narrow foundation, they gradually can extend the problem's domain, arguing that other, less melodramatic cases are another form of, really no different than, the moral equivalent of, or just the same as the original typifying examples, and that the problem is complex, with many facets demanding attention. Such expansive claims help keep the problem visible. Social movements cannot afford to succeed and then relax; once members believe a cause is won, they may drift away. Domain expansion and elaboration let movement leaders argue that the battle continues, that work remains to be done, and that the cause needs continued support. Similarly, extending the domain lets advocates offer the media new angles on a problem, encouraging continued coverage that can keep the problem visible.

Domain expansion is a tactic that also can be adopted by new advocates—those not involved in the initial campaign, but who hope to couple their own (often less popular) causes to an established social problem (Best 1990). Once child abuse achieved general recognition as a social problem, various advocates began claiming that the category ought to include parental smoking, circumcision, not buckling small children into car seats, and so on. Similarly, the growing acceptance of the term "hate crime" as a label for assaults on racial and religious minorities attracted claims from gay and lesbian activists who argued that attacks on homosexuals were also hate crimes; similar domain-expansion efforts continue by feminists, advocates for the disabled, and others hoping to further expand the domain of hate crimes. The campaign against hate crimes led to the first federal law equating homosexuals with other minorities—an important symbolic victory for gay and lesbian activists. This example suggests how advocates for potentially unpopular causes stand to gain through domain expansion.

Diffusion

The scope of social problems also can expand by geographic diffusion. Regardless of where a problem originates, advocates usually bring claims to national attention from the core media centers of New York, Los Angeles, or Washington: wilding emerged in New York, freeway violence and stalking in Los Angeles, and so on. Over time, as a new problem gains familiarity, concern spreads outward to the heartland and across institutions: policymakers pass state laws and local ordinances; regulatory agencies establish standards; private firms set internal policies; various professionals receive training in recognizing and dealing with the problem; local media run stories that play up the local angle; and so on. Through this process, social-problems imagery spreads: L.A.'s super-gangs' colors and drive-by shootings began being spotted in medium- and small-sized cities across the country, and local advocates insisted that these local gangs posed the same dangers as the Crips and Bloods. Disease metaphors—infections, contagions, epidemics, plagues—lend themselves to claims about the hazards of diffusion.

Less often, claims cross international boundaries (Jenkins 1992). Warnings about a huge satanic blood cult, committing tens of thousands of human sacrifices, countless acts of ritual abuse, and other occult crimes arose among conservative Christians in United States in the early 1980s, then spread to Great Britain, the Netherlands, Norway, and Australia later in the decade. Although religious advocates carried most of the claims about satanic criminals across international borders, once established in a new country, belief in satanists spread among some feminists, therapists, law-enforcement officials, and others. But this sort of determined effort to spread claims seems fairly uncommon. Equally interesting is the sheer number of other countries where claims of occult crime failed to get off the ground. In general, social-problems claims seem restricted to their countries of origin. Rarely do claims become the basis for official foreign policy (the limited success in enlisting other countries in the war on drugs suggests why this may be the case). American media may reach around the globe, but to the degree that they carry our social-problems claims, their messages may be discounted as applicable only to the United States. For example, beliefs that the United States tolerates especially high levels of violence and inequality may make foreign audiences perfectly willing to believe that serial murders or hate crimes are commonplace here, yet not be too worried about the same problems spreading to their own societies. As a result, even the English-speaking countries whose cultures most resemble that of the United States—Canada, Great Britain, and Australia—seem to ignore many claims that achieve considerable visibility here. However, as CNN and other U.S. news media reach a growing international audience, cross-national diffusion of claims may increase.

In addition, advocates sometimes practice a sort of diffusion across time, retrospectively claiming to discover social problems in the past.

They search the historical record for evidence of men's crimes against women, adults' abuse of children, and the like. Again, occult crime offers a nice example: antisatanist advocates find evidence of ritual abuse in Afro-Caribbean religions (voodoo, *santeria*, etc.), shamanism, witchcraft in all its forms (from witchcraft beliefs in preliterate societies to the European witch craze to today's Wiccans), the Gnostics, Illuminati, Freemasons, and Branch Davidians; they insist that, properly understood, all of these phenomena confirm the threat posed by contemporary satanists (Noblitt and Perskin 1995). While some social-problems claims trade on novelty, arguing that a terrible new threat has recently emerged, other advocates prefer to trace the history of problems, arguing that our enlightened age should take a stand against forms of suffering our predecessors ignored or took for granted.

Social problems' definitions, then, are rarely precise or static. Because most advocates avoid specifying the exact scope of a problem, problems tend to expand their domains and spread across space and time.

ORIENTATIONS TOWARD SOCIAL PROBLEMS

All claims about social problems establish an orientation, a way of looking at or thinking about whatever is at issue. This goes beyond the problem's scope: given the problem's domain, what sort of problem is it? For example, during the 1970s, feminist advocates began challenging the assumption that rape is a sex crime, arguing that rapists want dominance, not sex, and that rape should properly be considered a violent crime. Rape's domain—the actions that constitute rape—was not at issue; rather, advocates wanted to change people's orientation, how they thought about rape.

Orientation links social-problems claims to one another in several ways. First, enduring problems require that some advocates *assume ownership*. But ownership does not always ensure static orientations: over time, advocates may change their orientations, *expanding their rationales*. Often orientations reflect established ideologies, and advocates *extend their ideology* to encompass the new problem. In some cases, a problem's owners adopt an available *master frame*, thereby aligning the new problem with other, familiar problems. Finally, claims can—but rarely do—locate new social problems within *systems of interrelated social ills*.

Assuming Ownership

Although wilding and freeway violence attracted a great deal of attention, neither crime remained in the public spotlight for long. The difference between these short-lived crime problems and other new crimes that became institutionalized, such as stalking and hate crimes, is that institutionalization requires that someone assume ownership of the new problem (Gusfield 1981). Advocates who own a problem become the authorities on the topic: the media interview them; policymakers solicit their opinions; and so on. Most important, a problem's owners frame— that is, define the appropriate orientation toward—the problem, explaining what sort of problem this is. For example, complaints about the behaviors involved in stalking were not new, but they had been viewed as symptomatic of obsession or other individual psychological problems. The recent invention of the term "stalking," and the assumption of ownership of the stalking problem by the victims' rights and battered women's movements, redefined these behaviors as a new crime, often a form of domestic violence, another way that men exploit women. This new orientation quickly became the authoritative way to understand stalking; it created a framework within which the press could cover the issue, provided a foundation upon which legislators could construct anti-stalking laws, led agencies to fund research on stalking, and so on.

There is nothing automatic about social-problem ownership. There may be small, homogenous societies where all talk about social problems invokes a single orientation: the New England Puritans seem to have couched virtually all social commentary in religious language. But contemporary society offers an extensive, constantly changing menu of orientations from which to choose; social-problems claims can derive from a broad range of political philosophies, economic theories, psychological principles, religious orientations, schools of literary criticism, and so on. Within academia, there are debates among disciplines (e.g., economists vs. psychologists vs. sociologists), among schools within disciplines (e.g., within sociology, conflict theory vs. functionalism vs. constructionism), and even within schools (e.g., strict vs. contextual constructionism). Because complex, heterogeneous societies offer many alternative orientations for understanding social problems, assuming ownership is a dramatic, consequential step.

Until ownership is established, orientations toward social problems are unstable: recall the competing interpretations for freeway violence as variously a crime problem, a gun problem, a traffic problem, and so on. However, once advocates assume ownership, their orientation toward the problem becomes taken for granted, and, unless their ownership is contested, the possibility that a problem can be seen in multiple ways recedes from view. Established ownership creates a single, dominant orientation.

Rationale Expansion

In competing for and maintaining ownership of a social problem, advocates may find it advantageous to alter or expand the orientation they promote. Karl Kunkel (1995), for example, describes the shifting rhetoric of the Farm Animal Reform Movement (FARM), an organization opposed to factory farming that originally emphasized animal rights. When FARM discovered that relatively few people worry about the rights of cattle, pigs, and chickens, it began a process of rationale expansion, seeking additional arguments that might persuade more people. FARM coupled its animal-rights rhetoric to new warnings about both the health risks of eating factory-farm-raised meat and factory farming's harmful effects on the environment. Though animal rights remained their central concern, FARM's activists found it expedient to present health and environmental issues as supplementary orientations.

Like domain expansion, rationale expansion offers advocates a way of keeping their claims fresh and holding their current supporters' attention, while simultaneously trying to increase their own influence by attracting more adherents. Rationale expansion reminds us that claims must compete in the social-problems marketplace. It is not enough that advocates find their own orientations convincing; their audiences—the media, the public, and policymakers—must respond to their claims. Some orientations may be considered authoritative within a particular, segmented audience, but this need not lead to claims being generally accepted. For instance, although some conservative Christians readily accepted claims about occult crimes and ritual abuse, secular institutions proved more skeptical. On the other hand, an orientation can have broad support. Feminists maintain ownership over several problems involving new victims, and a vocal feminist presence in academia, law, and other institutions has helped advance their claims.

Ideological Extension

Many orientations toward social problems derive from more or less coherent ideologies, such as feminism, that invoke particular schemes for interpreting social life. These ideologies may be associated with political philosophies (e.g., liberalism, conservatism, Marxism), interest groups (e.g., feminism, religious fundamentalism), or professions (e.g., medicalization). Thus, Marxism views social problems as rooted in political economy, feminism finds their causes in patriarchy, and so on. Anyone familiar with an ideology can imagine how it might be used to interpret a particular social problem. Ideologies are useful because they offer relatively coherent interpretations of social life. At the same time, of course, by focusing our attention on some aspects of society, most ideologies treat other aspects as essentially irrelevant.

Heterogeneous societies support an array of ideologies whose adherents sometimes compete for ownership of particular social problems. Policy debates between liberals and conservatives, for example, are a familiar feature of the political landscape. The set of visible ideologies changes over time, as some groups become increasingly influential while others' importance fades. During the course of the twentieth century, for instance, the influence of physicians, psychiatrists, and the medical model rose while religious ideologies seemed to lose much of their clout.

The rise of the women's movement in the early 1970s, and the emergence of feminism as a coherent ideology, created an important new voice in policy debates. Feminist theory argues that patriarchal societies systematically place women at a disadvantage, and that many social problems have especially severe consequences for women. Feminist advocates have been ready to apply these insights to an ever-expanding set of social problems, including crime. Following the early campaigns to draw attention to rape and battering, feminists became active in promoting the causes of many of the new victims. For example, feminists played active roles in the victims' rights and battered women's movements that assumed ownership of the stalking problem; in the process, they redefined stalking as a crime that usually involved men victimizing women—an interpretation consistent with feminist claims about other forms of domestic and sexual violence. Not every bid for ownership is successful, of course: feminist efforts to have rape defined as a hate crime have had little success. But it is not uncommon for feminist interpretations to become influential; over the last twenty-five years, the ideology's influence has been extended to cover a broad range of social problems.

In part, this extension of feminist influence reflects the institutionalization of feminist ideology. For example, most colleges and universities now house women's studies programs that offer an institutional center for feminist theorists, but feminist interpretations also are taught by faculty—both male and female—in traditional humanities and social-sciences disciplines, in the helping professions, and in law and other pro-

fessional schools. Identifying a new problem or offering a fresh interpretation for a familiar problem is, of course, a traditional way to build
an academic career, and the diffusion of feminist scholars throughout
higher education has produced a vast literature of feminist interpretations (much of it published in journals devoted to the ideology), including claims about social problems. This broad institutional base supports the ideology's extension to claim ownership of additional social
problems.

Master Frames

Advocates' orientations offer frameworks for understanding social problems—what students of social movements call *collective action frames*
(Snow and Benford 1992). Social-movement frames should feature a
diagnosis (specifying the nature of the problem), a prognosis (how the
movement can solve the problem), and frame resonance (persuasive
rhetoric capable of mobilizing adherents to the cause). Obviously, there
is considerable overlap between social movements and the creation of
social problems: the diagnoses offered by movements are equivalent to
what we have been calling social-problems claims; the prognoses are
similar to policy proposals; and frame resonance resembles advocates'
efforts to create effective rationales, compelling examples, and so on.
Though not all social-problems claims come from social movements,
many do.

Like sociologists of social problems, social-movement scholars favor case studies of particular movements, each with its own collective
action frame. However, the concept of the *master frame* reveals links
among parallel movements. Master frames are broad orientations shared
by diverse movements. For example, the perceived legitimacy of demands for "equal rights" has served as a master frame of campaigns
by or on behalf of ethnic minorities, women, the disabled, gays and lesbians, fetuses, and even animals. "Master frames are generic; specific

collective action frames are derivative" (Snow and Benford 1992:138). In particular, "elaborated" master frames, such as "equal rights,"

> use language that is open to interpretation, can be used to address a large variety of social ills, and allows for a variety of collective action. . . . [The elaborated master frame's] flexible language makes it resistant to being made irrelevant by the course of events, and thus can be adopted by differing groups over a period of decades. Particularly for social movements that are coalitions of separate, loosely overlapping organizations, elaborated master frames hold the coalitions together even when there is not complete ideological agreement. (G. Williams and Williams 1995:194)

The notion of master frame can help us think about parallels among social-problems claims. The recent popularity of depicting new crimes in terms of random violence suggests the presence of a master frame; certainly the ideology of victimization offers a widespread master frame. These are cases where the dominant orientations toward different social problems bear a kind of family resemblance.

If nothing else, the visibility of social-problems claims fosters the emergence of master frames. Successful claims receive widespread promotion in the media, and they become generally familiar. This encourages advocates trying to promote new problems to model their claims on existing orientations. Although it helps if the advocates have kindred ideologies, this is not necessary. Note that the ideology of victimization is a master frame that has been adopted by a very diverse set of advocates, including liberals, political and religious conservatives, feminists, therapists, and social scientists. An elaborated master frame can encompass a wide variety of social-problem orientations.

Identifying Systems of Social Problems

The tendency to address social problems one at a time means that causal links among social problems often receive little attention. There are exceptions. The perceived concentration of social problems in the inner cities—poverty, single-parent families, high rates of violence, and so on—has produced rival claims about systems of social problems. In general, liberals argue that the central cities now offer fewer industrial jobs that can be filled by less-educated workers; this reduces incomes and makes it more difficult to establish stable, two-parent families, which in turn creates single-parent families and despair that, further, lead to crime and drug abuse; racism, physical segregation, and inadequate institutional supports for education and health care block the children of this new underclass from finding better job opportunities, so that things only get worse as the cycle continues (W. Wilson 1987). In contrast, conservative interpretations emphasize the role of social-service programs in weakening the family, religion, and other traditional institutions, replacing self-sufficiency with dependency, and fostering a dysfunctional culture of poverty that allows crime, drug abuse, poor achievement in school, and other problems to flourish (Murray 1984). But both orientations emphasize that the social problems of the underclass are systemic: particular problems exacerbate and are exacerbated by other problems.

It is remarkable how rarely such systemic interpretations figure into contemporary discussions of social problems. Most of the claims about new crimes, new victims, and new policies discussed in the earlier chapters do not present these social problems as part of a troubled, interconnected system of social ills. Again, the notions of random violence, melodramatic exploitation, and commonplace victimization discourage recognizing systems of social problems: if violent crime can strike anyone at any time, if evil villains attack innocent victims for inexplicable reasons, then there is no sense to be made of our problems, no need to look for larger patterns.

Systemic visions tend to be the products of coherent ideologies—liberalism, conservatism, feminism, and the like. Such grand theories are available to advocates, of course, but they seem to play a limited role in many contemporary discussions of social problems. In part, this may be because, although each theory has proponents, it also has opponents, and claims couched in ideological terms invite opposition from those less concerned with the problem at hand than with blocking the ideology. Thus, feminists might perceive stalking as part of a larger pattern of patriarchal oppression, or gay and lesbian activists might see attacks on homosexuals as a reflection of a heterosexist culture, but claims couched in those terms invite controversy and opposition. Far better to frame these problems as random, melodramatic criminal acts. Similarly, conservative Christians found that emphasizing the criminal (and downplaying the religious) aspects of occult crimes let them get their claims circulated by the secular media.

Note, too, that the media may view ideological debates as tired topics. Claims about a particular problem—a new crime or a new victim—seem fresh, but casting the same problem in familiar ideological terms threatens to turn the new problem into old news. Even the most ideological advocates may find it easier to advance their causes if they soft-pedal ideology. Avoiding systemic arguments and discussing problems one by one reduces controversy and makes it easier to promote claims.

CLAIMS IN THEIR
HISTORICAL CONTEXT

Americans also tend to ignore their social problems' histories. After all, a social problem seems immediate; it confronts us right now, and now is when we need to do something about it. Who cares what happened long ago? It can be startling to discover that the "new" problem currently featured on the front page bedeviled previous generations, too. History links social-problems claims in at least three ways: *cycles of concern* involve periodic waves of attention to a particular social problem; *recurring issues* involve parallel claims about similar yet distinct problems; while still other claims identify social problems as the *ironic consequences* of earlier, failed social policies.

Cycles of Concern

Some social problems seem to rise and fall in periodic waves of concern. Urban gangs, for example, have been the subject of concerned claims since at least the 1840s; the recent wave of intense concern resembles earlier waves in the 1950s, the 1920s–30s, and so on. Similarly, the current focus on pedophiles and sexual predators was preceded by two earlier twentieth-century campaigns against "sexual psychopaths" and molesters (Jenkins 1998). These are cases where essentially the same problem attracted considerable attention, faded from view, then again rose to prominence.

What accounts for this cyclical concern? Advocates usually assume that they're calling attention to a problem that has suddenly gotten worse, that they're responding to a "crime wave." But it is difficult to accurately measure changing levels of gang activity, sexual abuse, or most other social problems. Most criminologists view crime waves as fluctuations in the media attention given to crime, rather than shifts in the actual level of criminality. So what accounts for increased attention? Sometimes a melodramatic crime—the attack on the Central Park jogger—commands the media's notice and sets off a crime wave. But other crime waves are products of advocates' efforts to draw attention to a neglected problem or to promote their particular orientation for interpreting that problem. Thus, although there were already laws against assault and vandalism, the activists who campaigned for laws against hate crimes wanted to redefine those offenses in cases involving minority victims, to create a new classification for crimes motivated by hatred.

New cycles of concern frequently involve new advocates promoting new orientations. Thus, psychiatrists in the 1930s started what would become a successful campaign to medicalize sex crimes as the acts of sexual psychopaths, while more recent claims about sexual abuse and sexual predators have been mounted by feminists and conservatives who share a suspicion of psychiatry's effectiveness, and who call for more punitive measures against offenders. In a new wave of concern, a problem's previous owners may come under attack for not having done enough, or for doing the wrong thing; in contrast, their challengers offer a new orientation—a fresh approach, featuring different, more promising solutions—and ownership may change hands.

But what accounts for the other side of these waves, the periods when concern declines? Keeping the attention of the press, the public, and policymakers focused on a problem requires constant effort. Without fresh, newsworthy events to report, media attention tends to drift to other, more compelling stories, and the public and policymakers often follow the media's lead. Advocates must continually feed the demand for new material; in addition to holding press conferences and conducting demonstrations, they can sometimes keep an issue visible through domain expansion, diffusion, rationale expansion, or ideological extension. But every issue fades in time. Many advocates try to maintain public attention by escalating their claims, warning that things are bad and getting worse, but few problems can continue living up to this billing. Eventually, it becomes clear that gangs will not actually overrun and destroy the next generation, and we forget them and turn to the next threat.

Cyclical concerns imply intractable problems that won't go away. Unless the conditions that produce gangs disappear, gangs will remain a part of the urban landscape, available for periodic discovery. Since most policies intended to address the gang problem—for example, assigning youth workers to keep an eye on gang members, creating specialized police antigang units, or passing laws assigning stiffer penalties to gang-related crimes—do not confront the circumstances that produce gangs, gangs themselves are likely to continue to form. And, because fears of uncontrolled youths and deviant conspiracies seem to resonate within our culture, every so often gangs will reappear as a focus for intense concern.

Recurring Issues

Where cycles of concern involve periodic attention to the same social problem, in the related phenomenon of recurring issues, waves of attention focus on distinct troubles that belong to the same broad class of problems. Here, drug scares provide the obvious example. Since the second half of the nineteenth century, there have been numerous campaigns warning of the dangers posed by various drugs, including opium, morphine, alcohol, marijuana, tranquilizers, amphetamines, LSD, PCP, and so on. Advocates usually warn that abuse of the particular drug is rising and has terrible consequences, that the drug's users (often deviants, ethnic minorities, or rebellious youths) endanger the larger society, and that law enforcement needs new laws and more resources to fight this growing menace. Typically, a drug scare features alarming rhetoric and attracts considerable notice, then fades away. Later, another scare, often focused on a different drug, emerges. The recurring fears about rebellious youth subcultures (often typified by peculiar costumes and hairstyles, and troubling tastes in sex, drugs, and rock and roll) provide a parallel example.

Like cycles of concern about the same problem, recurring issues seem to identify problems that won't go away. These claims speak to central issues in our culture. Kai Erikson (1976:82) refers to

> an *axis of variation* that cuts through the center of a culture's space and draws attention to the diversities arrayed along it. . . . The identifying motifs of a culture are not just the *core values* to which people pay homage but also the *lines of point and counterpoint* along which they diverge. . . . In this view, every human culture can be visualized, if only in part, as a kind of theater in which certain contrary tendencies are played out. (Emphasis in original)

Recurring problems expose such axes of variation. Our culture both celebrates and fears contradictory values—such as leisure and work, individual freedom and conformity, and self-indulgence and self-control. These sources of ambivalence are revealed in social-problems claims. We both use and worry about the use of drugs, just as we both encourage youth to express their independence and worry when they do. The result is a peculiar pattern in which some phenomenon becomes a focus for concern (e.g., claims about a new drug problem lead to general alarm and the authorities cracking down), then fades, only to be rediscovered in a slightly different form (e.g., yet another new drug, billed as an even greater threat).

Ironic Consequences

Note, too, that policymakers' responses to a social problem sometimes lead to competing claims that the new social policies have ironic consequences, that they somehow create new problems or make the old ones worse (Marx 1981; Lowney and Best 1998). Thus, critics argue that efforts to eradicate illicit drugs serve to drive up prices, encouraging new dealers to enter the drug trade, thereby spreading drug use; or that deinstitutionalizing mental hospitals led to massive increases in the number of homeless mentally ill. Or consider the long-standing debate between educators arguing that phonics should be the centerpiece of reading instruction and those promoting sight reading, in which each group blames the other's influence for students' difficulties with reading. Again, there is the sense that some problems seem intractable, that none of the available policies can eradicate these problems, so that whichever choices are made provide a foundation for counterclaims.

Claims that point to the ironies of policy failures define current problems as products of past mistakes. In contrast, the claims generated by cycles of concern and recurring issues often seem to forget or ignore the past, drawing no connection between what has gone before and the current crisis. History, too, is a cultural resource, one that can—but need not—be invoked in social-problems claims.

WHAT WE SAY
ABOUT SOCIAL PROBLEMS

We depend on language to talk about—even to think about—social problems. The language we choose makes a difference: it shapes what we think about, and therefore how we deal with, our problems. New crimes, new victims, and new policies all emerge through our talk about social problems.

Sociologists tend to divorce language from the conditions they describe. More traditional sociologists act as though language were irrelevant; they treat social problems as objective conditions, and they propose to measure each problem's extent, identify its causes, and perhaps recommend solutions. But even the most objectivist sociologists need language if they are to think, identify, and propose: their language defines the domain they measure; it specifies the causes, the effects, and the intervening variables; and it spells out how and why proposed policies should work.

At the other extreme are those sociologists who pretend that social conditions are irrelevant, that sociologists should study language alone. Imagining themselves freed from the constraint that their work can or should accurately describe the world, they try to build analytic castles in the air, only to discover that language is itself a reflection of the society that uses it, dependent on the social structure they wish to ignore. They can no more jettison society than traditional sociologists can avoid language.

Language—culture—makes a difference. Individual social problems—the very notion that we have "social problems" (Schwartz 1997)—can be identified, defined, categorized only through language. Our language gives shape to problems, and lets us alter their shapes by redefining, expanding, reframing, changing ownership. Advocates choose language that can persuade, the media choose language that will have an impact, and policymakers choose language that can rally support, just as sociologists try to choose language that accurately describes and analyzes social problems. All these words depict actions and conditions in the social world, and we judge the words and respond to them based on how convincing those depictions seem.

Because language is important, it deserves critical attention. How we think and talk about social problems—about new crimes and new victims and new policies—demands to be better understood. Different kinds of social-problems talk have different advantages and disadvantages. Melodramatic depictions of social problems, for example, have great rhetorical power; they can arouse intense concern, but they do so by distorting our understanding of social life. Just as no social problem exists in isolation, unconnected from the surrounding patterns of social life, so the way we talk about a given problem has many links to other, familiar social problems—and to the larger culture—and those links influence what we understand and how we respond. This book has sought to explore some of the ways in which language shapes our understandings of—our worries about—crime, victimization, and social policy, and to offer some tools for critically assessing what we say and know.

As the twentieth century winds to a close, there is a striking mood of pessimism in this country. After all, a history of the United States during this century might be upbeat and optimistic, written to emphasize considerable social progress; compared to our predecessors at the last century's end, we have achieved longer life expectancies, a higher standard of living, a better-educated population, more equal opportunities, and on and on. And yet, when we talk about social problems, it is as though we redefine these developments as failures; instead of emphasizing how far we have come, we focus on how far we have to go. Talk about progress is unfashionable. Instead, we characterize our world as beset by random violence, as one in which new crimes flourish, one that callously tolerates the sufferings of new victims, one that can be saved only by declaring war on problems that are our deadly enemies. Such talk is consequential. It scares us and it threatens to paralyze us. After all, if things are awful and rapidly, inevitably getting worse, we can hardly expect to make them better. Recognizing the patterns in our talk about social problems is a necessary first step in coming to terms with both our language—and our problems.

NEW WAYS TO STUDY MEDIA COVERAGE OF SOCIAL PROBLEMS

Studies of emerging social problems usually examine coverage by the mass media; sometimes such coverage is the only data these studies analyze. The press and entertainment media have become the principal means of relaying social-problems claims to a broad audience, and sociologists tend to assume that claims presented in the media have both reached and gained considerable acceptance in the general population.

For decades, sociologists measured fluctuations in public attention to social problems by counting articles indexed in the *Reader's Guide to Periodical Literature* or the *New York Times Index*. For example, Howard S. Becker's classic study (1963) of the Marijuana Tax Act used an increase in *Reader's Guide* entries about marijuana in the 1930s as evidence of increased concern about the drug. These two indexes offered researchers several advantages: they appeared in essentially the same form for decades (thereby letting analysts measure long-term changes in coverage); they used detailed subject headings that were relatively consistent from year to year and relatively thorough (the *Times* index, in particular, has long been far more detailed than printed indexes available for other U.S. newspapers); and they were readily available in most libraries. To be sure, these two indexes were restricted to press coverage in some two hundred popular magazines and one newspaper, and the resulting data were imperfect and needed to be handled with some care (Beniger 1978), but researchers agreed there was nothing better available.

189

That is no longer necessarily true. There now are several other ways to measure media coverage of social problems, although sociologists have been slow to exploit them. At various points in this volume, I have made use of some of these resources. Here, I want to discuss working with some of these materials, both to let readers assess my evidence and to encourage other researchers to consider the advantages—and problems—of adopting these techniques. In particular, I want to discuss full-text databases (such as NEXIS), Vanderbilt University's Television News Archive, and printed transcripts of television and radio broadcasts. First, however, some general methodological issues demand attention.

MEASURING MEDIA CONTENT

Using an index, such as the *Reader's Guide* or the *New York Times Index*, to measure media coverage involves a set of assumptions. First, the analyst assumes that the index includes the appropriate media. The *Reader's Guide*, of course, indexes some two hundred popular magazines, a substantial number, but only a small fraction of all periodicals published. All indexes leave out more than they include, and researchers necessarily accept these limitations. (In contrast, there is a sense in which the *New York Times Index* includes too much. The *Times* often carries more detailed reporting than most other newspapers, and analysts should be careful when generalizing from the *Times's* coverage to the press as a whole.) Second, the mix of sources included in the index may change. If, for example, the number of periodicals covered by an index increases, then the number of stories listed under a particular heading—for example, "Crime"—might be expected to rise, even if the number of stories about crime published in each periodical remained constant. Similarly, the rise or fall of categories of periodicals (e.g., the failure of such general-interest weeklies as *Collier's* and *Look* in the 1950s and 1960s or the rise of computer magazines in the 1980s) can change the types of social-problems claims published and therefore indexed.

Third, periodicals change over time. In particular, since World War II, newspapers and magazines have been responding to the expansion of electronic media. The newsweeklies (e.g., *Time* and *Newsweek*) have had to react, first to the growth of television's local and network news, then to the emergence of C-SPAN, CNN, and other cable news channels, as well as to the expansion of televised reporting in magazine-format programs (e.g., *60 Minutes*). The news-magazines' original purpose—to provide a capsule summary of the week's key news for those too busy to keep up with the newspapers—has changed as more people watch more televised news, and, in turn, the newsweeklies' coverage of social problems reflects these shifts in the sorts of stories they publish. Similarly, newspaper coverage has changed for many of the same reasons, yet analysts who examine shifts in the level of press coverage over time usually ignore these fluctuations in the forms journalism takes.

Fourth, analysts who measure media content by examining indexes are at the mercy of the indexers' decisions. Will articles about carjacking be indexed under "Carjacking," or "Motor-Vehicle Theft," or "Violence," or "Crime," or—who knows? The names assigned to social problems change from time to time, and the headings used by indexers often—but not always—follow suit (Spector and Kitsuse 1977). Even if "carjacking" is today's term of choice, stories about such crimes probably used to be listed under other headings. Moreover, indexers usually list a particular story under only a few headings. When Susan Smith killed her sons, she claimed that they had been kidnapped by a carjacker. Probably few indexers listed that story under "Carjacking"; they undoubtedly considered other headings (e.g., "Homicide") more appropriate. Ideally, an index uses a consistent set of rules in classifying stories from one issue—or one year—to the next, but this need not be so (particularly for new indexing services that have not yet developed stable routines and procedures), and researchers must take care rather than simply assuming that an index is consistent.

Fifth, the emergence of several new indexing services raises the issue of the quality of the indexing. Until relatively recently, the *New York Times Index* was far superior to the indexes for other newspapers because it used many, detailed headings and included even very brief articles. In contrast, most newspaper indexes used fewer—and therefore less precise—headings, and failed to index many shorter stories. Researchers could feel confident that the *Times* index was both reasonably reliable and reasonably valid, but other indexes fell far short of this ideal.

What I have just presented is not a complete list of the problems involved in using indexes to measure media content, but it ought to serve as a warning. Usually, however, analysts ignore these problems in reporting their research. They seem to make an implicit assumption that indexes provide a straightforward measure of media content. This assumption is clearly flawed; even the most familiar indexes, the *Reader's Guide* and the *New York Times Index*, have limitations that ought to be taken into account. However, far more serious problems confront researchers using some of the new reference tools.

NEXIS AND OTHER FULL-TEXT DATABASES

Some of the limitations of indexes are circumvented in full-text databases, such as NEXIS and Broadcast News Service. These databases are electronic, rather than printed, indexes; they must be accessed through computer terminals (many libraries have special terminals for this purpose). Basically, NEXIS is a huge computerized database that contains most of the editorial contents of many major newspapers and magazines. (NEXIS does not include such pictorial or noneditorial matter as advertisements, photographs, charts, comic strips, the classified section, and the like.) Broadcast News Service (available on CD-ROM) contains the verbal contents of recent news broadcasts on ABC, CNN, PBS, and NPR. Full-text databases let researchers search for *every* article or program that used a particular word or set of words. For example, you can search for "carjacking" and locate every article in the database in which that word appears. Usually, the analyst does not search the entire database, restricting the search to particular sources, perhaps a single newspaper or magazine. On the one hand, this is an incredibly powerful research tool. You can discover, for example, that the word "carjacking" appeared in fifty-two pieces in the *New York Times* during 1992.

On the other hand, researchers must use full-text databases such as NEXIS with caution. Whereas "carjacking" probably has few noncriminal referents, searching for, say, "stalking" turns up references to mycologists "stalking wild mushrooms" and linebackers "stalking running backs," uses of the metaphor "stalking horse," and the like, and a search for references to "wilding" uncovers stories about people named Wilding. The choice of a search term also makes a difference: searching for "gang AND initiation AND rite" will produce more stories than searching for "gang initiation rite," because the former does not require that the words appear together in a single phrase; but neither search term will uncover stories that refer to, say, "gang initiation rituals." In short, selecting search terms is a consequential decision; it requires some thought.

It is also important to appreciate that many databases are continually expanding to incorporate more sources with each passing year. NEXIS covered relatively few newspapers and magazines in 1980, but included many more ten years later. A researcher, then, cannot merely count the number of references that appear in all sources over a series of years, because the database covers more sources with each passing year. Thus, even if a term appeared at a constant rate (e.g., one story per source per year), indexing more sources would lead to more stories using the term being identified in each successive year. One solution I have used is to restrict the analysis to a few major newspapers and magazines that were included in the database throughout some given period of years.

There are other problems with using full-text databases to measure media coverage. Because these are relatively new databases, they do not allow analyses of coverage extending back before 1980, at best. Unrestricted NEXIS searches may uncover multiple instances of the same story being printed in different papers, or in different editions of the same paper. Searches for some topics (e.g., "O. J. Simpson" during 1994–95) can identify far more stories than any analyst can (or could want to) examine. And, of course, like printed indexes, full-text databases index a limited set of sources; researchers must be sure they understand what is—and what is not—included. In general, coverage of mainstream sources tends to be relatively good, while coverage of alternative sources is both thin and rather spotty. In short, although searching full-text databases frees the researcher from the traditional dependence on indexers' accuracy and reliability, this new technique requires an understanding of the nature of such databases.

VANDERBILT UNIVERSITY'S
TELEVISION NEWS ARCHIVE

Vanderbilt University's Television News Archive is better known, but poorly understood and often ineffectively used by social researchers. Since 1968, Vanderbilt University has been videotaping the nightly news broadcasts of the three major television networks. (The broadcasts that are indexed have expanded over time; e.g., ABC's *Nightline* was added in 1988, *CNN Prime News* in 1989.) For a fee, scholars can borrow videotaped copies of selected stories from the archive. In order to help researchers locate stories of interest, the archive offers a brief abstract of each story covered on each indexed broadcast. From 1968 to 1994, these abstracts were published in the *Television News Index and Abstracts*—a printed monthly guide that can be found in many libraries. However, its entries are not especially informative; for example, an abstract for a story on stalking may indicate that the story contains an estimate for the number of stalkers, without telling what the estimate is. (Presumably, this is to encourage interested researchers to find out by paying the fee and borrowing the videotaped story from the archive.)

Television News Index and Abstracts was awkwardly indexed: headings seemed to change from year to year, and even month to month, so that a story about carjacking might be indexed under only a single heading, and, depending on the month, that heading might be "Carjacking," or "Violence," or even "Crime." Researchers who simply treat *Television News Index and Abstracts* as another index and chart year-by-year changes in the number of stories reported in the index do not seem to appreciate that the erratic indexing makes such comparisons of dubious value. Similarly, authors who use the abstracts as though they adequately summarize the stories' contents ignore the fact that the abstracts contain only minimal—and sometimes misleading—information.

Recently, the Television News Archive stopped publishing a printed index and established an up-to-date Web site (http://tvnews.vanderbilt.edu) that permits searching all the abstracts, from 1968 to the most recent broadcasts. Although this eliminates the problems with erratic indexing, researchers must understand that their searches will cover only the contents of the abstracts, not the full contents of the news stories. The wording of the abstract now determines what searches can locate.

It is far more effective to use the index or the Web site to locate stories, and then order and view the videotape. Often, of course, it is visual imagery that gives television news stories much of their power. It is relatively easy to analyze printed words, and more difficult to find ways to analyze pictures—especially moving pictures. Still, the Television News Archive offers a remarkable resource—roughly three decades of visual records—that sociologists have been slow to exploit.

TRANSCRIPTS OF TELEVISION AND RADIO BROADCASTS

A growing proportion of television and radio programs now sell copies: videotapes of television episodes, audiotapes of radio broadcasts, or printed transcripts of broadcasts. Usually there is a brief announcement at the end of the broadcast, giving an address from which copies can be ordered. In addition, the transcripts for many popular programs are handled by two major services—Burrelle's Information Services and Journal Graphics. Interested researchers can contact those services and ask for a list of all available programs dealing with particular topics. (At least until recently, however, the services did not have especially useful indexes of their inventories, so that calling to request transcripts of, say, all broadcasts concerning stalking doubtless missed some relevant programs—another example of the analyst at the indexers' mercy.)

Printed transcripts of televised broadcasts, of course, reveal little or nothing about what viewers saw, and they may not always accurately record what listeners heard. Transcripts are only as accurate as the transcribing process, and many transcripts betray signs of hasty work—for example, spelling errors, evidence that the transcriber did not understand what was being said, and so on. Yet, although imperfect, transcripts let researchers recover media messages that used to be ephemeral.

TOWARD MORE COMPLETE RECORDS
OF MEDIA CONTENT

Traditional analyses of the *Reader's Guide* and the *New York Times Index* probably represented the best available ways to measure media coverage through roughly 1980. But their value now seems more limited: the *Times*'s audience, though influential, was never large, and newsmagazines seem to be losing much of their influence. At a minimum, researchers need to make efforts to trace coverage in a broader range of newspapers and in televised news—the regular news broadcasts and the feature stories covered in magazine-format programs—as well as the treatment on reality shows, talk shows, and so on.

Stories in other newspapers and electronic broadcasts used to be difficult or impossible to retrieve, but it is becoming possible to locate a broader range of coverage about different social problems. Not only does the much-bandied "information explosion" represent an increase in the amount of information; it also involves improvements in our ability to locate and recover particular bits of information. As full-text databases, videotapes, and transcripts become increasingly available to researchers, opportunities to assess a broad range of media coverage should improve. However, traditional methodological issues will not vanish; researchers must continue to confront questions of sampling, validity, and reliability.

NOTES

CHAPTER 1: RANDOM VIOLENCE

1. For a general treatment of moral panics, see Goode and Ben-Yehuda 1994. The concept originated among British sociologists of deviance, and many of the principal case studies are British (S. Cohen 1980; Hall et al. 1978; Jenkins 1992). Historians have shown that moral panics have had essentially the same dynamics (i.e., sensational press coverage coupled with outraged posturing by political figures) since at least the mid–nineteenth century (Adler 1996; Davis 1980; Pearson 1983; Sindall 1990). For an early eighteenth-century example, see Statt 1995.

2. On serial murders, see, for example, Jenkins 1994; on freeway violence, Best 1991; on hate crimes, Jacobs and Henry 1996, Jenness 1995a, 1995b; on "random drug violence," Brownstein 1991, 1996; on stalking, Lowney and Best 1995; on rape, Rose 1977, Matthews 1994; on missing children, Best 1990; on child molestation and sexual predators, Jenkins 1998, Websdale 1996; on gangs and gang initiation rites, Best and Hutchinson 1996, Jackson 1993, Zatz 1987; on kids and guns, Best forthcoming; on assaults on the elderly, Fishman 1978. Most of these studies adopt a constructionist approach to the study of social problems, focusing on how and why the particular issue came to public attention (Spector and Kitsuse 1977; Holstein and Miller 1993; Best 1995).

3. I collected these data from NEXIS, a full-text database, using "random

violence" as search words. Because NEXIS continually expands the list of indexed sources, I restricted my search to major news sources that had been in the database since 1985. Such searches are necessarily crude: my search may have located irrelevant articles (e.g., those dealing with other countries or using the expression to refer to noncriminal topics), and it will have overlooked articles that used slightly different expressions (e.g., "random criminality" or "senseless violence"). Still, the data show a clear pattern in the press's use of the expression "random violence." (For a more detailed discussion of my methods, see the appendix.)

4. On the importance of typifying examples in shaping our understanding of social problems involving violence, see Best 1990, J. Johnson 1995, and Loseke 1992. R. Gibson and Zillman's experimental subjects (1994) read a purported newsmagazine story about carjacking; regardless of the story's other contents, "extremely exaggerated exemplars" (i.e., typifying examples involving the victims' deaths) made the subjects more likely to consider carjacking a serious national problem.

5. Basu's story also served as a typifying example for carjacking stories in *Time* (Gup 1992), *U.S. News & World Report* (Witkin 1992), *People* (Treen and Nugent 1992), and *Ladies' Home Journal* (Gross 1993), and in evening network news broadcasts on ABC (September 14, 1992) and NBC (September 16, 1992).

6. Some feminist theorists indict males generally for being prone to or benefiting from criminal violence. In Susan Brownmiller's famous assessment (1975: 5), rape "is nothing more or less than a conscious process of intimidation by which *all men* keep *all women* in a state of fear" (emphasis in original). In *Men Are Not Cost-Effective*, June Stephenson (1995:360) advocates a tax for males as a "'user fee' since men are using the criminal justice system almost exclusively."

7. There are several reasons for picking this example. Criminologists view homicide victimization statistics as being more accurate than other crime statistics: considered the most serious crime, homicide is less likely to go unreported; and the fact that a dead body must be accounted for also helps insure that the crime will be noticed and recorded. In fact, there are two separate record-keeping systems that track homicides: criminal justice records of crimes reported to the police (tracked nationally in the Federal Bureau of Investigation's *Uniform Crime Reports*); and public-health records of death registrations (tracked nationally by the National Center for Health Statistics). The two sets of data tell essentially the same story, although because the NCHS uses a slightly broader definition of homicide, its statistics consistently list somewhat more

deaths and many experts consider those data more complete. The analysis and figures that follow use data compiled from NCHS records; the data set appears in MacKellar and Yanagishita 1995:16–19. Statistics for crime rates calculated by the FBI are from Maguire and Pastore 1996:324. For a detailed analysis exploring essentially the same homicide patterns in one major city, see Block and Christakos 1995.

8. Classifying people as "nonwhite" groups African-Americans, Asian-Americans, and American Indians into a single category (MacKellar and Yanagishita 1995:6). These three groups have very different overall homicide rates. During 1989–91, the overall homicide rates were as follows: blacks, 38.8 per 100,000; Asian-Americans, 5.5; American Indians, 11.7; whites, 5.7. This means that the differences between the homicide rates of whites and blacks are even greater than the differences between rates for whites and nonwhites discussed in this chapter.

9. For these reasons, criminologists usually avoid referring to "random violence." Anderson et al. (1996) are an exception. After describing patterns in contemporary violence, they do use the term—presumably for its rhetorical impact.

10. J. Katz (1988) explores offenders' reasoning behind crimes ranging from shoplifting to serial murder.

11. It is far easier to find data about crime and race than about crime and class. Crime and arrest reports routinely classify victims and offenders by race (which criminal justice agencies usually treat as a set of straightforward categories, ignoring the complexities posed by mixed heritages and so on). In contrast, it is more difficult to assess class (i.e., should it be measured by an individual's [or the individual's parents'] income, education, or job title?), and official statistics rarely categorize individuals by class. Instead, most social scientists use race as a proxy for class, assuming that the difference between, say, black and white homicide victimization rates actually represents class, rather than racial, differences.

CHAPTER 2:
FROM INCIDENTS TO INSTANCES

1. These themes appeared in various 1989 articles and columns published in *Newsday* and the *New York Times*, which I located through a NEXIS search for "wilding."

2. NEXIS searches for "wilding" in the *New York Times* located one to five articles per year for the period 1991–95. These counts exclude nonrelevant articles (e.g., those mentioning people named Wilding). Similarly, *Newsweek*, *Time*, and *U.S. News & World Report* mentioned wilding in a total of fifteen stories in 1989, eleven stories in 1990, and zero to five stories per year during 1991–95. Criminologists made little use of the term; though Cummings (1993) describes a "wilding gang" during the 1980s, it is not clear that the young criminals he studied used that expression.

3. Two years later, researchers from the Centers for Disease Control (CDC) finally offered some evidence that summertime "roadway firearm assaults" in Los Angeles did rise in 1987. They searched law-enforcement records for reported incidents involving "the shooting or brandishing of a firearm at occupants of a moving vehicle on any freeway, highway, or surface street," then eliminated cases deemed gang related or "the result of preexisting domestic quarrels" (Onwuachi-Saunders et al. 1989:2262). They found 137 incidents in 1987 (49 on freeways)—an increase over 1985 (32 incidents, 4 on freeways) and 1986 (91 incidents, 15 on freeways).

4. In 1996, advocates in the United States and Great Britain began promoting the term "road rage" to describe aggressive driving (Furedi 1997). The term promised to serve a variety of ends—for example, justifying calls for freeway construction (Wald 1997), and even publicizing routine traffic patrols: "Troopers are especially looking for drivers engaged in the kind of activities that anger fellow motorists and spur what has come to be known as 'road rage,' such offenses as speeding, tailgating, driving under the influence and improper lane use" (Wuerz 1998).

5. Social scientists often characterize crime waves as myths (cf. Bell 1962: 151–74; Kappeler et al. 1996:31–51). The classic case studies (Fishman 1978; Hall et al. 1978) describe how reporters manufacture crime waves by interpreting incidents as part of a larger trend. Historians have found the same process at work in the nineteenth century (Adler 1996; Pearson 1983; for a famous firsthand account, see Lincoln Steffens's "I Make a Crime Wave" [1931]), and even in the eighteenth century (King 1987).

6. Problematizing cases—categorizing a particular case as an instance of a broader problem—can be seen as the flip side of typification (Best 1995), in which a dramatic case is used to illustrate a larger, often more mundane social problem.

7. There are limits; not every crime gets problematized. The revelations about Jeffrey Dahmer did not lead to press coverage of the cannibalistic-serial-murderer problem. Presumably this reflected some assessment that Dahmer's case was unique.

8. Novaco (1987) noted an important flaw in this explanation: "The road assaults are not being done by commuters." Many incidents occurred not during heavily congested rush hours, but at night or on weekends—a pattern common to other violent crimes. For instance, four of the five fatalities attributed to freeway violence occurred on weekend nights—two in a single incident at an intersection with a stop sign (i.e., not on a freeway). The CDC researchers found that "more than two thirds (69%) of the 1987 assaults occurred outside of the hours of peak traffic flow," although they "found a positive association between freeway congestion and freeway firearm assaults" (Onwuachi-Saunders et al. 1989:2264).

9. There are many studies of press coverage of crime. For some recent examples, see Barak 1994; Benedict 1992; Chermak 1995; McCormick 1995; *Media Studies Journal* 1992; Sasson 1995a. These works usually focus on either which crimes receive coverage or the orientations the press adopts in reporting crimes.

10. On MADD as a social movement, see Reinarman 1988; J. McCarthy and Wolfson 1996; Weed 1991, 1993. Gusfield (1981, 1996) and Ross (1992) note that drunk driving might be characterized in other ways—that instead of blaming killer drunks, we might blame the manufacturers of cars or alcohol, those who serve the drinks that produce intoxication, arrangements for available transportation, and so on.

CHAPTER 3: BEYOND INSTANCES

1. Before the term "stalking" emerged, the popular press sometimes described women annoyed by prolonged following or harassment. Magazine articles called these behaviors "a form of sexual harassment," "obsession," or "psychological rape" (Wilcox 1982; Mithers 1982), characterizing the male harassers as obsessive, compulsive, often passive in nature but rarely violent, with a limited range of sexual expression and low self-esteem (Heil 1986; Wilcox 1982). While holding the harasser responsible for his behavior, the articles simultaneously suggested that some victims subtly encouraged their harassers,

and some women acknowledged partial culpability (*Good Housekeeping* 1980: 34). Victims complained that they felt terror, yet got little help from the criminal justice system. In retrospect, these articles can be seen as early claims about what would become the stalking problem. For a more detailed history of stalking, see Lowney and Best 1995.

2. The stalking problem did not emerge automatically in response to a well-publicized crime against a celebrity victim. There had been other such cases. The 1982 stabbing of the actress Theresa Saldana, her recovery, and her founding of the self-help group Victims for Victims received extensive publicity: Saldana played herself in a 1984 NBC made-for-TV movie (*Victims for Victims*) and wrote a book about her experiences (Reilly 1982; Saldana 1986). Only following Schaeffer's death in 1989, as California prepared to parole Saldana's attacker (who had continued to threaten her) (Bacon 1989), did Saldana's case become a typifying example in claims about, first, star-stalking, and later, general stalking. Earlier accounts treated the attack on Saldana as an example of violent crime and its effects on victims, rather than focusing on its stalking-like qualities; there was no particular emphasis placed on Saldana's awareness, prior to the attack, that she was being pursued and might be in danger. In spite of its rich potential as a typifying example, Saldana's case did not lead to claims about the stalking problem.

3. The first national survey to attempt to measure the extent of stalking—conducted some years later and adopting a broad definition of stalking—indicated that 1.4 million victims (including 400,000 men) experienced stalking each year (Tjaden 1997).

4. This figure of 38 percent—often repeated—apparently came from an unpublished study of the first seventy-four case files from the LAPD's TMU. The study classified victims as highly recognized celebrities (17 percent), lesser-known entertainment figures (32 percent), former employers or other professionals (13 percent), and ordinary citizens (38 percent) (Morin 1993:127–28). However, the published version of this research did not include this classification, instead noting: "none of the [study's] cases involved domestic violence situations" (Zona et al. 1993:896). Nonetheless, advocates routinely used the 38 percent figure as evidence of the link between stalking and domestic violence.

5. This is the earliest appearance of the term in NEXIS's file for major newspapers; the *New York Times* did not refer to hate crimes until 1987. The expression "bias crime" preceded, but was largely replaced by, "hate crime."

For example, the New York police formed a Bias Incident Investigating Unit in 1980 to investigate synagogue vandalism; the unit began investigating attacks on gays in 1985 (Jacobs 1992).

6. The methodology of these studies virtually guaranteed that successive reports would show assaults increasing. Typically, a local gay/lesbian organization would solicit accounts of incidents from victims and then release a report summarizing the data; the publicity given to that report made the following year's solicitation easier and encouraged more victims to report, making it likely that the next report would show increased violence, and therefore get even more press coverage. Typically, neither the reports nor the resulting media coverage paid much attention to these methodological problems. Reporting of this sort has a long history, dating back at least to the NAACP campaign to publicize the number of lynchings. By the 1980s, several religious and ethnic organizations (e.g., the ADL) had begun issuing statistical reports about violence against their groups.

7. By 1995, thirty-two states had passed some sort of hate-crime law, although these laws varied a great deal in nature and scope. Though all thirty-two states specified race-motivated assaults as criminal, and thirty-one mentioned religion, only eleven referred to sexual orientation (Jenness and Broad 1997).

8. In 1994, antiwhite incidents composed the second-largest category of the 5,932 reported incidents. Percentages were as follows: antiblack, 37 percent; antiwhite, 17 percent; anti-Jewish, 15 percent; anti-gay/lesbian/bisexual, 11 percent (Maguire and Pastore 1996:349). On police departments' methods of classifying and investigating hate crimes, see Martin 1995, 1996.

9. Hood (1995) describes a "hate crime" in a university library—the hiding of bound volumes of women's studies periodicals on other shelves, and the defacing of some journals—and the reaction to it.

CHAPTER 4: GANGS, CONSPIRACIES, AND OTHER CULTURAL RESOURCES

1. What Los Angeles–inspired gang imagery existed prior to the 1980s focused largely on exotic features of Mexican-American gangs (e.g., zoot suits).

2. This does not mean that the Los Angeles audience somehow has "more

advanced" tastes than the rest of the country. Locally produced films and re-cordings are more often test-marketed and initially released there, and, since most popular-culture industries overproduce (Hirsch 1972), the reactions of Los Angeles audiences influence popular-culture producers' decisions about dis-tributing and marketing. Thus, many recordings are initially distributed in southern California; if a major L.A. radio station begins playing a new song, a recording company may decide to promote that song more aggressively, thereby improving its prospects for becoming a national hit. But the same sort of filtering presumably could occur in, say, Des Moines—if only producers re-leased their new products there.

  3. For social scientists accustomed to using the terms "core" and "periph-ery" (e.g., in world systems theory), these words may imply a system of political and economic domination—an implication I do not intend. Similarly, scholars of human geography refer to hierarchical innovation diffusion, meaning that innovations typically begin in the largest population centers and disseminate to less-populated communities. My point is that, although advocates find it easiest to begin or soon move to the Big Three media centers, this is neither because those cities are centers of political domination nor simply because they are large, but rather because they are the principal centers for the media that make it pos-sible to disseminate claims nationally.

An analogous process seems to operate internationally. During the 1980s, U.S. concerns about sexual abuse, especially ritual abuse and satanism, were in effect exported to Great Britain (Jenkins 1992), the Netherlands (Rossen 1990), Norway (Dyrendal 1998), and Australia (Richardson 1996). As an inter-national media center, the United States serves as a core country for social-problems claims, particularly for Canada and Western Europe, although the spread of CNN and other U.S. news media may expand the regions that ef-fectively fall within the periphery of the United States. That is, claims that X is a problem in the United States may inspire parallel claims that X is a problem in this or that other country. Of course, it is easiest to disseminate claims when language and cultural differences are modest. It is more difficult to identify social-problems claims moving from other countries to the United States—for example, instances of claims that originate elsewhere ("X is a prob-lem here") being adopted in the United States ("X is also a problem in the United States"). More often, American media disseminate claims about social problems *in* other countries (e.g., arguing that the United States should be concerned about child labor in the Third World, or the destruction of tropical rain forests); the advocates making these claims hope to enlist U.S. foreign policy to influence other countries' social policies—a more traditional form of core-periphery influence.

4. Of course, fears about deviant conspiracies also appear frequently in other cultures. Often, such conspiracies involve outsiders—especially ethnic or religious minorities—banding together in a conspiratorial alliance that conceals yet connects apparently unrelated acts of deviance. Dedicated to advancing the deviant cause, the conspirators are a powerful yet invisible social force who commit terrible crimes against society's most vulnerable members. Examples include Christian claims about ritualized child sacrifice by Jews (the "Blood Libel"), witches, and other heretics, as well as first-century Romans' belief that Christians initiated new members in rituals that included sacrificing and eating infants (Dundes 1991; B. Ellis 1983; Moore 1987; Stevens 1991).

5. Consider this prescient description, written half a century before the recent fears about automatic weapons and drive-by shootings: "In the old days rival gangs would shoot for hours at each other without serious damage being done. But the victim of the modern gang is sprayed with a hundred bullets a minute and is certainly marked for death beyond hope" (Howe 1933:5–6).

CHAPTER 5: THE NEW VICTIMS

1. Orrin E. Klapp's *Heroes, Villains, and Fools* (1962) was more interested in cataloging social types than in explaining their emergence. In a recent review of the literature on role change, Ralph Turner (1991:88) notes the absence of sociological studies of changes in value roles "like the hero, traitor, criminal, and saint."

2. For reasons discussed below, advocates calling attention to some of these problems reject the label "victim" because it implies passivity or powerlessness, preferring other, more supportive, empowering terms, such as "survivor." Since this renaming is part of the process I analyze, I have chosen to use the more traditional term.

3. Much of the discussion that follows also applies to societal reactions to new disorders that may not be blamed on interpersonal victimization, such as attention deficit/hyperactivity disorder and other learning disorders, chronic

fatigue syndrome, and Gulf War syndrome. That is, although their advocates may not speak of "victimization," both the ideological underpinnings for claims describing these disorders and syndromes and their institutional supports resemble the ideological and institutional supports for claims about other new victims (Showalter 1997). Parallel patterns also appear in debates about the harms caused by tobacco, breast implants, and other recently constructed hazards.

4. In placing both generally accepted and widely disputed claims under the same heading, I do not mean to imply that all claims about new victims are equally true or false. This analysis seeks to understand how contemporary claims get made; for this purpose, the truth of particular claims is irrelevant. Constructionist analysts of social problems routinely adopt this stance (Spector and Kitsuse 1977). Although there has been considerable debate about whether analysts can avoid all assumptions about the objective world (Woolgar and Pawluch 1985; Holstein and Miller 1993), most constructionist research concentrates on claims rather than on the social conditions about which claims are made.

5. Victims' rights was not the only victim-related social issue on which feminists found themselves allied with political conservatives. Their most notable collaboration involved opposition to pornography. For the right, pornography was a moral and criminal issue; decisions by the same Warren Court that had expanded protection for criminal defendants let pornographers operate with little interference. For feminists, not only did pornography constitute symbolic and (within the sex industry) real objectification and exploitation of women; it inspired rape. Both camps concentrated their attacks on marginal pornographic genres—for example, child pornography, violent pornography, and snuff films— where charges of victimization were least open to dispute (D. Downs 1989). Similarly, feminists and conservatives joined in opposition to pedophiles, sexual predators, and even satanic ritual abuse. In each case, an emphasis on victims' suffering provided the rhetorical foundation for an alliance. Framing these social problems in other terms, such as emphasizing their structural causes, presumably would have made it far harder for feminists and conservatives to make a common cause.

6. Wagner (1997) argues that such claims threaten powerful interests and that, in response, a "new temperance" ideology tends to blame individuals who ignore the risks inherent in their lifestyles. These models can conflict, as in the debate over whether smokers or tobacco companies are to blame (and therefore

legally responsible) for illnesses caused by prolonged smoking. However, claims about new victims address a much broader range of social problems than do calls for a new temperance.

7. In 1992, the National Crime Victimization Survey (NCVS)—the principal federal measure of criminal victimization—was revised to make it more inclusive:

> *Questions were added* to let respondents know that the interviewer is interested in a board spectrum of incidents, not just those involving weapons, severe violence, or violence perpetrated by strangers. *New methods of cuing* respondents about potential experiences with victimizations increased the range of incident types that are being reported to interviewers. And *behavior-specific wording* has replaced criminal justice terminology to make the questions more understandable. (Bachman and Saltzman 1995:1; emphasis in original)

These changes had the effect of markedly increasing reported rates of victimization; NCVS respondents who answered the more inclusive survey reported 44 percent more crimes of violence, and 157 percent more rapes (Kinderman et al. 1997). Of course, the resulting increases can be interpreted as either real increases in victimization or artifacts of the new measures. When the Centers for Disease Control has adopted more inclusive definitions of AIDS, activists and the press have tended to treat the resulting increases in reported cases as evidence of spreading infections (Fumento 1990).

8. This psychological emphasis reflects the modern perception that the real self is primarily a product of individual experiences and impulses, rather than institutional ties (R. Turner 1976). This individualism makes our culture more receptive to claims that experiences of victimization have lasting consequences.

9. Imagery of good, innocent victims did not originate with advocates. The "ideal victim" (Christie 1986) is a cultural icon who appears in ordinary citizens' depictions of crime (Madriz 1997).

10. Lofland (1969:141) suggests that labeling deviants is facilitated when there is "a large number of alternatively sufficient indicators." Presumably this principle holds for other labels as well.

11. The notion of "backlash" experienced a revival in the late 1980s. According to NEXIS, references to "backlash" appeared in an average 145 *New York Times* stories per year during 1982–86; 229 stories per year in 1987–91; and 283 stories per year in 1992–96. For discussions of backlash against

new-victim movements, see Hechler's *The Battle and the Backlash: The Child Sex Abuse War* (1998); Myers's *The Backlash: Child Protection under Fire* (1994); and especially Faludi's *Backlash: The Undeclared War against American Women* (1991). As all three subtitles indicate, victim advocates often couple the term to the sort of militarized rhetoric examined in chapter 7.

12. At the same time, the label "victim" may be embraced by those who find it less discrediting than alternative terms. Thus, Victims of Child Abuse Laws (VOCAL) represents individuals accused of child abuse. The fact that there is another VOCAL—Victims of Clergy Abuse Linkup—suggests that advocates favor the term "victim" to characterize suffering inflicted by powerful institutions, such as the legal system or organized religion (Jenkins 1996).

CHAPTER 6: THE VICTIM INDUSTRY

1. According to Showalter (1997:17): "Hysterical epidemics require at least three ingredients: physician-enthusiasts and theorists; unhappy, vulnerable patients; and supportive cultural environments." Jean-Martin Charcot, the nineteenth-century French proponent of hysteria, is the classic example of the first category, noteworthy precisely because his work was considered to meet the standards of scientific inquiry of his time.

2. For example, Patai and Koertge (1994) argue that women's studies programs promote an "oppression sweepstakes" that rewards identification with victimization.

3. Some sociologists are uncomfortable with calling the self-help or recovery movement a "social movement"; they prefer to restrict that term's use to campaigns aimed explicitly at changing society rather than individuals.

4. Patai (1997) argues that contemporary higher education has established a "sexual harassment industry."

5. Sociologists writing about celebrity tend to focus on entertainment figures and, less often, politicians, and particularly on the processes of manufacturing celebrities (see, e.g., J. Gamson 1994). In *Symbolic Leaders*, Klapp (1964: 51) argues that celebrities play roles in public dramas, including the role of "popular victims":

> A sad story, bullying or oppression, certain kinds of illness . . . —these can engulf the public in a wave of sympathy and concern. However, the most practical effects of victims are to stir movements for aid and reform and to help develop welfare institutions.

CHAPTER 7: DECLARING WAR
ON SOCIAL PROBLEMS

1. Like social problems, social policies are socially constructed. Whereas political scientists have developed constructionist interpretations of policy-making (cf. Edelman 1988; Rochefort and Cobb 1994; Schneider and Ingram 1993; Stone 1988), sociologists have paid less attention to policy claims.

2. Other countries favor other rhetoric, and are far less likely to declare war on social problems. Jun Ayukawa informs me that, in Japan, militarized metaphors would not be considered appropriate descriptions for social policy. Japanese media sometimes speak of "eradicating" or "exterminating" crime, but usually restrict such extreme language to discussions of crime in other countries, or to Japanese crimes involving firearms or drugs.

3. As Edelman notes elsewhere (1977:32–35), political rhetoric usually characterizes groups of people, rather than social conditions, as enemies. Ibarra and Kitsuse (1993:47–48) call for the study of "motifs" in social-problems rhetoric. They seem to equate motifs with metaphors, and include declaring war on their list of examples.

4. This list is based on common perceptions; it includes those major conflicts that concentrated government and public attention and consumed substantial resources against powerful opposition—that is, the conflicts generally perceived to have been wars, regardless of whether there was a formal declaration of war. Obviously, this list ignores a variety of lesser armed conflicts, including military campaigns against various Native American peoples and assorted minor foreign invasions/police actions/occupations. (For a longer list of American wars, see Aho 1994:95.) I have excluded these other conflicts precisely because they rarely became the focus for either extensive federal government action or public opinion. However, expanding my list of wars would not alter my argument; these other campaigns also tended to be short and victorious.

5. It is interesting that this successful campaign used less dramatic, albeit militarized, rhetoric to mobilize support: the "March of Dimes" suggests long-term, steady progress rather than a brief, all-out push to victory.

REFERENCES

Acland, Charles R. 1995. *Youth, Murder, Spectacle: The Cultural Politics of "Youth in Crisis."* Boulder, Colo.: Westview.

Adler, Jeffrey S. 1996. "The Making of a Moral Panic in 19th-Century America: The Boston Garroting Hysteria of 1865." *Deviant Behavior* 17:259–78.

Aho, James A. 1994. *This Thing of Darkness: A Sociology of the Enemy.* Seattle: University of Washington Press.

Albelda, Randy, Nancy Folbre, and the Center for Popular Economics. 1996. *The War on the Poor: A Defense Manual.* New York: New Press.

Alcoff, Linda, and Laura Gray. 1993. "Survivor Discourse: Transgression or Recuperation?" *Signs* 18:260–90.

American Psychiatric Association. 1987. *Diagnostic and Statistical Manual of Mental Disorders.* 3d ed., revised. Washington, D.C.: American Psychiatric Association.

Anderson, James F., Terry Grandison, and Laronistine Dyson. 1996. "Victims of Random Violence and the Public Health Implication." *Journal of Criminal Justice* 24:379–91.

Angle, Paul M. 1952. *Bloody Williamson.* New York: Knopf.

Armstrong, Scott. 1987. "Southern California Freeway Shootings Test Drivers, Police." *Christian Science Monitor* (August 3): 3–4.

Asbury, Herbert. 1927. *The Gangs of New York.* New York: Knopf.

Axthelm, Pete. 1989. "An Innocent Life, a Heartbreaking Death." *People* 32 (July 31): 60–62, 64, 66.

Bachman, Ronet, and Linda E. Saltzman. 1995. "Violence against Women: Estimated from the Redesigned Survey." *Bureau of Justice Statistics Special Report* (August).

Bacon, Doris. 1989. "Vicious Crime, Double Jeopardy." *People* 31 (June 5): 44, 46–49.

———. 1990. "When Fans Turn into Fanatics . . . ." *People* 33 (February 12): 103, 105–6.

Bainbridge, William Sims. 1991. "Social Construction from Within: Satan's Process." In *The Satanism Scare*, edited by James T. Richardson, Joel Best, and David G. Bromley, 297–310. Hawthorne, N.Y.: Aldine de Gruyter.

Barak, Gregg, ed. 1994. *Media, Process, and the Social Construction of Crime*. New York: Garland, 1994.

Bass, Ellen, and Laura Davis. 1988. *The Courage to Heal*. New York: Harper & Row.

Beardsley, Tim. 1994. "A War Not Won." *Scientific American* 270 (January): 130–38.

Beattie, Melody. 1987. *Codependent No More*. New York: Harper/Hazelton.

Beck, Melinda. 1992. "Murderous Obsession." *Newsweek* 120 (July 13): 60–62.

Becker, Howard S. 1963. *Outsiders*. New York: Free Press.

Bell, Daniel. 1962. *The End of Ideology*. Rev. ed. New York: Collier.

Benedict, Helen. 1992. *Virgin or Vamp: How the Press Covers Sex Crimes*. New York: Oxford University Press.

Beniger, James R. 1978. "Media Content as Social Indicators: The Greenfield Index of Agenda-Setting." *Communication Research* 5:437–53.

Bennett, William J., John J. DiIulio, Jr., and John P. Walters. 1996. *Body Count: Moral Poverty . . . and How to Win America's War against Crime and Drugs*. New York: Simon and Schuster.

Ben-Yehuda, Nachman. 1980. "The European Witch Craze of the 14th to 17th Centuries." *American Journal of Sociology* 86:1–31.

Bernstein, Nina. 1989. "Needles in Angry Hands." *Newsday* (December 20): 4.

Berrick, Jill Duerr, and Neil Gilbert. 1991. *With the Best of Intentions: The Child Sexual Abuse Prevention Movement*. New York: Guilford Press.

Bertram, Eva, Morris Blachman, Kenneth Sharpe, and Peter Andreas. 1996. *Drug War Politics*. Berkeley: University of California Press.

Best, Joel. 1990. *Threatened Children: Rhetoric and Concern about Child-Victims*. Chicago: University of Chicago Press.

———. 1991. "'Road Warriors' on 'Hair-Trigger Highways': Cultural Resources and the Media's Construction of the 1987 Freeway Shootings Problem." *Sociological Inquiry* 61:327–45.

———. Forthcoming. "Random Risks or Patterned Problems: Constructing Violence as a Threat to Children."

———, ed. 1995. *Images of Issues: Typifying Contemporary Social Problems.* 2d ed. Hawthorne, N.Y.: Aldine de Gruyter.

Best, Joel, and Mary M. Hutchinson. 1996. "The Gang Initiation Rite as a Motif in Contemporary Crime Discourse." *Justice Quarterly* 13:383–404.

Billiter, Bill. 1987. "Traffic Dispute Results in Third Freeway Shooting." *Los Angeles Times* (July 20): I-3.

Blain, Michael. 1994. "Power, War, and Melodrama in the Discourses of Political Movements." *Theory and Society* 23:805–37.

Block, Carolyn Rebecca, and Antigone Christakos. 1995. "Major Trends in Chicago Homicide: 1965–1994." *Illinois Criminal Justice Information Authority Research Bulletin* (September).

Blumstein, Alfred. 1995. "Youth Violence, Guns, and the Illicit-Drug Industry." *Journal of Criminal Law and Criminology* 86:10–36.

Bradburn, Wayne E., Jr. 1992. "Stalking Statutes." *Ohio Northern University Law Review* 19:271–88.

Bradshaw, John. 1988. *Bradshaw On: The Family.* Deerfield Beach, Fla.: Health Communications.

Brenner, Martin. 1987. "Power to the Freeway Wimps." *Los Angeles Times* (August 5): II-7.

Breslin, Jimmy. 1989. "Crime Rooted Where Force Meets Force." *Newsday* (April 23): 2.

Bricklin, Mark. 1993. "Let's Declare War on Breast Cancer!" (editorial). *Prevention* 145 (September): 39–40, 42.

Bromley, David G. 1991. "Satanism: The New Cult Scare." In *The Satanism Scare,* edited by James T. Richardson, Joel Best, and David G. Bromley, 49–72. Hawthorne, N.Y.: Aldine de Gruyter.

Brown, J. David. 1991a. "Preprofessional Socialization and Identity Transformation." *Journal of Contemporary Ethnography* 20:157–78.

———. 1991b. "The Professional Ex-." *Sociological Quarterly* 32:219–30.

Brownmiller, Susan. 1975. *Against Our Will: Men, Women, and Rape.* New York: Simon and Schuster.

Brownstein, Henry H. 1991. "The Media and the Construction of Random Drug Violence." *Social Justice* 18 (4): 85–103.

————. 1996. *The Rise and Fall of a Violent Crime Wave: Crack Cocaine and the Social Construction of a Social Problem.* Guilderland, N.Y.: Harrow and Heston.

Brunvand, Jan Harold. 1993. *The Baby Train.* New York: Norton.

————. 1995. "'Lights Out': A Faxlore Phenomenon." *Skeptical Inquirer* 19 (March): 32–37.

Bumiller, Kristin. 1988. *The Civil Rights Society: The Social Construction of Victims.* Baltimore: Johns Hopkins University Press.

Bureau of Justice Assistance. 1996. *Regional Seminar Series on Developing and Implementing Antistalking Codes.* Washington, D.C.: U.S. Department of Justice.

California Council on Criminal Justice. 1989. *Final Report of the State Task Force on Gangs and Drugs.* Sacramento.

California Office of Criminal Justice Planning. 1989. *Occult Crime.* Sacramento.

Caputi, Jane. 1987. *The Age of Sex Crime.* Bowling Green, Ohio: Bowling Green State University Popular Press.

Carlton, Jim. 1990. "Driver Escapes Injury in Freeway Shooting." *Los Angeles Times* (June 12): B-5.

Cartalk [on-line]. 1996. "Southern California Freeway Shooting Schedule." Cartalk.com/Mail/Letters/4.

Chermak, Steven. 1995. *Victims in the News: Crime and the American News Media.* Boulder, Colo.: Westview.

Chicago Tribune. 1991. "Police Need Help to Stop Stalkers" (editorial). November 18, p. I-18.

Christie, Nils. 1986. "The Ideal Victim." In *From Crime Policy to Victim Policy,* edited by Ezzat A. Fattah, 17–30. London: Macmillan.

Cloward, Richard A., and Lloyd E. Ohlin. 1960. *Delinquency and Opportunity.* New York: Free Press.

CNN Prime News. 1993. "Michigan Legal System Takes Stalking Very Seriously." January 1. Journal Graphics transcript no. 273.

Cohen, Albert K. 1955. *Delinquent Boys.* New York: Free Press.

Cohen, Stanley. 1980. *Folk Devils and Moral Panics: The Creation of the Mods and Rockers.* Rev. ed. New York: St. Martin's.

Congressional Record. 1992. 102d Cong., 2d sess. Vol. 138, pt. 97.

Connor, Walter. 1972. "The Manufacture of Deviance: The Case of the Soviet Purge, 1936–1938." *American Sociological Review* 37:403–13.

Conrad, Peter. 1992. "Medicalization and Social Control." *Annual Review of Sociology* 18:209–32.

Cosgrove, Stuart. 1990. "Erotomania." *New Statesman & Society* 3 (July 27): 31–32.

Cowell, Carolyn. 1992. "It Was the Half a Mouse That Did It." *Newsday* (April 9): 4.

Crouch, Ben, and Kelly Damphousse. 1991. "Law Enforcement and the Satanism-Crime Connection: A Survey of 'Cult Cops.'" In *The Satanism Scare*, edited by James T. Richardson, Joel Best, and David G. Bromley, 191–204. Hawthorne, N.Y.: Aldine de Gruyter.

Culliton, Barbara J. 1976. "Mrs. Lasker's War." *Harper's* 252 (June): 60.

Cummings, Scott. 1993. "Anatomy of a Wilding Gang." In *Gangs*, edited by Scott Cummings and Daniel J. Monti, 49–73. Albany: State University of New York Press.

Currie, Elliott P. 1968. "Crimes without Criminals." *Law and Society Review* 3 (August): 7–32.

Dannen, Frederic. 1995. "The Thin White Line." *New Yorker* 71 (July 31): 30–34.

Davis, Jennifer. 1980. "The London Garotting Panic of 1862." In *Crime and the Law: The Social History of Crime in Western Europe since 1500*, edited by V. A. C. Gatrell, Bruce Lenman, and Geoffrey Parker, 190–213. London: Europa.

Dean, Paul. 1987. "Defensive Driving." *Los Angeles Times* (August 5): V-1.

de Becker, Gavin. 1997. *The Gift of Fear: Survival Signals That Protect Us from Violence.* Boston: Little, Brown.

DeKeseredy, Walter S. 1995. "Enhancing the Quality of Survey Data on Woman Abuse: Examples from a National Canadian Study." *Violence against Women* 1:158–73.

Derber, Charles. 1996. *The Wilding of America: How Greed and Violence Are Eroding Our Nation's Character.* New York: St. Martin's.

Dershowitz, Alan M. 1994. *The Abuse Excuse, and Other Cop-Outs, Sob Stories, and Evasions of Responsibility.* Boston: Little, Brown.

Dietz, Park Elliott, Daryl B. Matthews, Daniel Allen Martell, Tracy M. Stewart, Debra R. Hrouda, and Janet Warren. 1991. "Threatening and Otherwise Inappropriate Letters to Members of the United States Congress." *Journal of Forensic Sciences* 36:1445–68.

Dietz, Park Elliott, Daryl B. Matthews, Cindy Van Duyne, Daniel Allen Martell, Charles D. H. Parry, Tracy Stewart, Janet Warren, and J. Douglas

Crowder. 1991. "Threatening and Otherwise Inappropriate Letters to Hollywood Celebrities." *Journal of Forensic Sciences* 36:185–209.

Dollard, J., N. E. Miller, L. W. Doob, O. H. Mowrer, and R. R. Sears. 1939. *Frustration and Aggression.* New Haven: Yale University Press.

Donahue. 1992. "Love Stalkers Would Rather See Ex Dead Than with Someone Else." November 25. Journal Graphics transcript no. 3607.

Dorken, Herbert, ed. 1986. *Professional Psychology in Transition.* San Francisco: Jossey-Bass.

Douglas, Mary, and Aaron B. Wildavsky. 1982. *Risk and Culture.* Berkeley: University of California Press.

Downs, Anthony. 1972. "Up and Down with Ecology—The 'Issue-Attention Cycle.'" *Public Interest* 28:38–50.

Downs, Donald Alexander. 1989. *The New Politics of Pornography.* Chicago: University of Chicago Press.

———. 1996. *More Than Victims: Battered Women, the Syndrome Society, and the Law.* Chicago: University of Chicago Press.

Dundes, Alan, ed. 1991. *The Blood Libel Legend.* Madison: University of Wisconsin Press.

Dyrendal, Asbjørn. 1998. "Media Constructions of 'Satanism' in Norway, 1988–1997." *FOAFTale News* 43:2–5.

Economist. 1996. "Gangs in the Heartland." Vol. 339 (May 25): 29–30.

Edelman, Murray. 1971. *Politics as Symbolic Action.* New York: Academic Press.

———. 1977. *Political Language: Words That Succeed and Policies That Fail.* Orlando, Fla.: Academic Press.

———. 1988. *Constructing the Political Spectacle.* Chicago: University of Chicago Press.

Elias, Robert. 1986. *The Politics of Victimization: Victims, Victimology, and Human Rights.* New York: Oxford University Press.

———. 1993. *Victims Still: The Political Manipulation of Crime Victims.* Newbury Park, Calif.: Sage.

Ellis, Bill. 1983. "De Legendis Urbis: Modern Legends in Ancient Rome." *Journal of American Folklore* 96:200–208.

———. 1991. "Legend-Trips and Satanism: Adolescents' Ostensive Traditions as 'Cult' Activity." In *The Satanism Scare,* edited by James T. Richardson, Joel Best, and David G. Bromley, 279–95. Hawthorne, N.Y.: Aldine de Gruyter.

Ellis, David. 1993. "Nowhere to Hide." *People* 39 (May 17): 62–66, 68, 71–72.

Elson, John. 1994. "Closing the Last Chapter." *Time* 143 (February 21): 68.

Elwood, William N. 1994. *Rhetoric in the War on Drugs.* New York: Praeger.

Englehardt, Tom. 1995. *The End of Victory Culture.* New York: Basic Books.

Erikson, Kai T. 1976. *Everything in Its Path: Destruction of Community in the Buffalo Creek Flood.* New York: Simon and Schuster.

Faller, Kathleen Coulborn. 1994. "Child Sexual Abuse Allegations." *Violence Update* 4 (February): 1–2, 4, 8, 10–11.

Fallers, Lloyd A. 1954. "A Note on the 'Trickle Effect.'" *Public Opinion Quarterly* 18:314–21.

Fallows, James. 1989. "Containing Japan." *Atlantic Monthly* 263 (May): 40–54.

Faludi, Susan. 1991. *Backlash: The Undeclared War against American Women.* New York: Anchor.

Federal Bureau of Investigation. 1990. *Hate Crime Data Collection Guidelines.* Washington, D.C.

———. 1994. *Crime in the United States, 1993: Uniform Crime Reports.* Washington, D.C.

Felson, Richard B. 1991. "Blame Analysis: Accounting for the Behavior of Protected Groups." *American Sociologist* 22:5–23.

Fine, Gary Alan, and Lazaros Christoforides. 1991. "Dirty Birds, Filthy Immigrants, and the English Sparrow War: Metaphorical Linkage in Constructing Social Problems." *Symbolic Interaction* 14:375–93.

Fishman, Mark. 1978. "Crimes Waves as Ideology." *Social Problems* 25:531–43.

FOAFTale News. 1993a. "Ankle Slashers at the Mall." Vol. 29:10–11.

———. 1993b. "'Lights Out' Gang Initiation." Vol. 31:5–6.

———. 1993c. "Blood Initiation Weekend." Vol. 31:6.

48 Hours. 1992. "Stalker." March 4. Burrelle's Information Services transcript.

Freedman, Estelle B. 1987. "'Uncontrolled Desires.'" *Journal of American History* 74:83–106.

Fumento, Michael. 1990. *The Myth of Heterosexual AIDS.* New York: Basic Books.

Furedi, Frank. 1997. *Culture of Fear.* London: Cassell.

Furio, Joane. 1993. "Can New State Laws Stop the Stalkers?" *Ms.* 3 (January): 90–91.

Gagne, Patricia. 1996. "Identity, Strategy, and Feminist Politics: The Case of Battered Women Who Kill." *Social Problems* 43:77–93.

Gamson, Joshua. 1994. *Claims to Fame: Celebrity in Contemporary America.* Berkeley: University of California Press.

Gamson, William, and Andre Modigliani. 1989. "Media Discourse and Public Opinion on Nuclear Power." *American Journal of Sociology* 95:1–37.

Gans, Herbert J. 1995. *The War against the Poor: The Underclass and Antipoverty Policy.* New York: Basic Books.

Gates, Daryl F. 1987. "Highway Hostility Must Be Stopped." *Los Angeles Times* (August 23): V-5.

Gellman, Susan. 1991. "Sticks and Stones Can Put You in Jail, but Can Words Increase Your Sentence? Constitutional and Policy Dilemmas of Ethnic Intimidation Laws." *UCLA Law Review* 39:333–78.

Geraldo. 1990. "Tracking the Star Stalkers." March 20. Journal Graphics transcript no. 654.

Gerol, Mark. 1994. "The New Arms Race" (letter to the editor). *Time* 143 (January 10): 6.

Gest, Ted. 1987. "Rambo's Brothers Cruise Clogged Expressways." *U.S. News & World Report* 103 (August 10): 6.

Gibson, James William. 1994. *Warrior Dreams: Paramilitary Culture in Post-Vietnam America.* New York: Hill and Wang.

Gibson, Rhonda, and Dolf Zillman. 1994. "Exaggerated versus Representative Exemplification in News Reports." *Communication Research* 21:603–24.

Gilbert, James. 1986. *A Cycle of Outrage: America's Reaction to the Juvenile Delinquent in the 1950s.* New York: Oxford University Press.

Gilbert, Neil. 1994. "Miscounting Social Ills." *Society* 31 (March): 18–26.

———. 1997. "Advocacy Research and Social Policy." *Crime and Justice* 22: 101–48.

Gillam, Jerry. 1987. "Bills Signed to Combat Violence on the Freeways." *Los Angeles Times* (September 27): I-21.

Gilligan, Matthew J. 1992. "Stalking the Stalker." *Georgia Law Review* 27:285–342.

Gitlin, Todd. 1980. *The Whole World Is Watching.* Berkeley: University of California Press.

Goldman, Abigail. 1996. "Series of Attacks on Cars Continue on Area Freeways." *Los Angeles Times* (September 25): A-1.

Goldman, John J. 1989. "Gang Assault on Woman Stuns N.Y." *Los Angeles Times* (April 24): I-15.

Gonzales, Monica. 1987. "Motorist Mayhem." *Wall Street Journal* (August 3): 1, 14.

Goode, Erich, and Nachman Ben-Yehuda. 1994. *Moral Panics.* Cambridge, Mass.: Blackwell.

Good Housekeeping. 1980. "My Ex-Husband Won't Leave Me Alone." Vol. 190 (March): 32–34, 39, 42.

Goodwin, Michael. 1993. "Stalked?" *Woman's Day* 56 (March 16): 49–50, 52.

Gorelick, Steven M. 1989. "'Join Our War': The Construction of Ideology in a Newspaper Crimefighting Campaign." *Crime and Delinquency* 35:421–36.

Greenblatt, Sidney Leonard. 1977. "Campaigns and the Manufacture of Deviance in Chinese Society." In *Deviance and Social Control in Chinese Society,* edited by Amy Auerbacher Wilson, Sidney Leonard Greenblatt, and Richard Whittingham Wilson, 82–120. New York: Praeger.

Gross, Andrea. 1993. "Danger on the Road." *Ladies' Home Journal* 110 (February): 48, 54.

Gup, Ted. 1992. "A Savage Story." *Time* 140 (September 21): 55.

Gusfield, Joseph R. 1981. *The Culture of Public Problems: Drinking-Driving and the Symbolic Order.* Chicago: University of Chicago Press.

————. 1996. *Contested Meanings: The Construction of Alcohol Problems.* Madison: University of Wisconsin Press.

Hacking, Ian. 1986. "Making Up People." In *Reconstructing Individualism,* edited by Thomas C. Heller, Morton Sosna, and David E. Wellbery, 222–36. Stanford, Calif.: Stanford University Press.

Hall, Stuart, Chas Critcher, Tony Jefferson, John Clarke, and Brian Roberts. 1978. *Policing the Crisis: Mugging, the State, and Law and Order.* London: Macmillan.

Haller, Mark H. 1990. "Illegal Enterprise." *Criminology* 28:207–35.

Harry, Joseph. 1982. "Derivative Deviance: The Cases of Extortion, Fag-Bashing, and Shakedown of Gay Men." *Criminology* 19:546–64.

Hechler, David. 1988. *The Battle and the Backlash: The Child Sex Abuse War.* Lexington, Mass.: Lexington.

Heil, Andrea. 1986. "Lovesick." *Mademoiselle* 92 (December): 128–30, 136–38.

Herek, Gregory M. 1989. "Hate Crimes against Lesbians and Gay Men." *American Psychologist* 44:948–55.

Herek, Gregory M., and Kevin T. Berrill, eds. 1992. *Hate Crimes: Confronting Violence against Lesbians and Gay Men.* Newbury Park, Calif.: Sage.

Herman, Judith Lewis. 1992. *Trauma and Recovery.* New York: Basic Books.

Hicks, Robert D. 1991a. "The Police Model of Satanic Crime." In *The Satanism Scare*, edited by James T. Richardson, Joel Best, and David G. Bromley, 175–89. Hawthorne, N.Y.: Aldine de Gruyter.

———. 1991b. *In Pursuit of Satan: The Police and the Occult*. Buffalo, N.Y.: Prometheus.

Hilgartner, Stephen, and Charles L. Bosk. 1988. "The Rise and Fall of Social Problems." *American Journal of Sociology* 94:53–78.

Hirsch, Paul M. 1972. "Processing Fads and Fashion: An Organization-Set Analysis of Cultural Industry Systems." *American Journal of Sociology* 77: 639–59.

Hofstadter, Richard. 1966. *The Paranoid Style in American Politics, and Other Essays*. New York: Knopf.

Holmes, Ronald M. 1989. *Profiling Violent Crimes*. Newbury Park, Calif.: Sage.

———. 1993. "Stalking in America." *Journal of Contemporary Criminal Justice* 9:317–27.

Holstein, James A., and Gale Miller. 1990. "Rethinking Victimization." *Symbolic Interaction* 13:103–22.

———, eds. 1993. *Reconsidering Social Constructionism: Debates in Social Problems Theory*. Hawthorne, N.Y.: Aldine de Gruyter.

Hood, Jane C. 1995. "Some Didn't Call It Hate: Multiple Accounts of the Zimmerman Library Incident." *Violence against Women* 1:228–40.

Howe, Louis McH. 1933. "Uncle Sam Starts after Crime." *Saturday Evening Post* 199 (July 29): 5–6.

Hughes, Robert. 1993. *Culture of Complaint: The Fraying of America*. New York: Oxford University Press.

Ianni, Francis A. J. 1972. *A Family Business*. New York: Russell Sage Foundation.

Ibarra, Peter R., and John I. Kitsuse. 1993. "Vernacular Constituents of Moral Discourse." In *Reconsidering Social Constructionism*, edited by James A. Holstein and Gale Miller, 25–58. Hawthorne, N.Y.: Aldine de Gruyter.

Inciardi, James A. 1992. *The War on Drugs II*. Mountain View, Calif.: Mayfield.

Ingrassia, Michele. 1993. "Stalked to Death?" *Newsweek* 122 (November 1): 27–28.

———. 1994. "Open to Attack." *Newsweek* 123 (January 17): 46–47.

Irvine, Leslie J. 1995. "Codependency and Recovery: Gender, Self, and Emotions." *Symbolic Interaction* 18:121–44.

Jackson, Patrick. 1993. "Moral Panic and the Response to Gangs in California." In *Gangs*, edited by Scott Cummings and Daniel J. Monti, 257–75. Albany: State University of New York Press.

Jacobs, James B. 1992. "Rethinking the War against Hate Crimes: A New York City Perspective." *Criminal Justice Ethics* 11 (summer): 55–61.

———. 1993. "Should Hate Be a Crime?" *Public Interest* 113:3–14.

Jacobs, James B., and Jessica S. Henry. 1996. "The Social Construction of a Hate Crime Epidemic." *Journal of Criminal Law and Criminology* 86:366–91.

Jacobs, James B., and Kimberly A. Potter. 1997. "Hate Crimes: A Critical Perspective." *Crime and Justice* 22:1–50.

Jefferson, David J. 1992. "A Harvard Doctor Offers Trauma Relief for UFO 'Abductees.'" *Wall Street Journal* (May 14): A-1, A-10.

Jencks, Christopher. 1992. *Rethinking Social Policy*. New York: HarperCollins.

Jenkins, Philip. 1992. *Intimate Enemies: Moral Panics in Contemporary Great Britain*. Hawthorne, N.Y.: Aldine de Gruyter.

———. 1994. *Using Murder: The Social Construction of Serial Homicide*. Hawthorne, N.Y.: Aldine de Gruyter.

———. 1996. *Pedophiles and Priests*. New York: Oxford University Press.

———. 1998. *Molesters: The Cycle of Sex Offender Panics*. New Haven: Yale University Press.

Jenness, Valerie. 1995a. "Social Movement Growth, Domain Expansion, and Framing Processes: The Gay/Lesbian Movement and Violence against Gays and Lesbians as a Social Problem." *Social Problems* 42:145–70.

———. 1995b. "Hate Crimes in the United States: The Transformation of Injured Persons into Victims and the Extension of Victim Status to Multiple Constituencies." In *Images of Issues*, edited by Joel Best, 2d ed., 213–37. Hawthorne, N.Y.: Aldine de Gruyter.

Jenness, Valerie, and Kendal Broad. 1997. *Hate Crimes: New Social Movements and the Politics of Violence*. Hawthorne, N.Y.: Aldine de Gruyter.

John and Leeza. 1992. Videotaped broadcast. December.

Johns, Christina Jacqueline. 1992. *Power, Ideology, and the War on Drugs*. New York: Praeger.

Johnson, David R. 1979. *Policing the Urban Underworld: The Impact of Crime on the Development of the American Police, 1800–1887*. Philadelphia: Temple University Press.

Johnson, John M. 1995. "Horror Stories and the Construction of Child Abuse." In *Images of Issues*, edited by Joel Best, 2d ed., 17–31. Hawthorne, N.Y.: Aldine de Gruyter.

Johnson, Lyndon Baines. 1971. *The Vantage Point: Perspectives on the Presidency, 1963–1969*. New York: Holt, Rinehart and Winston.

Johnston, Jerry. 1989. *The Edge of Evil: The Rise of Satanism in North America.* Dallas: Word.

Johnston, Lonn. 1987. "Stress on Freeways Sparks 'War Out There.'" *Los Angeles Times* (July 21): I-3. ·

Kaminer, Wendy. 1992. *I'm Dysfunctional, You're Dysfunctional*. Reading, Mass.: Addison Wesley.

Kappeler, Victor E., Mark Blumberg, and Gary W. Potter. 1996. *The Mythology of Crime and Criminal Justice*. 2d ed. Prospect Heights, Ill.: Waveland.

Katz, Alfred H. 1993. *Self-Help in America: A Social Movement Perspective.* New York: Twayne.

Katz, Jack. 1988. *Seductions of Crime*. New York: Basic Books.

Kaufman, Michael T. 1989. "Park Suspects." *New York Times* (April 26): A-1.

Kaus, Mickey. 1987. "Gunplay on the Freeway." *Newsweek* 110 (August 10): 18.

Keen, Sam. 1986. *Faces of the Enemy: Reflections of the Hostile Imagination*. San Francisco: Harper & Row.

Kelly, Liz. 1988. "What's in a Name? Defining Child Sexual Abuse." *Feminist Review* 28:65–73.

Kendall, John. 1987. "Death Raises Level of Fear on Highways." *Los Angeles Times* (July 26): I-1.

Kendall, John, and Jack Jones. 1987. "4 Men, Woman Held in Highway Shooting Death." *Los Angeles Times* (July 29): I-1, 20.

Kindermann, Charles, James Lynch, and David Cantor. 1997. "Effects of the Redesign on Victimization Estimates." *Bureau of Justice Statistics National Crime Victimization Survey* (April).

King, Peter. 1987. "Newspaper Reporting, Prosecution Practice, and Perceptions of Urban Crime: The Colchester Crime Wave of 1765." *Continuity and Change* 2:423–54.

Kingdon, John. 1984. *Agendas, Alternatives, and Public Policies*. Boston: Little, Brown.

Kinsley, Michael. 1995. "The Spoils of Victimhood." *New Yorker* 71 (March 27): 62–69.

Kirk, Stuart A., and Herb Kutchins. 1992. *The Selling of DSM*. Hawthorne, N.Y.: Aldine de Gruyter.

Klapp, Orrin E. 1962. *Heroes, Villains, and Fools*. Englewood Cliffs, N.J.: Prentice-Hall.

————. 1964. *Symbolic Leaders: Public Dramas and Public Men*. Chicago: Aldine.

Klein, Malcolm W. 1995a. *The American Street Gang*. New York: Oxford University Press.

————. 1995b. "Street Gang Cycles." In *Crime*, edited by James Q. Wilson and Joan Petersilia, 217–36. San Francisco: Institute for Contemporary Studies.

Kraska, Peter B., and Victor E. Kappeler. 1997. "Militarizing American Police: The Rise and Normalization of Paramilitary Units." *Social Problems* 44: 1–18.

Kunkel, Karl R. 1995. "Down on the Farm: Rationale Expansion in the Construction of Factory Farming as a Social Problem." In *Images of Issues*, edited by Joel Best, 2d ed., 239–56. Hawthorne, N.Y.: Aldine de Gruyter.

Lamb, Sharon. 1996. *The Trouble with Blame: Victims, Perpetrators, and Responsibility*. Cambridge: Harvard University Press.

Lanning, Kenneth V. 1989. "Satanic, Occult, Ritualistic Crime." *Police Chief* 56 (10): 62–83.

Lardner, George, Jr. 1992. "The Stalking of Kristen." *Washington Post* (November 22): C-1–3.

Larry King Live. 1990. "Telephone Terrorism." September 10. Journal Graphics transcript no. 126.

————. 1994. "What About Nicole Simpson?" June 22. Journal Graphics transcript no. 1153.

Larson, Bart, and Wendell Amstutz. 1995. *Youth Violence and Gangs*. Rochester, Minn.: National Counseling Resource Center.

Larson, Bob. 1989. *Satanism: The Seduction of America's Youth*. Nashville: Thomas Nelson.

Laskey, John A. 1996. "Gang Migration: The Familial Gang Transplant Phenomenon." *Journal of Gang Research* 3 (2): 1–15.

Lemann, Nicholas. 1988. "The Unfinished War." *Atlantic Monthly* 262 (December): 37–49, 52–56.

Lens, Sidney. 1969. *Poverty: America's Enduring Paradox; A History of the Richest Nation's Unwon War*. New York: Crowell.

Leonard, Thomas C. 1986. *The Power of the Press: The Birth of American Political Reporting*. New York: Oxford University Press.

Lipsky, Michael, and Steven Smith. 1989. "When Social Problems Are Treated as Emergencies." *Social Service Review* 63:5–25.

Lloyd, Robin M. 1992. "Negotiating Child Sexual Abuse." *Social Problems* 39: 109–24.

Lobue, Ange. 1987. "Mayhem on the Freeways." *U.S. News & World Report* 103 (September 28): 9.

Lofland, John. 1969. *Deviance and Identity*. Englewood Cliffs, N.J.: Prentice-Hall.

Loftus, Elizabeth, and Katherine Ketcham. 1994. *The Myth of Repressed Memory: False Memories and Allegations of Sexual Abuse*. New York: St. Martin's.

Los Angeles Times. 1987a. "Guns and Tire Irons" (editorial). August 6, p. II-10.

———. 1987b. "Guns in Cars" (editorial). August 23, p. II-4.

Loseke, Donileen R. 1992. *The Battered Woman and Shelters*. Albany: State University of New York Press.

———. 1993. "Constructing Conditions, People, Morality, and Emotion." In *Constructionist Controversies*, edited by Gale Miller and James A. Holstein, 207–16. Hawthorne, N.Y.: Aldine de Gruyter.

Lowney, Kathleen S. 1994. "Speak of the Devil: Talk Shows and the Social Construction of Satanism." *Perspectives on Social Problems* 6:99–128.

———. 1995. "Teenage Satanism as Oppositional Youth Subculture." *Journal of Contemporary Ethnography* 23:453–84.

Lowney, Kathleen S., and Joel Best. 1995. "Stalking Strangers and Lovers: Changing Media Typifications of a New Crime Problem." In *Images of Issues*, edited by Joel Best, 2d ed., 33–57. Hawthorne, N.Y.: Aldine de Gruyter.

———. 1998. "Floral Entrepreneurs: Kudzu as Agricultural Solution and Ecological Problem." *Sociological Spectrum* 18:93–114.

Luckenbill, David F. 1977. "Criminal Homicide as a Situated Transaction." *Social Problems* 25:176–86.

———. 1984. "Character Coercion, Instrumental Coercion, and Gun Control." *Journal of Applied Behavioral Science* 20:181–92.

Lukas, J. Anthony. 1989. "Wilding—as American as Tom Sawyer." *New York Times* (May 28): IV-15.

MacKellar, F. Landis, and Machiko Yanagishita. 1995. *Homicides in the United States: Who's at Risk?* Washington, D.C.: Population Reference Bureau.

Madriz, Esther. 1997. *Nothing Bad Happens to Good Girls: Fear of Crime in Women's Lives*. Berkeley: University of California Press.

Maguire, Kathleen, and Ann L. Pastore. 1996. *Bureau of Justice Statistics Sourcebook of Criminal Justice Statistics—1995*. Washington: Bureau of Justice Statistics.

Marsteller, A. L. 1996. "A Social Construction of a Gang Problem." Paper delivered at the annual meeting of the Academy of Criminal Justice Sciences, Las Vegas, Nev., March.

Martin, Susan. 1995. "'A Cross Burning Is Not Just an Arson': Police Social Construction of Hate Crimes in Baltimore County." *Criminology* 33:303–26.

———. 1996. "Investigating Hate Crimes: Case Characteristics and Law Enforcement Responses." *Justice Quarterly* 13:455–80.

Marx, Gary T. 1981. "Ironies of Social Control: Authorities as Contributors to Deviance through Escalation, Nonenforcement, and Covert Facilitation." *Social Problems* 28:221–46.

Matthews, Nancy A. 1994. *Confronting Rape: The Feminist Anti-rape Movement and the State*. New York: Routledge.

Maury Povich Show. 1992. "A Stalker's Victim Discusses Her Ordeal." August 20. Journal Graphics transcript no. 247.

Maxson, Cheryl L. 1993. "Investigating Gang Migration: Contextual Issues for Intervention." *Gang Journal* 1 (2): 1–8.

Maxson, Cheryl L., Kristi J. Woods, and Malcolm W. Klein. 1996. "Street Gang Migration: How Big a Threat?" *National Institute of Justice Journal* 230:26–31.

McCarthy, Colman. 1984. "Mayor Flynn and Friend." *Washington Post* (July 14): A-19.

McCarthy, John D., and Mark Wolfson. 1996. "Resource Mobilization by Local Social Movement Organizations: Agency, Strategy, and Organization in the Movement against Drinking and Driving." *American Sociological Review* 61:1070–88.

McCarthy, John D., and Mayer N. Zald. 1977. "Resource Mobilization and Social Movements." *American Journal of Sociology* 82:1212–41.

McCormick, Chris, ed. 1995. *Constructing Danger: The Mis/Representation of Crime in the News*. Halifax, Nova Scotia: Fernwood.

McCoy, Alfred W., and Alan A. Block, eds. 1992. *War on Drugs: Studies in the Failure of U.S. Narcotics Policy*. Boulder, Colo.: Westview.

McDonald, R. Robin. 1994. "Where Are You Safe?" *Atlanta Journal and Constitution* (November 15): B-6.

McGuire, Thomas G. 1980. "Markets for Psychotherapy." In *Psychotherapy: Practice, Research, Policy*, edited by Gary R. Vandenbos, 187–245. Beverly Hills, Calif.: Sage.

McLellan, Dennis. 1987. "Ganging Up." *Los Angeles Times* (November 30): II-1.

Media Studies Journal. 1992. "Crime Story" (special issue). Vol. 6 (winter).

Meyer, David S., and Joshua Gamson. 1995. "The Challenge of Cultural Elites: Celebrities and Social Movements." *Sociological Inquiry* 65:181–206.

Miller, Bryan. 1993. "Thou Shalt Not Stalk." *Chicago Tribune Magazine* (April 18): 14–16, 18, 20.

Mills, C. Wright. 1959. *The Sociological Imagination*. New York: Oxford University Press.

Mithers, Carol Lynn. 1982. "Can a Man Be Too Mad about You?" *Mademoiselle* 88 (October): 36.

Moore, R. I. 1987. *The Formation of a Persecuting Society*. New York: Blackwell.

Morin, Karen S. 1993. "The Phenomenon of Stalking." *San Diego Justice Journal* 1:123–62.

Morville, Dawn A. 1993. "Stalking Laws." *Washington University Law Quarterly* 71:921–35.

Moscovici, Serge. 1987. "The Conspiracy Mentality." In *Changing Conceptions of Conspiracy*, edited by Carol F. Graumann and Serge Moscovici, 151–69. New York: Springer-Verlag.

Moynihan, Daniel Patrick. 1993. "Defining Deviancy Down." *American Scholar* 62 (winter): 17–30.

Muehlenhard, Charlene L., Irene G. Powch, Joi L. Phelps, and Laura M. Giusti. 1992. "Definitions of Rape: Scientific and Political Implications." *Journal of Social Issues* 48:23–44.

Mulhern, Sherrill. 1991. "Satanism and Psychotherapy." In *The Satanism Scare*, edited by James T. Richardson, Joel Best, and David G. Bromley, 145–72. Hawthorne, N.Y.: Aldine de Gruyter.

Murray, Charles. 1984. *Losing Ground: American Social Policy, 1950–1980*. New York: Basic Books.

Myers, John E. B., ed. 1994. *The Backlash: Child Protection under Fire*. Thousand Oaks, Calif.: Sage.

Nardi, Peter M., and Ralph Bolton. 1991. "Gay-Bashing." In *Targets of Violence and Aggression*, edited by R. Baenninger, 349–400. New York: Elsevier.

Nathan, Debbie, and Michael Snedeker. 1995. *Satan's Silence: Ritual Abuse and the Making of a Modern American Witch Hunt.* New York: Basic Books.

National Institute of Justice. 1993. *Project to Develop a Model Anti-stalking Code for States.* Washington, D.C.: U.S. Department of Justice.

Nelson-Rowe, Shan. 1995. "The Moral Drama of Multicultural Education." In *Images of Issues,* edited by Joel Best, 2d ed., 81–99. Hawthorne, N.Y.: Aldine de Gruyter.

Newton, Michael. 1992. *Serial Slaughter: What's behind America's Murder Epidemic?* Port Townsend, Wash.: Loompanics Unlimited.

New York Times. 1989. "Outbreak of Road Shootings Plagues Detroit." February 12, p. 27.

Noblitt, James Randall, and Pamela Sue Perskin. 1995. *Cult and Ritual Abuse.* Westport, Conn.: Praeger.

Novaco, Raymond W. 1987. "Highway Violence Has Numerous Triggers." *Los Angeles Times* (August 2): V-5.

Ofshe, Richard, and Ethan Watters. 1994. *Making Monsters: False Memories, Psychotherapy, and Sexual Hysteria.* New York: Scribner's.

Olson, Walter K. 1991. *The Litigation Explosion.* New York: Plume.

O'Neal, Gwendolyn S. 1997. "Clothes to Kill For." *Sociological Inquiry* 67: 336–49.

Onwuachi-Saunders, E. Chukwudi, Deborah A. Lambert, Polly A. Marchbanks, Patrick W. O'Carroll, and James A. Mercy. 1989. "Firearm-Related Assaults on Los Angeles Roadways." *Journal of the American Medical Association* 262:2262–64.

Oprah. 1991. "Roseanne & Tom Arnold." November 1. Journal Graphics transcript no. 1345.

———. 1992. "Stalking." May 1. Burrelle's Information Services transcript.

———. 1994. "Women in Fear for Their Lives." January 21. Burrelle's Information Services transcript.

Pacific Law Journal. 1990. "Selected 1990 Legislation." 22:500–501.

Patai, Daphne. 1997. "The Making of a Social Problem: Sexual Harassment on Campus." *Sexuality and Culture* 1:219–56.

Patai, Daphne, and Noretta Koertge. 1994. *Professing Feminism.* New York: Basic Books.

Patterson, James T. 1987. *The Dread Disease: Cancer and Modern American Culture.* Cambridge: Harvard University Press.

Pearson, Geoffrey. 1983. *Hooligan: A History of Respectable Fears.* London: Macmillan.

Pellegrini, Ann. 1990. "Rape Is a Bias Crime." *New York Times* (May 27): E-13.

Perez, Christine. 1993. "Stalking." *American Journal of Criminal Law* 20:264–280.

Pezdek, Kathy, and William P. Banks, eds. 1996. *The Recovered Memory/False Memory Debate.* San Diego: Academic Press.

Pilisuk, Marc, and Phyllis Pilisuk, eds. 1973. *How We Lost the War on Poverty.* New Brunswick, N.J.: Transaction.

Pitt, David E. 1989. "Jogger's Attackers Terrorized at Least 9 in 2 Hours." *New York Times* (April 22): I-1.

Pollitt, Katha. 1993. "Not Just Bad Sex." *New Yorker* 69 (October 4): 220–24.

Powers, Richard Gid. 1983. *G-Men: Hoover's FBI in American Popular Culture.* Carbondale: Southern Illinois University Press.

Priest, George L. 1990. "The New Legal Structure of Risk Control." *Daedalus* 119 (fall): 207–27.

Prothrow-Stith, Deborah. 1991. *Deadly Consequences.* New York: HarperCollins.

Quindlen, Anne. 1990. "A Bias Crime." *New York Times* (May 6): E-23.

Reilly, Sue. 1982. "A Rising Star Lives to Shine Again . . . ." *People* 18 (November 8): 155–56.

Reinarman, Craig. 1988. "The Social Construction of an Alcohol Problem: The Case of Mothers Against Drunk Drivers and Social Control in the 1980s." *Theory and Society* 17:91–120.

———. 1994. "The Social Construction of Drug Scares." In *Constructions of Deviance,* edited by Patricia A. Adler and Peter Adler, 92–104. Belmont, Calif.: Wadsworth.

———. 1995. "The Twelve-Step Movement and Advanced Capitalist Culture: The Politics of Self-Control in Postmodernity." In *Cultural Politics and Social Movements,* edited by Marcy Darnovsky, Barbara Epstein, and Richard Flacks, 90–109. Philadelphia: Temple University Press.

Reuter, Peter. 1983. *Disorganized Crime.* Cambridge: MIT Press.

Rice, John Steadman. 1992. "Discursive Formation, Life Stories, and the Emergence of Co-dependency: 'Power/Knowledge' and the Search for Identity." *Sociological Quarterly* 33:337–64.

Richardson, James T. 1997. "The Social Construction of Satanism: Understanding an International Social Problem." *Australian Journal of Social Issues* 32:61–85.

Richardson, James T., Joel Best, and David G. Bromley, eds. 1991. *The Satanism Scare*. Hawthorne, N.Y.: Aldine de Gruyter.

Rieff, David. 1991. "Victims, All?" *Harpers* 283 (October): 49–56.

Rivkin, Jacqueline. 1990. "Recovery Stores: A Sense of Mission." *Publishers Weekly* (November 23): 26, 28.

Roberts, Steven V. 1994. "Finding a Voice in the Sounds of Silence." *U.S. News & World Report* 117 (December 5): 8.

Rochefort, David A., and Roger W. Cobb, eds. 1994. *The Politics of Problem Definition*. Lawrence: University of Kansas Press.

Roiphe, Katie. 1993. *The Morning After: Sex, Fear, and Feminism on Campus*. Boston: Little, Brown.

Rose, Vicki McNickle. 1977. "Rape as a Social Problem: A Byproduct of the Feminist Movement." *Social Problems* 25:75–89.

Rosenberry, Pete. 1996. "It's War: A Crash Course on Gangs in Williamson County." *Southern Illinoisan* (January 30): 1-A, 7-A.

Ross, H. Laurence. 1992. *Confronting Drunk Driving*. New Haven: Yale University Press.

Rossen, Benjamin. 1990. "Moral Panic: The Story of Oude Pekela." Unpublished English translation of a Dutch document.

Royko, Mike. 1987. "California 'Trend' Strictly a Misfire." *Chicago Tribune* (August 4): 3.

Rudy, David. 1991. "The Adult Children of Alcoholics Movement." In *Society, Culture, and Drinking Patterns Reexamined*, edited by David Pittman and Harrison White, 716–32. New Brunswick, N.J.: Rutgers Center of Alcohol Studies.

Russell, Edmund P., III. 1996. "'Speaking of Annihilation': Mobilizing for War against Human and Insect Enemies, 1914–1945." *Journal of American History* 82:1505–29.

Ryan, William. 1971. *Blaming the Victim*. New York: Random House.

Safran, Claire. 1992. "A Stranger Was Stalking Our Little Girl." *Good Housekeeping* 215 (November): 185, 263–66.

Sagan, Carl. 1996. *The Demon-Haunted World: Science as a Candle in the Dark*. New York: Ballantine.

Sagarin, Edward. 1969. *Odd Man In: Societies of Deviants in America*. New York: Quadrangle.

Saldana, Theresa. 1986. *Beyond Survival*. New York: Bantam.

Salisbury, Harrison. 1958. *The Shook-Up Generation.* Greenwich, Conn.: Fawcett Crest.

Sally Jessy Raphael. 1993a. "I Was Stalked Like an Animal." May 19. Journal Graphics transcript no. 1227.

———. 1993b. "If I Can't Have Him No One Can." June 22. Journal Graphics transcript no. 1254.

———. 1994. "Miss America Stalked." February 15. Journal Graphics transcript no. 1420.

San Francisco Chronicle. 1987. "Limiting Guns in Motor Vehicles" (editorial). August 21, p. 72.

Saporta, Maria. 1994. "Staunch Advocate of Urban Living Having Second Thoughts after Drive-By Attack." *Atlanta Journal and Constitution* (March 15): D-1.

Sasson, Theodore. 1995a. *Crime Talk: How Citizens Construct a Social Problem.* Hawthorne, N.Y.: Aldine de Gruyter.

———. 1995b. "African American Conspiracy Theories and the Social Construction of Crime." *Sociological Inquiry* 65:265–85.

Sauter, Van Gordon. 1987a. "No Shelter from Freeway Violence." *Los Angeles Times* (June 26): V-1.

———. 1987b. "Too Much Ado about Freeway Shootings?" *Los Angeles Times* (August 3): II-5.

Schaum, Melita, and Karen Parrish. 1995. *Stalked: Breaking the Silence on the Crime of Stalking in America.* New York: Pocket Books.

Schiller, Dan. 1981. *Objectivity and the News: The Public and the Rise of Commercial Journalism.* Philadelphia: University of Pennsylvania Press.

Schneider, Ann, and Helen Ingram. 1993. "Social Construction of Target Populations." *American Political Science Review* 87:334–47.

Schwartz, Hillel. 1997. "On the Origin of the Phrase 'Social Problems.'" *Social Problems* 44:276–96.

Scott, Wilbur J. 1993. *The Politics of Readjustment.* Hawthorne, N.Y.: Aldine de Gruyter.

Segal, Jonathan. 1989. "Erotomania Revisited." *American Journal of Psychiatry* 146:1261–66.

Sheley, Joseph F., and James D. Wright. 1995. *In the Line of Fire: Youth, Guns, and Violence in Urban America.* Hawthorne, N.Y.: Aldine de Gruyter.

Sherman, William. 1994. "Stalking." *Cosmopolitan* 216 (April): 198–201.

Sherry, Michael S. 1995. *In the Shadow of War: The United States since the 1930s.* New Haven: Yale University Press.

Showalter, Elaine. 1997. *Hystories: Hysterical Epidemics and Modern Media.* New York: Columbia University Press.

Sidel, Ruth. 1996. *Keeping Women and Children Last: America's War on the Poor.* New York: Penguin.

Simmel, Georg. 1950. "The Secret Society." In *The Sociology of Georg Simmel,* edited and translated by K. H. Wolff, 345–76. New York: Free Press.

Sindall, Rob. 1990. *Street Violence in the Nineteenth Century: Media Panic or Real Danger?* Leicester, Great Britain: Leicester University Press.

Skolnick, Jerome H. 1994. "Wild Pitch: 'Three Strikes, You're Out' and Other Bad Calls on Crime." *American Prospect* 17 (spring): 30–37.

Skolnick, Jerome H., Theodore Correl, Elizabeth Navarro, and Roger Rabb. 1990. "The Social Structure of Street Drug Dealing." *American Journal of Police* 9 (1): 1–41.

Smith, Ann W. 1988. *Grandchildren of Alcoholics.* Deerfield Beach, Fla.: Health Communications.

Smith, Michael D. 1994. "Enhancing the Quality of Survey Data on Violence against Women: A Feminist Approach." *Gender and Society* 8:109–27.

Snow, David A., and Robert D. Benford. 1992. "Master Frames and Cycles of Protest." In *Frontiers in Social Movement Theory,* edited by Aldon D. Morris and Carol McClurg Mueller, 133–55. New Haven: Yale University Press.

Snyder, Howard N., and Melissa Sickmund. 1995. *Juvenile Offenders and Victims: A Focus on Violence.* Washington, D.C.: Office of Juvenile Justice and Delinquency Prevention.

Sontag, Susan. 1989. *AIDS and Its Metaphors.* New York: Farrar, Straus and Giroux.

Spector, Malcolm, and John I. Kitsuse. 1977. *Constructing Social Problems.* Menlo Park, Calif.: Cummings.

Stallings, Robert A. 1990. "Media Discourse and the Social Construction of Risk." *Social Problems* 37:80–95.

———. 1995. *Promoting Risk: Constructing the Earthquake Threat.* Hawthorne, N.Y.: Aldine de Gruyter.

Statt, Daniel. 1995. "The Case of the Mohocks: Rake Violence in Augustan London." *Social History* 20:179–99.

Steffens, Lincoln. 1931. *The Autobiography of Lincoln Steffens.* New York: Harcourt, Brace.

Stephenson, June. 1995. *Men Are Not Cost-Effective: Male Crime in America.* New York: Harper Perennial.

Stevens, Phillips, Jr. 1991. "The Demonology of Satanism." In *The Satanism Scare*, edited by James T. Richardson, Joel Best, and David G. Bromley, 21–39. Hawthorne, N.Y.: Aldine de Gruyter.

Stewart, Jill. 1987. "2nd Freeway Shooting Incident Is Investigated." *Los Angeles Times* (June 24): II-1.

Stone, Deborah A. 1988. *Policy Paradox and Political Reason.* New York: Harper-Collins.

———. 1989. "Causal Stories and the Formation of Policy Agendas." *Political Science Quarterly* 104:281–300.

Swidler, Ann. 1986. "Culture in Action." *American Sociological Review* 51:273–86.

Sykes, Charles J. 1992. *A Nation of Victims: The Decay of the American Character.* New York: St. Martin's.

Tharp, Mike. 1992. "In the Mind of a Stalker." *U.S. News & World Report* 112 (February 17): 28–30.

Thrasher, Frederic M. 1927. *The Gang.* Chicago: University of Chicago Press.

Time. 1987. "Homicide on the Highway." Vol. 130 (November 23): 31.

Tindle, Thomas C. 1996. "Evil in E'Ville: Media Treatment of the Gang Issue in a Medium-Sized, Midwestern City." Master's thesis, Southern Illinois University at Carbondale.

Tjaden, Patricia. 1997. "The Crime of Stalking: How Big Is the Problem?" *National Institute of Justice Research Preview* (November).

Tobias, J. J. 1967. *Crime and Industrial Society in the 19th Century.* New York: Schocken.

Toobin, Jeffrey. 1994. "The Man Who Kept Going Free." *New Yorker* 70 (March 7): 38–48, 53.

Trebach, Arnold S., and Scott Ehlers. 1996. "The War on Our Children." *Drug Policy Letter* 30:13–17.

Treen, Joe, and Tom Nugent. 1992. "Carjackers Don't Always Draw the Line at Murder." *People* 38 (November 23): 52–55.

Trippett, Frank. 1987. "Highway to Homicide." *Time* 130 (August 17): 18.

Tucher, Andie. 1994. *Froth and Scum: Truth, Beauty, Goodness, and the Ax Murder in America's First Mass Medium.* Chapel Hill: University of North Carolina Press.

Turner, Patricia A. 1993. *I Heard It through the Grapevine: Rumor in African-American Culture*. Berkeley: University of California Press.

Turner, Ralph H. 1976. "The Real Self: From Institution to Impulse." *American Journal of Sociology* 81:989–1016.

———. 1990. "Role Change." *Annual Review of Sociology* 16:87–110.

Turque, Bill. 1992. "A New Terror on the Road: Carjacking Puts Fear in the Driver's Seat." *Newsweek* 120 (November 23): 31.

U.S. House. 1985. Subcommittee on Criminal Justice, Committee on the Judiciary. *Hate Crime Statistics Act: Hearings*. 99th Cong., 1st sess., March 21.

———. 1986. Subcommittee on Criminal Justice, Committee on the Judiciary. *Anti-Gay Violence: Hearings*. 99th Cong., 2d sess., October 9.

U.S. Senate. 1988. Subcommittee on the Constitution, Committee on the Judiciary. *Hate Crime Statistics Act of 1988: Hearings*. 100th Cong., 2d. sess., June 21.

———. 1992. Committee on the Judiciary. *Antistalking Legislation: Hearings*. 102d Cong., 2d. sess., September 29.

———. 1993. Committee on the Judiciary. *Antistalking Proposals: Hearing*. 103d Cong., 1st sess., March 17.

———. 1994. Subcommittee on the Constitution, Committee on the Judiciary. *The Hate Crimes Statistics Act: Hearings*. 103d Cong., 2d sess., June 28.

Vigil, James Diego. 1996. "Street Baptism: Chicano Gang Initiation." *Human Organization* 55:149–53.

Wagner, David. 1997. *The New Temperance: The American Obsession with Sin and Vice*. Boulder, Colo.: Westview.

Wald, Matthew L. 1997. "Temper Cited as Cause of 28,000 Road Deaths a Year." *New York Times* (July 18): A-14.

Waldorf, Dan. 1993. "When the Crips Invaded San Francisco—Gang Migration." *Gang Journal* 1 (4): 11–16.

Walinsky, Adam. 1995. "The Crisis of Public Order." *Atlantic Monthly* 276 (July): 39–41, 44, 46–49, 52–54.

Warshaw, Robin. 1988. *I Never Called It Rape*. New York: Harper & Row.

Washington Post. 1987. Editorial cartoon. August 3, p. A-14.

Websdale, Neil S. 1996. "Predators: The Social Construction of 'Stranger-Danger' in Washington State as a Form of Patriarchal Ideology." *Women and Criminal Justice* 7 (2): 43–68.

Weed, Frank J. 1991. "Organizational Mortality in the Anti-Drunk-Driving

Movement: Failure among Local MADD Chapters." *Social Forces* 69:851–68.

———. 1993. "The MADD Queen: Charisma and the Founder of Mothers Against Drunk Driving." *Leadership Quarterly* 4:329–46.

———. 1995. *Certainty of Justice: Reform in the Crime Victim Movement.* Hawthorne, N.Y.: Aldine de Gruyter.

Weeks, Elaine Lunsford, Jacqueline M. Boles, Albeno P. Garbin, and John Blount. 1986. "The Transformation of Sexual Harassment from a Private Trouble into a Public Issue." *Sociological Inquiry* 56:432–55.

Wilcox, Barbara. 1982. "Psychological Rape." *Glamour* 80 (October): 232–33, 291–96.

Will, George. 1992. "From MEOW to Meow." *Newsweek* 119 (February 10): 82.

Williams, Gwyneth I., and Rhys H. Williams. 1995. "'All We Want Is Equality': Rhetorical Framing in the Fathers' Rights Movement." In *Images of Issues,* edited by Joel Best, 2d ed., 191–212. Hawthorne, N.Y.: Aldine de Gruyter.

Williams, Rhys H. 1995. "Constructing the Public Good: Social Movements and Cultural Resources." *Social Problems* 42:124–44.

Wilson, James Q. 1994. "What to Do about Crime." *Commentary* 98 (September): 25–34.

———. 1997. *Moral Judgment: Does the Abuse Excuse Threaten Our Legal System?* New York: Basic Books.

Wilson, William Julius. 1987. *The Truly Disadvantaged: The Inner City, the Underclass, and Public Policy.* Chicago: University of Chicago Press.

Witkin, Gordon. 1992. "Willing to Kill for a Car: Auto Theft Is Booming, and Carjacking Makes It a Deadly Menace All Over." *U.S. News & World Report* 113 (September 21): 40, 42, 44.

Woititz, Janet Geringer. 1983. *Adult Children of Alcoholics.* Deerfield Beach, Fla.: Health Communications.

Woolgar, Steve, and Dorothy Pawluch. 1985. "Ontological Gerrymandering." *Social Problems* 32:214–27.

Wright, Susan. 1993. "Blaming the Victim, Blaming Society, or Blaming the Discipline: Fixing Responsibility for Homelessness." *Sociological Quarterly* 34:1–16.

Wuerz, Scott. 1998. "State Police 'See Everything.'" *Southern Illinoisan* (February 15): 3-A.

Zangrando, Robert L. 1980. *The NAACP Crusade against Lynching, 1909–1950.* Philadelphia: Temple University Press.

Zarefsky, David. 1986. *President Johnson's War on Poverty: Rhetoric and History.* Tuscaloosa: University of Alabama Press.

Zatz, Marjorie S. 1987. "Chicano Youth Gangs and Crime: The Creation of a Moral Panic." *Contemporary Crises* 11:129–58.

Zawitz, Marianne W., Patsy A. Klaus, Ronet Bachman, Lisa D. Bastian, Marshall M. DeBerry, Jr., Michael R. Rand, and Bruce M. Taylor. 1993. *Highlights from 20 Years of Surveying Crime Victims: The National Crime Victimization Survey, 1973–92.* Washington, D.C.: Bureau of Justice Statistics.

Zevitz, Richard G., and Susan R. Takata. 1992. "Metropolitan Gang Influence and the Emergence of Group Delinquency in a Regional Community." *Journal of Criminal Justice* 20:93–106.

Zona, Michael A., Kausshal K. Sharma, and John Lane. 1993. "A Comparative Study of Erotomanic and Obsessional Subjects in a Forensic Sample." *Journal of Forensic Sciences* 38:894–903.

INDEX

Compositor: Prestige Typography
Text: 10/15 Janson
Display: Janson
Printer and Binder: Haddon Craftsmen, Inc.